PENGUIN BOOKS

THE MOON'S A BALLOON

David Niven was one of Britain's best-known actors and, in later years, a bestselling author – his autobiography, *The Moon's a Balloon*, first published in 1971, has sold over 5 million copies worldwide. Often remembered for playing the archetypal English gentleman, he made ninety films during a career that stretched over forty years.

David Niven was born in London in 1910. Losing his father in the First World War, his childhood was quite unsettled until he attended Stowe School. After passing out from the Royal Military College at Sandhurst he gained a commission with the Highland Light Infantry, serving for a time in Malta. He resigned his commission at the age of twenty-three and took off for Canada and the United States, where for three years he tried his hand at a variety of jobs before heading west to Hollywood. Of his pre-war films the best-known is probably *The Prisoner of Zenda* (1937). When war broke out Niven returned to England and rejoined the army, this time in the Rifle Brigade. In 1946 Niven was widowed after the tragic death of his first wife, Primmie. Over the next twenty years he went on to make some of his best films, including the Oscar-winning *Separate Tables*, *Around the World in Eighty Days*, *Casino Royale*, *The Guns of Navarone*, *Please Don't Eat the Daisies* and *Death on the Nile*. A natural storyteller, he published his first novel, *Round the Rugged Rocks*, in 1951 and his two volumes of autobiography, *The Moon's a Balloon* (1971) and *Bring on the Empty Horses* (1975), were instant bestsellers. His last book, *Go Slowly, Come Back Quickly*, was published in 1981. David Niven died in July 1983, survived by his second wife and his four children.

DAVID NIVEN

———

THE MOON'S A BALLOON

PENGUIN BOOKS

PENGUIN BOOKS

UK | USA | Canada | Ireland | Australia
India | New Zealand | South Africa

Penguin Books is part of the Penguin Random House group of companies
whose addresses can be found at global.penguinrandomhouse.com.

First published by Hamish Hamilton 1971
Published in Penguin Books 1994
Reissued in this edition 2016

042

Printed and bound in Great Britain by Clays Ltd, Elcograf S.p.A.

A CIP catalogue record for this book is available from the British Library

ISBN: 978–0–140–23924–9

www.greenpenguin.co.uk

for
Kira Triandpyllapopulous

who knows if the moon's
a balloon, coming out of a keen city
in the sky—filled with pretty people?
(and if you and i should

get into it, if they
should take me and take you into their balloon,
why then
we'd go up higher with all the pretty people

than houses and steeples and clouds:
go sailing
away and away sailing into a keen
city which nobody's ever visited, where

always
      it's
           Spring) and everyone's
in love and flowers pick themselves

e. e. cummings

List of Illustrations

INTRODUCTION

EVELYN WAUGH penned these words: 'Only when one has lost all curiosity about the future has one reached the age to write an autobiography.'

It is daunting to consider the sudden wave of disillusionment that must have swept over such a brilliant man and caused him to write such balls.

Nearer the mark, it seems to me, is Professor John Kenneth Galbraith of Harvard University who wrote: 'Books can be broken broadly into two classes: those written to please the reader and those written for the greater pleasure of the writer. Subject to numerous and distinguished exceptions, the second class is rightly suspect and especially if the writer himself appears in the story. Doubtless, it is best to have one's vanity served by others; but when all else fails, it is something men do for themselves. Political memoirs, biographies of great business tycoons *and the annals of aging actors* sufficiently illustrate the point.'

The italics are mine.

I apologise for the ensuing name dropping. It was hard to avoid it.

People in my profession, who, like myself, have the good fortune to parlay a minimal talent into a long career, find all sorts of doors opened that would otherwise have remained closed. Once behind those doors it makes little sense to write about the butler if Chairman Mao is sitting down to dinner.

DAVID NIVEN
Cap Ferrat A.M.

CHAPTER ONE

NESSIE, when I first saw her, was seventeen years old, honey-blonde, pretty rather than beautiful, the owner of a voluptuous but somehow innocent body and a pair of legs that went on for ever. She was a Piccadilly whore. I was a fourteen-year-old heterosexual schoolboy and I met her thanks to my stepfather. (If you would like to skip on and meet Nessie more fully, she reappears on page 41.)

I had a stepfather because my father, along with 90 per cent of his comrades in the Berkshire Yeomanry, had landed with immense panache at Suvla Bay. Unfortunately, the Turks were given ample time to prepare to receive them. For days, sweltering in their troopships, the Berkshire Yeomanry had ridden at anchor off shore while the High Command in London argued as to the best way to get them on the beach. Finally, they arrived at their brilliant decision and the troops dutifully embarked in the ship's whalers. On arrival they held their rifles above their heads, cheered, and gallantly leaped into the dark waist-high water. A combination of barbed wire beneath the surface and machine guns to cover the barbed wire, provided a devastating welcome.

Woodpigeons were calling on a warm summer evening and my sister, Grizel, and I were swapping cigarette cards on an old tree trunk in the paddock when a red-eyed maid came and told us our mother wanted to see us and that we were not to stay too long.

After a rather incoherent interview with our mother, who was French, and had trouble explaining what 'missing' meant, we returned to the swapping of cigarette cards and resumed our perusal of endless trains lumbering along a distant embankment loaded with guns and waving young men ... 1915.

I am afraid my father's death meant little or nothing to me at the time; later it meant a great deal. I was just five years old and had not seen him much except when I was brought down to be shown off before arriving dinner guests or departing fox-hunting companions. I could always tell which

13

were which because the former smelled of soap and perfume and the latter of sweat and spirits.

I lived with Grizel in a nursery presided over by a warm enveloping creature, Whitty.

Rainy days were spent being taught Highland reels by a wounded piper of the Argyll and Sutherland Highlanders, and listening to a gramophone equipped with an immense horn. Our favourite record had 'The Ride of the Valkyrie' on one side and, on the other, a jolly little number for those days, called 'The Wreck of the Troopship'. We were specially fascinated by the whinnying of the horses as the sharks moved in (the troops were on the way to the South African War).

Occasionally, I was taken to the hospital in Cirencester to 'do my bit'. This entailed trying not to fidget or jump while V.A.D.s practised bandaging any part of me they fancied.

The war days sped by and the house in Gloucestershire was sold. So, too, was one we had in Argyllshire. Everyone, my mother included, was under the misapprehension that my father was very rich. He had cheerfully gone off to war like a knight of old, taking with him as troopers his valet, his under-gardener and two grooms. He also took his hunters, but these were exchanged for rifles in Egypt en route and my father, his valet and one groom were duly slaughtered.

It transpired that he was hugely in debt at the time.

We soon moved to London to a large, damp house in Cadogan Place. Straw had been laid in the street when we arrived to make things quieter for someone dying next door. The sweaty, hearty, red-faced, country squires were replaced by pale, gay, young men who recited poetry and sang to my mother. She was very beautiful, very musical, very sad and lived on cloud nine.

A character called 'Uncle Tommy'* soon made his appearance and became a permanent member of her entourage. Gradually the pale, gay young men gave way to pale, sad, older men.

'Uncle Tommy' was a second line politician who did not fight in the war. A tall, ramrod straight creature with

* Sir Thomas Comyn-Platt. Liked to be known as the mystery man of the Conservative Party. Contested Portsmouth Central in the Election of 1926.

14

immensely high, white collars, a bluish nose and a very noisy cuff-link combination which he rattled at me when I made an eating error at mealtime.

I don't believe he was very healthy really. Anyway he got knighted for something to do with the Conservative Party and the Nineteen Hundred Club, and Cadogan Place became a rendezvous for people like Lord Willoughby de Broke, Sir Edward Carson, K.C., and Sir Edward Marshall Hall, K.C. I suppose it bubbled with the sort of brilliant conversation into which children these days would be encouraged to join, but, as soon as it started, Grizel and I were sent up to a nursery which had a linoleum floor and a string bag full of apples hanging outside the window during the winter. Grizel, who was two years older than me, became very interested during this period in the shape and form of my private parts; but when after a particularly painful inspection, I claimed my right to see hers too, she covered up sharply and dodged the issue by saying, 'Well, it's a sort of flat arrangement.'

The Germans raided London. High in the night sky, I saw a Zeppelin in flames.

One day my mother took me to buy a pair of warm gloves. Some Fokkers came over and everyone rushed into the street to point them out to each other. Then as the possibility of what might be about to drop out of the Fokkers dawned on them they rushed back indoors again.

My mother didn't leave the glove shop. She was busy giving a discourse on the superior quality of French gloves when the manager said, 'This place will come down like a pack of cards.' By this time the Fokkers must have been fifty miles away but I was nevertheless lugged across the street and we joined an undignified Gadarene swine movement down the steps of the Knightsbridge Tube station. One woman had a parrot. Another had hysterics and between screams, ate handsful of marmalade out of a stone jar, a spectacle I found highly enjoyable.

Uncle Tommy's marriage to my mother coincided with my sixth birthday. The wedding took place at All Saints, Sloane Street. Purple with embarrassment, I was press-ganged into being a page and pressure-fed into a primrose coloured suit with mother-of-pearl buttons, a white lace collar, shorts and socks.

15

I did everything I could do to wreck the show and fidgeted and picked my nose till an aquiline creature, later identified as the famous Margot Asquith, came and knelt in the aisle to comfort me. I decided she was a witch and again and again informed the congregation of this discovery in a shrill treble.

I was removed and Uncle Tommy, forever politically sensitive, treated me from that moment on with frosty distaste.

My eldest brother, Henri (known as Max), was a naval cadet at Dartmouth, longing to get into the war. My elder sister, Joyce, was at home helping my mother and Grizel had gone away to boarding school in Norfolk. I was the youngest. And, overcoming my mother's apprehensions, 'Tommy' soon saw to it that I was packed off to a boarding school near Worthing.

Apart from the Chinese, the only people in the world who pack their sons off to the tender care of unknown and often homosexual schoolmasters at the exact moment when they are most in need of parental love and influence, are the British so-called upper and middle classes.

I had not long been at boarding school before I discovered that life could be hell. There was a great deal of bullying and for a six-year-old, the spectacle of a gang of twelve-year-olds bearing down, cracking wet towels like whips, can be terrifying.

For the most part, the masters were even more frightening. It would be charitable to think that they were shell-shocked heroes returned from the hell of Mons and Vimy, but it seems more probable that they were sadistic perverts who had been dredged up from the bottom of the educational barrel at a time of acute manpower shortage.

One, a Mr. Croome, when he tired of pulling ears half way out of our heads (I still have one that sticks out almost at right angles thanks to this son of a bitch), and delivering, for the smallest mistake in declension, back-handed slaps that knocked one off one's bench, delighted in saying, 'Show me the hand that wrote this', and then bringing down the sharp edge of a heavy ruler across the offending wrist.

He took the last class on Friday evening and I remember praying every week that he would die before then so that I could somehow reach the haven of Saturday and Sunday and the comparative safety of the weekend.

I don't think I have ever been so frightened of a human being in my life. Once he made me lean out of a fourth floor window – a stupefying height for a little boy – then he shut the window across the small of my back, ordered two equally terrified boys to hold my feet and laid into me mightily with a cane. All this for some mistake in – 'common are saceredos dux vates parens et conjux . . .'

Years later, when I was at Sandhurst and playing in the Rugby football fifteen, big enough and ugly enough to take care of myself, I had an overpowering urge to see the bastard again, face to face.

I went down to the school, filled with vindictiveness. I don't know what I intended to do really, but when I got there I found the school deserted; its prison-like exercise yard full of rubbish and old newspapers. The fourth floor window, out of which I had dangled, was broken and open to the rain – it didn't even look very high.

My mother, at the time, however, would not believe my tales of woe or rather Uncle Tommy persuaded her that they were nonsense, telling her that all boys exaggerated and that anyway she could not be expected to know anything about English schools.

After two years of this purgatory, I got a large and painful boil as a result of the bad food. 'Oh!' said the matron, 'that's nothing, don't make such a fuss!', and lopped off the top of it with a pair of scissors. The ensuing infection was pretty horrible and put me in hospital.

The next term, I was removed and sent to Heatherdown at Ascot.

At this point, I don't believe my mother was actually taking in washing, but, as sure as hell, she was sending very little out, and it must have been a fearful drain on her resources. Heatherdown was far more expensive than Worthing; certainly only a token subscription to the family coffers was being made by Uncle Tommy and she still had her thumb in the dyke of my father's debts, but I was blissfully unconscious of all this and wallowed in my good fortune.

Heatherdown was a very different cup of tea, very carriage-trade, very protected and, compared to Worthing, very soft, very snobbish. Everybody went from there to Eton. Gone were the sadistic masters and the school bullies tying small

17

boys to hot radiators; no more scissor-wielding matrons; no more ex-naval cooks with finger nails like toe nails doling out their nauseous confections; and, receding like a bad dream, were the flinty playground and the evil-smelling doorless lavatories, open to the elements and to the helpful advice of schoolmates.

Instead, I found a world of cleanliness and kindly masters; motherly matrons; green playing fields; a lake; delicious food and a swimming pool. In short ... schoolboy heaven.

The only grown-ups who hit me were the headmaster who, under great provocation, occasionally uncorked a dose of the cane; and a dear old gentleman who taught divinity, called Mr. Hodgson, who sometimes brandished a clothes brush known as 'Dixon and Parker' because if, as rarely happened, he hit someone with it, the name of the maker was left imprinted on the bum.

After the appalling apprenticeship of Worthing, I could not believe that life could be so perfect. Released from fear and oppression, the whole thing went to my head.

Almost nine, I became something of a clown. This was hastened on when, for some strange reason, my balls dropped three years earlier than they should have done.

I was in the choir at the time, the possessor of a voice of guileless purity. Sometimes I was entrusted with solo passages and it was on such an occasion, and in front of a full house, that disaster struck.

Ascot Sunday – parents staying for the race meeting in smart country houses nearby had filled the chapel to capacity. Alone, I was piping my way through 'There is a green hill far away, without a city wall'. ... Suddenly, on the word 'wall' a fearful braying sound issued from the angelic face of the soloist. I tried for the note again: this time it sounded like a Rolls-Royce klaxon of the period. The paper-thin discipline of the choir quickly disintegrated ... repressed laughter became contagious and finally, general.

Immediately after chapel, I was caned by the headmaster – Sammy Day. He had once played cricket for England and still had one of the best late cuts in the business. It hurt a lot and, considering the medical evidence that was from then on permanently with me, was rather unfair.

Boys are terrible snobs and I was annually unnerved when

the school list came out, to see some of my contemporaries sniggering because in between the young marquesses and dukes with their splendid addresses, was –

Niven, D. Rose Cottage, Bembridge, I.W.

It had become necessary for the house in London to be sold and our permanent address was now as advertised – a converted fisherman's cottage which had a reputation for unreliability. When the East wind blew, the front door got stuck and when the West wind blew, the back door could not be opened – only the combined weight of the family seemed to keep it anchored to the ground. I adored it and was happier there than I had ever been, especially because, with a rare flash of genius, my mother decided that during the holidays she would be alone with her children.

Uncle Tommy was barred – I don't know where he went – to the Carlton Club, I suppose.

After the sudden descent of my testicles, I was removed from the choir as a bad risk and became the 'bellows man' and the musical success of each service (we suffered through two a day) depended entirely on my prowess behind the organ. This was a position of great trust, but the newly found clown in me could not resist the opportunities it offered. For a small price – two chocolate whirls, one Cadbury's Milk Flake or a brace of Turkish delights – I could be bribed to let the air out of the bellows on important occasions. The whole school, on the selected day, would be in the know and would sit through an endless sermon hugging itself with delicious anticipation.

It took careful preparation but I could generally arrange matters so that a rude noise could be subtly injected into the proceedings, usually just after an Amen. I could redress the situation rapidly by quick pumping and only the connoisseurs could detect that it was not a mistake ... the boys were all connoisseurs.

Once I tried it when the Bishop of Ripon was in the middle of a special address. This was my masterpiece and also my downfall but the bribes were mountainous.

It was a highly technical job and involved surreptitiously and noiselessly keeping the bellows half-filled for several minutes after the end of the preceding hymn. I had intended to let this air out in a series of well-spaced small squeaks

19

and trills thus keeping the boys happy during what promised to be a long, trying period, but something went wrong and it all came out at once and on a most unfortunate cue ... a quotation from Proverbs 7, 'I have perfumed my bed with myrrh, aloes and cinnamon. . . .'

It was as if the bellows could not contain themselves any longer – a tremendous fart rent the air. All was confusion.

The school was infiltrated with informers and I was soon dealt with once more by the long-suffering Sammy Day.

I loved Heatherdown and tried hard to uphold the agricultural standards of the landed gentry with whom I was rubbing shoulders.

Every summer on the First Sunday After the Derby (it is not thus described in the Book of Common Prayer but so many boys of noble birth had racehorse owner fathers that at Heatherdown, it far outranked Rogation Sunday, the Sunday after Advent, and the Twenty-first Sunday after Trinity) a prize was given to the boy with the most beautiful garden. Each boy had one about the size of a lavatory mat in a small commercial hotel, but immense ingenuity and forethought was displayed by the owners. Actually, these allotments were status symbols of the worst kind, and boys whose family estates employed an army of gardeners proudly displayed the most exotic flowers and shrubs, delivered for planting hot from the family greenhouses while the more modest smallholders nurtured colourful annuals and arranged them in intricate patterns.

I could only manage a bi-annual crop of mustard and cress.

The year that Humorist won the Derby saw that rare phenomenon, a drought in England, and my crop, carefully timed for the Flower Show, failed, burned to a crisp.

By now the self-appointed jester to the upper classes, I decided to fill the gap, and creeping out of the dormitory after dark, I made my way downstairs and flitting from tree to tree in the moonlight, arrived at a well-known gap in the wall which separated Heatherdown from Heathfield – the girls' school next door.

From preliminary reconnaissance, I knew that this gap opened on to the kitchen garden. I selected a huge vegetable marrow plant, pulled it up by the roots and once safely back on the male side of the wall, hid it behind a piece of corrugated iron.

It took some while and several near heart attacks but I finally made it back to bed. The next morning I retrieved the marrow and in the hubbub caused by the arrival of other boys' parents in Daimlers and Rolls-Royces, managed to plant my prize on my poor piece of desert.

It didn't go down very well. The Countess of Jersey – one of the parents – presented the prizes.

She didn't give one to me and later, I was caned again by a no longer affable Sammy Day: not for making a nonsense of the Flower Show which could have been justified – but for *stealing* which put a totally different connotation on the thing.

After this, I went rapidly downhill from popular school clown to unpopular school nuisance. Striving to maintain my waning reputation, I fell in the lake and nearly drowned, purposely split the seat of my trousers on the school walk through Ascot and was caught trying to get into the Race-course – a hideous crime. Poor Brian Franks, a Bembridge friend, near death's door with pneumonia at Wixenford, a school nearby, received from me on the day of his 'crisis', a large chocolate box inside which was a smaller box, then a smaller box and so on down the scale to a match box with a piece of dog's mess in it.

Not a funny joke, especially for the Matron who opened it, but then I didn't know Brian was ill.

Brian* overcame his illness and my gift and has remained a life-long friend but the Matron took a dim view, the smoke signals went up between Wixenford and Heatherdown and Sammy Day decided that his school could get along without me.

I was ten and a half when I was expelled.

* Later as a Lieut.-Col. in the Special Air Services in World War II, Brian, for great gallantry after being dropped behind the German lines, was decorated with the D.S.O. and M.C. It is rather depressing to think that his mother complained to mine because I told him the facts of life when we were both ten years old. He, not believing this phenomenal piece of news, had asked her for up-to-date information.

CHAPTER TWO

THERE is a Chinese proverb to the effect that when everything in the garden is at its most beautiful, an ill wind blows the seeds of weeds and suddenly, when least expected, all is ugliness.

The decision to remove me from Heatherdown, I am sure, was not taken lightly because in those days expulsion from school was tantamount to ruin for a boy of my age. Public schools with bulging waiting lists could pick and choose among far more desirable applicants and any boy without a public school education started life at an incalculable disadvantage. Sure enough my mother soon received a polite letter from Mr. Tuppy Headlam for whose house at Eton I had hopefully been entered, saying that unfortunately, he had decided that he was going to have to 'shorten his entry list etc. etc.'

But of this I knew nothing. It was the end of term anyway, and in the excitement I noticed no chill on the part of Sammy Day, nor any of the other masters, as I said goodbye and went off whooping and hollering with the rest of the boys to board the school train for the trip to London.

On arrival at Waterloo Station, the shouting, laughing hysterically happy boys were clutched to parental bosoms while eyes were averted from filthy nails, grease spots and ink stains.

I braced myself for my usual encounter with 'Tommy'. He was enlisted on these occasions to meet the school train at one platform, collect my trunk and see me safely ensconced in a third-class compartment on the train for Portsmouth Harbour where my mother would be waiting to take me on the ferry across the Solent to Ryde and thence to my beloved Rose Cottage, Bembridge, I.W. Once this had been accomplished, Tommy's contribution to the proceedings ended.

'Tommy' was easily identifiable. Above his beetling eyebrows and Duke of Wellington nose, he wore a top hat, the wont of his ilk whenever the King was in London. He bore down upon me, uttered no word of greeting and with an imperious gesture of his umbrella commanded me to follow.

22

Everything so far had been perfectly normal. He hardly ever wasted conversation on me, so the silent march through the station following a porter with my trunk gave me no sense of foreboding.

Soon I was alone in a sooty compartment that smelled of stale smoke and orange peel, watching the retreating figure of my step-father stalking towards the exit. Hanging out of the window I saw him pause and speak to the guard and point in my direction. The guard nodded his understanding. Soon we were off.

I sat back and savoured the delicious aroma of my compartment, then, after examining the framed, faded pictures of Freshwater Bay and Shanklin, I snuggled into my corner seat, gazed out of the window and gave myself up to delicious anticipation of the four weeks' holiday ahead.

My mother had beautiful teeth and a beautiful smile. I imagined her standing by the barrier, the Harbour behind her, waiting for me. Would I run to meet her as I longed to do? No, I thought, the little kids at Waterloo had looked pretty soppy doing that; I would play the whole thing cool – saunter, that's what I'd do, saunter, and then suddenly, shove out my hand and give her the wooden bracket I had made for her in the carpentry class. I had clutched this bracket in my hand wrapped in brown paper ever since I left Heatherdown.

Two hours later, the green Hampshire countryside gave way to the drab outskirts of Portsmouth and as the train slowed down for its first stop, Portsmouth Town, I looked down into the busy heart of the city – another five minutes, ten at the most and I would see my mother and the holidays really would start. I wondered if the tyres of my bicycle were flat and if Grizel and Joyce were there and above all if Brian Franks was back from Wixenford yet. Max I knew was away on a six months' training cruise as a cadet on H.M.S. *Thunderer* but I squirmed with excitement, little knowing that the Chinese wind had blown a whole car load of weeds into my garden and I was, at that very moment, waist deep in nettles.

The train stopped. The guard opened the door, jerked his thumb in my direction and addressed someone behind him. 'That's the little bastard.'

A gigantic man in a trench coat with a magenta coloured face and tufts of hair sprouting on his cheek bones, filled the doorway.

'Get your things,' he commanded, 'you are coming with me.'

'No, sir,' I quavered, 'my mother is waiting for me at the next stop.'

'Don't argue, get your bloody things.'

Stupefied with fear, I cowered into my corner.

'Oh, Christ!' said the man to the guard, 'get his bloody things down, will you? I'll lug him out.'

With that, while the guard lowered my suitcase and mackintosh, this huge creature picked me up bodily. I grabbed wildly at the luggage rack as I was carried out and dropped my mother's bracket. I don't think I fought much or even cried. I was paralysed with terror.

I was dragged along the platform, outside into the station yard and shoved into an ancient car.

'What are you doing with that little boy?' asked a woman with a baby.

'Mind your own fucking business,' was the answer. I noticed a heavy smell of spirits.

Through Portsmouth we lurched and out to the genteel suburbs of Southsea. I now sobbed uncontrollably. My brain refused to consider what could be happening to me. I cried for my mother.

'Stop that bloody noise and when you do, I'll tell you where you're going.'

My sobs dried up into a snivelling kind of hiccups.

'First of all, you have been expelled from Heatherdown because you are a dirty little shit. You are not going home for the holidays, you are staying here with me and if you don't behave yourself, I'll tan the arse off you – Any questions?'

I shall always remember Southsea Common: flat, greasy, wet and windswept, with a dejected flock of dirty sheep morosely munching its balding surface.

Halfway across he stopped the car and slapped me hard several times across the face.

'Stop it, for Christ's sake ... You're not a bloody girl.'

I was still whimpering with fear when we arrived at a

dreary house in a shoddy row. Grimy net curtains and an aspidistra filled half of a bleak downstairs window which looked on to a brick path and a muddy garden: the other half was filled by the curious faces of half a dozen boys.

Commander Bollard ran a school for 'difficult' boys.

I don't know how my stepfather found him. He was an unlovable man who fulminated constantly against the terrible injustice he had suffered by being 'axed' from the Navy when a promising Lieutenant-Commander. Now he and his thin-lipped, blue-veined, tweedy, terribly 'refained' wife added to his meagre pension and indulged their mutual passion for pink gin by taking in a dozen or so boarders.

The boarders were without exception pretty hard cases. Nearly all had been expelled from one or more schools and despairing parents had committed them to the tender care of Commander and Mrs. Bollard, hoping that stern discipline would work where kindness or indifference had so far failed.

A few eventually pulled themselves together and clawed their way back to acceptance by lesser public schools. Others ran away and joined the merchant navy. Several ended up in Borstal.

The gallant Commander laid about him with a will on the smallest excuse, and there was hardly a bottom in the house that did not bear witness to his Dickensian brutality.

We were treated like young criminals and soon began to feel that we might as well behave like them. Pocket money was not allowed as part of our 'cure', but extra food was essential because the gin-sodden labours of Mrs. Bollard only half-filled our bellies.

The house was a three-storeyed rabbit warren and terribly over-populated, but oh! it was clean. We scrubbed and re-scrubbed every inch of it daily. It must have been the only building in existence where the wooden floors were holy-stoned twice a day. Oil lamps had to be spotless too – there was no electric light – and an ill-trimmed wick was evil-smelling evidence of highly punishable inefficiency.

The ghastly dining-room was called the 'Gun Room', the kitchen 'the Galley', the cellar 'the Brig' and so forth. We did not sleep in hammocks but on wooden shelves, four to a room. The Commander and his wife prowled about at night in stockinged feet hoping to catch us talking.

25

A couple of grey-faced ex-schoolmasters came every day to give us almost continuous lessons and there were no games. Saturday afternoons were free and we made full use of them.

One of the few useful things I learned there was the Morse Code which the Commander taught himself. I suspect it was all he knew but it made it unnecessary to speak when talking after lights out. It did, however, make flashlights and batteries an essential part of our survival kit. These were procured in the same way as food – by stealing.

On Saturday afternoons, 'the ship's company', as the Commander liked to refer to his charges, split up into highly organised gangs of four to six and went shop-lifting for chocolate, condensed milk, cakes, batteries, flashlights, and other essentials.

Every day was torture for me. I received no word from my mother and when once I borrowed enough money, sevenpence I believe, to put through a telephone call to wish her a happy Easter, somebody at Rose Cottage hung up as soon as they heard my voice. Feeling a complete outcast and worst of all, within sight of Bembridge seven miles away across the water, I gradually became the best and most dedicated 'front man' in the establishment.

'Curly' and 'Dusty' were the two unchallenged gang leaders. I worked mostly in Curly's group. A large foxy-faced boy with a mop of sandy hair, protruding teeth and freckles, he called the shots on Saturdays. He was a brilliant organiser.

On Saturday mornings he decided exactly what was to be lifted during the afternoon and it was never an excessive amount – food for consumption during the coming week or saleable goods to provide purchasing power. Curly knew a 'fence' in Southampton who worked with smugglers in the merchant navy and with the exception of our most ambitious effort, a 'hot' motorcycle, which had to be dumped in a chalk quarry on the Downs, this man took everything we had to offer.

One Saturday I was paid the supreme compliment of being chosen to travel with Curly on the bus to Southampton to visit the 'fence'.

Curly had decided that as summer was coming on, thin cotton shirts and singlets would be most acceptable to the 'fence's' regular customers – sailors heading for the Indian

Ocean, Dakar or Panama. We lifted that day about two dozen saleable articles. As front man for candy, cigarettes and buns, my job was simple: to open big blue eyes wide and engage the owner of a tobacconist's or cake shop in long conversation about the price of various items which I hoped to be able to buy for my crippled uncle in hospital. While this was going on, one or two of the rest of the gang pocketed necessities from the far end of the counter. It was easy, in the small shops but the big stores, with the possibility of store detectives, called for a more advanced technique – the marbles.

Once I saw that 'the lifters' were exactly in position for their grab, I burst a large paper bag full of glass marbles. The crash of falling glass turned all heads – many willing souls stooped to aid the poor little boy who even on occasions could summon up a few tears of embarrassment.

We never 'worked' the same store twice.

Three weeks passed and as a relief from the Commander's crude and vicious discipline – I once spent a whole day in 'the brig': alone in the darkness of the cellar listening to the rats scrabbling about among piles of old newspapers around me – Saturday afternoons became oases in the desert of my loneliness.

Thrashed by the Commander for the smallest offence, ill-fed, apparently deserted by the family, expelled from a well-known school and facing my future through a bead curtain of question marks, I was, after ten years of life, already at a very low ebb.

But if, Dear Reader, you should think that I was a victim of circumstances, a magnet for bad luck, or just plain 'hardly done by', I beg you also to consider the possibility that I was a thoroughly poisonous little boy.

After a month under the command of Commander Bollard, his wife one day came to find me. A cigarette permanently waggled from her tight mouth. Her upper lip was yellow.

'May husbind wants yew,' she announced.

I followed her to the 'Captain's Cabin' – a dreadful little study full of leather furniture and old navy lists. Around the place plenty of bottles were in evidence – none held sailing ships.

The Commander lounged behind his desk.

'All right, you little bugger, you have been sprung. Get packed, don't steal anybody else's stuff because you go through Customs here before you leave – you're catching the three o'clock ferry to the Island.'

My heart nearly stopped beating. I could hardly believe it. I rushed upstairs and started packing furiously, terrified that he would change his mind.

No mother met the ferry on which I was dumped unceremoniously by the gallant Commander. With a strange last-minute change of character, he thrust a stick of Southsea Rock into my hand along with my ticket.

On the short train trip to Bembridge I reflected on what sort of welcome would be awaiting me.

It was my ally, Grizel, very distressed, bless her, who met me and as we walked up the hill to the cottage, she filled me in as to my immediate fate.

I was to be sent into the Navy, if they would have me and if I could pass the exam, about two years hence.

'How is Mum? Is she very angry with me?'

'I think she is terribly unhappy about Heatherdown. They wouldn't have you at Eton after being expelled, you know.'

I had a poor welcome at Rose Cottage, but it was no worse than I had expected. My mother was in her room. I went upstairs with leaden feet and watery knees.

Coldly she went over my miserable performance at Heatherdown – the damage was done, she said, but it was far more serious than I realised – I wouldn't be able to get into anything now. The Navy might take me but everything depended on getting very high marks in the exam: if I got those they might overlook my being expelled from school.

My mother explained that I had been brought over from Portsmouth, not for a holiday but to repack my trunk and leave the very next morning for Penn Street, in Buckinghamshire, where 'Uncle Tommy' had arranged for me to go to a crammer's who would try to get me past the entrance examination for Dartmouth.

Another of 'Uncle Tommy's' selections? I quailed at the thought but I couldn't see that things could get very much worse than they had been lately so after a silent family supper, I borrowed Grizel's bicycle and pedalled up to the

Mill House where Brian Franks lived, knowing I would find a sympathetic ear.

Still shaky from his illness, Brian gave me an eye-witness account of the opening of my gift. It seemed that the Matron had unwrapped the box with quite a flourish and the contents had flown into a medicine cabinet whence it had been extracted with forceps.

Brian said he had begun to feel better from that moment.

I have noticed again and again that when things are really black and one feels that they can't possibly get any worse – they often do. This time, however, things improved.

The crammer at Penn Street was the Vicar – the Reverend Arthur Browning, a magnificent looking grandson of Robert Browning – clear, blue eyes and white, wavy hair.

Chorus: 'It's the roast beef of old England
That makes us what we are today!'
Verse: 'What makes the Vicar's hair so nice and wavy?
It's simply becos he was brought up on the gravy,
Of the Roast Beef of old Engerlund
That makes us wot we are today.'

etc. etc.

So we dutifully and sycophantically warbled at the village fete, a week after I arrived.

Sycophantically because, beneath his benign and exotic exterior, he was an evil-tempered, vain old tyrant. The parents uniformly adored him: the boys without exception loathed him.

The Victorian vicarage nestled next to the Victorian church in a damp dell, enfolded by dripping beechwoods, part of the well-known pheasant shoot of Lord Howe's Penn House estate, three miles away.

Mrs. Browning was a plump partridge of a woman who wore pince-nez which were attached to a little chain. These in turn were controlled by a spring concealed inside a round enamel receptacle pinned to her generous left bosom.

There was a nice sporting master called Mr. Keeble who took us for long walks to Amersham and bicycle rides to Beaconsfield, and a nice scholarly old gentleman called Mr. Woodcock whose ill-fitting false teeth had a distressing habit of flying out on to the carpet or into the soup. At the village fete they became embedded in a macaroon.

Ma Browning was immensely greedy and the high fees paid by our parents enabled her to provide a very good 'board' indeed. She had a brace of pretty daughters aged eighteen and twenty whose woollen bloomers hung in steaming festoons in the bathroom and an elder son who enlivened Sunday luncheons by arriving flushed and late with garrulous business friends from London.

All in all, with the exception of 'Pa' Browning's rages, which were the twittering of little birds compared to the exhibitions of Mr. Croome and Commander Bollard, Penn Street vicarage was a very pleasant interlude.

I worked hard but many of Pa Browning's tantrums were certainly brought on when it became apparent to him that mathematics of all sorts would for ever be beyond me.

It began to look probable that the Royal Navy would not entrust the navigation of several million pounds' worth of battleship and several hundred lives to an officer who could not work out his position; but there was still some hope as the most important part of the naval entrance exam was said to be the interview by the Board of Admirals, and many encouraging stories were in circulation to prove that he who impressed the Admirals personally was well on his way to conquering the written papers.

There were about a dozen boys at the vicarage, some of my age trying to pass the common entrance exam to public schools and an older group who had finished with school and were trying to pass examinations for universities. Some of these had been removed under a cloud from public schools.

Having been expelled myself from Heatherdown, I had a certain amount in common with these, but not nearly so much as one large ex-Etonian thought. At first I was flattered by his attentions and was naïve enough to think he liked me for myself. He took me for bicycle rides and stood me ice-cream cornets by the gross. Then one day he took me for a walk in the beechwoods.

It was a very dreary experience and the laws on homosexuality being what they still are, I am certainly not going into it in any great detail here. Suffice to say that I came out

30

of the wood with a ten and sixpenny second-hand accordion which I had admired in a junk shop in Loudwater.

I think I had visions of owning a whole orchestra. In any event, I could not wait to tell everyone how easy it was to obtain musical instruments.

I was interrogated by Pa Browning and a large, black taxi came and took the large ex-Etonian away.

The day of the naval entrance exam finally dawned. I was scrubbed from head to toe and, shining like a new sixpence, was dumped with several hundred other applicants in a forbidding morgue of a building, next to Burlington Arcade.

My French, English, history and geography were all pretty reliable and I had been primed with a few questions in arithmetic, algebra and geometry that Pa Browning was sure would come up. I had those answers down pat, but above all I was rehearsed in how to behave in front of the Admirals.

'Be quick and intelligent without being smug or cheeky,' said Pa Browning.

'If you don't know the answer to a question – make one up quickly – don't just dither. Remember above all the boy who was asked to give the names of the three most famous Admirals in British naval history – "Admiral Nelson, sir; Admiral Drake, sir; and I didn't quite catch your name sir".'

The first exam was the medical one.

Half a dozen at a time, we were stripped naked and to test our hearts, made to climb ropes without using our legs; then the usual tapping of knees and peering into ears, mouths and eyes took place.

Finally, 'get on your marks as though you were going to run a hundred yards'. Once in position, a large hand grabbed our testicles from the rear. 'Cough!' came the order. One poor little brute thought the man said 'Off!' and leaped eagerly forward. He was still being rubbed with ice when I was fully dressed and waiting to be summoned by the Admirals.

A bemedalled Master-at-Arms approached me in the ante-room.

'All right you, you're next, now go and sit at that desk. You'll find a pencil and paper there. You have five minutes to write a funny story – got it?'

I repressed my urge to indulge in lavatory humour and I

don't remember what I wrote but it was certainly plagiarism in its finest form as I had read it the day before in an old *Punch*.

Clasping my funny story, I followed the Master-at-Arms into a long panelled room. Seated round a table was a drift of Admirals. One or two wore beards; all were bound to the elbows with gold braid and clanking with medals.

They seemed rather bored. One took my funny story and read it then passed it to his neighbour. Out of the corner of my eye I watched it progress as questions were fired at me.

'Have you had any relations in the Navy?'

I dug up a distant cousin who fought at Jutland.

'How does a petrol engine work?'

I knew.

'What was the number of the taxi you came in, this morning?'

'I walked, sir.'

'There is a blank map on the wall over there, go and point out Singapore.'

I jabbed a desperate finger in the region of Bangkok.

'Why do you want to go into the Navy?'

'I want to be an Admiral, sir.'

(I think I overdid it a bit there.)

After a few more fairly inane questions to which I gave answers of equal non-distinction, the most heavily bearded of the Admirals spoke up.

'One last question – why were you expelled from Heatherdown?'

That really rocked me but I should have realised they would have done their homework.

There was no point in trying to work round that one so I put on what I hoped was 'the boy stood on the burning deck' expression –

'I put some dog's mess in a box, sir, and sent it to a sick friend.'

It sounded quite awful the way I said it and a long silence followed my announcement.

'You thought that was funny?'

'Yes, sir.'

'But your headmaster did not – correct?'

'Yes, sir.'

'I see. Well, fortunately, we don't have dogs aboard ship.'

Hearty laughter greeted this sally, and I was so grateful to the old man. I quite oddly said,

'Thank you, sir.'

I believe I passed the interview and I was bullish after most of the written papers. The last one to confront me was mathematics.

Not one of the carefully learned problems so confidently predicted by Pa Browning came up and my total score in the subject was 28 out of a possible 300.

Not unnaturally, the Royal Navy decided that it could rub along without me. So, aged twelve and a half, it was 'back to the old drawing board'.

CHAPTER THREE

THE English public schools have been operating for a long time: some for a very long time indeed. Eton was founded in 1440, and Winchester even earlier, in 1378. Rugby, where that horrible little boy picked up a soccer ball and charged off with it, started in 1567 and Oundle, ten years before that. Cheltenham and Marlborough, having opened their doors for the first time in the early eighteen-forties, were probably the youngest additions to the well-known list, until in 1923, Stowe came along.

Stowe School was established not, as were the others, by Kings, Archbishops or Lord Mayors but by a consortium of educators and hard-headed businessmen who saw the possibilities for a new public school and hoped to make a good thing out of it.

Stowe House, the vast Georgian home of the extinct Dukes of Buckingham, had become the debt-ridden property of a kinsman – the Master of Kinloss.

He, like my father, was slaughtered during the war to end all wars, and his mother, like mine, was forced to liquidate.

The consortium obtained this magnificent house and several hundred acres of grounds. Clough Williams-Ellis, the architect of Portmeirion in North Wales, was enlisted to transform it. A prospectus was issued and Stowe was on its way heralded as 'the New Great Public School'.

In these early post-war years, a whole stratum of suddenly well-to-do industrialists found the established public schools, to which they longed to send their sons, already bulging at the seams, so the consortium had no problem whatever in finding clients. Discovering a young aggressive headmaster with new ideas was far more difficult. They made a most fortunate choice – a young housemaster from Lancing College – J. F. Roxburgh.

In May of 1923, the school opened with less than a hundred boys. Somewhere in the depths of the Carlton Club, 'Tommy' heard rumblings; they could have been fulminations because a leading article in *The Times* and the Headmaster of

Eton, Edward Lyttelton, in that year both opined that instead of starting a new public school it would be far more sensible to enlarge the facilities of the old ones. Whatever they were, the rumblings sank in. Pa Browning was instructed to investigate this last resort and in July, I was sent over to Stowe, 30 miles in the dilapidated village taxi, to be interviewed by 'J.F.' Roxburgh.

Stowe must be the most beautiful school in England. Golden stone colonnades, porticos by Vanbrugh, sweeping lawns, huge lakes, long green valleys, glorious avenues, a Corinthian arch, a Palladian bridge and scores of assorted grottoes and 'temples d'amour' from each of which, through spectacular beech woods, rides open up to show other more fascinating 'follies'. Robert Adam, Grinling Gibbons, Kent, Valdré and Borra combined to produce glowing, beautifully proportioned interiors. Roxburgh, in his first public speech as Headmaster, said, 'Every boy who goes out from Stowe will know beauty when he sees it for the rest of his life.'

How true, but the apprehensive, small boy who waited in the Headmaster's flower-filled garden on that warm summer evening, saw nothing of the architectural and landscaped beauties around him. All he knew was that he had never in all his life wanted anything so much as to be accepted for that school – it just felt right and he longed passionately to be part of it.

Roxburgh finally appeared. Very elegant, he seemed, with a spotted bow tie, very tall, curly hair parted in the middle.

He came out through the french windows of his study and crooked his finger at me. Then he smiled, put an arm round my shoulders and led me to a stone bench.

'Now, my dear man,' he said, 'you seem to have had a lot of ups and downs – tell me about it.'

I don't pretend to have total recall but I do remember those words – I will never forget them.

He listened sympathetically as I told him my version of my life so far. When I had finished, he remained silent for what seemed like an eternity. Then he stood up and said, 'I'll walk with you to the car.' On the way through the school, he showed me the Assembly Hall and the Library and pointed out the fabulous view from the top of the South Front steps across sloping, green pastures to a lake, then up to the

35

towering Corinthian arch. Several times he spoke to boys who passed us, each time addressing them by their Christian names.

When he reached the ancient taxi, he looked down at me and smiled again, then he said, 'There will be two hundred new boys coming next term and you will be in Chandos House. Your housemaster will be Major Haworth.'

I mumbled something then climbed into the taxi and wept.

In September I arrived at Stowe along with the other new boys. As we outnumbered the old boys by two to one, everybody, masters included, for the first couple of weeks, sported pieces of white cardboard pinned to their coats showing their name in bold print, rather like a dentists' convention in Chicago.

One of Roxburgh's better new ideas was to break with the traditional prison garb of the older establishments; no top hats, stiff collars or straw boaters for us ... the boys wore grey flannel suits on weekdays and blue suits on Sunday.

Rules were sensible and good manners were encouraged: for instance hands had to be removed from pockets when passing masters or visiting parents. There were no 'bounds' and boys were allowed to have bicycles. As, however, one had to pedal three miles to get out of the school grounds, this was a little more strenuous than it sounded.

I could not believe my good fortune. The boys seemed nice and friendly albeit as bemused for the first few days as I was and Major Haworth, lately a company commander at Sandhurst, was one of the kindest and gentlest of men.

People are sharply divided about their schooldays and contrary to what one tells one's children about their being the best days of one's life, most people remember them with distaste.

Stowe, in those early days, was different from any other school. At the start, we were all the same age − around thirteen. Within four years, as the number of boys swelled from three hundred to five hundred, there was an annual intake of younger ones but somehow it seemed as though we all grew up together and I for one enjoyed the whole thing immensely. Inevitably, my inherent weakness of not being able to stand prosperity got me into trouble, but for the first couple of years, I was a fairly reliable citizen.

Roxburgh dominated the scene and I worshipped the man.

The first to notice some special interest being shown by a boy, Roxburgh nurtured it, fostered it and made the boy feel a little bit special because of it. How he did this, I shall never know, but he made every single boy at that school feel that they, and what they did, were of real importance to the Headmaster. Boys were always addressed by their first names and encouraged to build radio sets, to fence and play golf and tennis besides the usual school games, to paint, play the piano or the bagpipes and to keep pets, though this last got a little out of control as the boys grew older and instead of rabbits and ferrets being the status symbols, monkeys, bears, hyenas and skunks filled the cages. Finally, the school zoo was shut down for reasons of noise and smell.

I played the trombone and the drum in the school band and started a house magazine, to which 'J.F.' subscribed, called *The Chandosian*. I also by the age of fourteen fell in love once more with milk chocolate and became almost entirely conical in shape. My nickname was Podger or Binge and I went bright pink after Rugger. Another boy, named Smallman, was even fatter than I was; his nickname was unoriginal – 'Tiny'. 'Tiny' Smallman was very large indeed and we both became self-conscious about our physical defects. Tiny found an ad in a boys' paper and we spent our pocket money on strange tubes containing a foul-smelling green paste which, when rubbed on to the stomach or bottom, was guaranteed to reduce it in size. After football, we waited till the others had left the changing room rather than take a shower in public.

Because of my shape, I was enlisted in the school plays, usually playing a mushroom or something fairly unobtrusive ... I got the call of the greasepaint, however, and before I left, I was running the school concerts and giving myself all the best parts.

I studied fairly hard, though permanently stymied by mathematics, and my immediate goal was the School Certificate, a public exam for which one sat between 15 and 16 and which, provided one obtained enough 'credits', was comparable with 'O' and 'A' levels today. One of the 'credits' which one had to obtain in order to get the School Certificate

37

was mathematics, so from a very early date 'J.F.' saw to it that I took special tuition to try and defeat the monster.

My long-term goal, thanks to some pretty nifty salesmanship by Major Haworth, became the Royal Military College, Sandhurst, followed by a commission in the Argyll and Sutherland Highlanders.

School, between thirteen and fifteen, therefore, presented no great problems and the holidays, too, went along very nicely during this period of formation. Tommy being persona non grata at Rose Cottage, the summers were bliss: for Christmas Grizel and I were packed off to spend the holiday at Nanpanton, in Leicestershire, with the Paget family — where the children, Peter and Joan, were of identical vintage.

Their father, Edmund, was, with a splendid figure named Algy Burnaby, joint-Master of the Quorn Hunt; Barbara, their mother, was a garrulous, gossipy, enchanting, shop-talking, fox huntress who rode side-saddle under a top hat bigger than Tommy's, swore like a trooper and, along with the rest of her family, never could grasp the fact that Grizel and I were not actually afraid of horses — we were just too impecunious to hunt. We loved the Pagets.

Easter holidays in English schools being short — three weeks — Tommy would arrange to be away while my mother found a variety of places in which to house us. Sometimes, it was Bembridge, but Rose Cottage was barely habitable at that time of year. Once we were sent to a sister of Tommy's who lived in a noisome little flat in Portsmouth — far too near the Bollards and the scenes of my crimes for comfort — but the worst was when Tommy decided to be a real estate tycoon.

He bought a poky little house in a back street behind Windsor Castle. It was a dark panelled purgatory, whose sole charm lay in the fact that it had once belonged to Nell Gwyn and much Royal thrashing around was said to have gone on in the four-poster upstairs. It poured with rain for the entire holiday and Grizel and I, wearing overcoats, played Mah-Jongg in semi-darkness for three weeks. I hope I never again have to set eyes on the Bamboos, the Flowers, the Winds, the Seasons and all those miserable Dragons. I couldn't wait to get back to Stowe.

The memorable Easter holiday of this period came just after my fourteenth birthday.

Tommy's real estate operations found us, for a while, the inhabitants of 110 Sloane Street, a small house of many floors which shook as the buses went past the door: petrol-driven red Metropolitan buses, numbers 19 and 22 and – far more fascinating to me because they were driven by steam – the white Nationals, No. 30.

My brother, who had left the Navy because of chronic sea sickness and sensibly switched to the Army, was abroad with his regiment in India. Joyce and Grizel both had tiny bedrooms but there was no room for me so I slept in a minute cubicle in a boarding-house in St. James's Place, some distance away.

Every night after dinner, I walked to Sloane Square, boarded a 19 or a 22 headed for Piccadilly, got off at the Ritz Hotel and proceeded down St. James's Street to my iron bed, wooden floor, stained jug and basin and po under the bed.

The next morning, I had to be back for breakfast at eight o'clock and I was given fourpence a day for the round trip. Even my rudimentary mathematics could work out that by walking four miles a day, I could save almost half a crown a week.

I enjoyed my nocturnal travels very much and soon gave up going straight from Sloane Street to St. James's Place and took to going all the way down Piccadilly to Piccadilly Circus to watch the electric signs.

Every night, I became more adventurous and after a week or so, I knew the area bounded by Park Lane, Oxford Street, Regent Street and Pall Mall like the back of my hand. This was a pretty safe area for a fourteen-year-old, indeed, it never crossed my mind that it could be otherwise, and apart from being spoken to a few times by strange men who asked me if I would like to go home with them to meet their dogs or see their paintings, I tramped around unhindered.

It seemed to me perfectly normal for a boy to be walking around the West End of London at night so I saw nothing out of the ordinary in the number of girls who were doing the same thing: cloche hats, flesh-coloured stockings and the forerunner of the mini-skirt being the vogue, I saw a vast amount of female legs and ankles twinkling their way up and down the same streets that I frequented.

Bond Street was a great favourite of mine because many of the shops were lit up all night, and I made it a point, after watching BOVRIL, IRON JELLOIDS and OWBRIDGE'S LUNG TONIC change colours in Piccadilly Circus, to check on how things looked in the windows of Gerrards, Aspreys and Ciro Pearls.

Some of the girls, I noticed, were walking every night on the same streets and I was soon on nodding terms with them though I didn't understand at all the remarks made as I passed, nor the giggles that followed me.

One night, in Bond Street, I noticed a really superior pair of legs in front of me and I became so fascinated by them that I followed them for quite a distance. The girl seemed to have many friends and stopped and spoke to them from time to time.

The next night, I skipped going to watch the electric signs, and went looking for those legs instead. I searched up and down Bond Street and cased the side streets too, Clifford Street, Savile Row and even Burlington Street, the scene of my naval defeat.

Just as I was about to give up, the girl came out of a house right in front of me and walked rapidly off towards Piccadilly. I followed and when she stopped on a corner to talk to a couple of lady friends, I crossed the street and pretended to look into a shop window. I managed to get a fairly good view of her face. She was laughing and talking ... very lively, very gay, and her face looked beautiful in an open, fresh, English rose kind of way – blonde, blue eyes, high colour – you know the sort of thing.

She stayed there talking to her friends and as I didn't want to be conspicuous, I moved off towards my boarding house.

When I woke up in the morning I knew I must be in love. At least, I suspected that I was because I could think of nothing else but this girl. The day dragged on interminably, a shopping morning with my mother and in the afternoon, playing among the stunted, grimy bushes of the gardens opposite our house with some stunted, grimy, Spanish children.

That night, after dinner, I didn't walk, I was in a hurry. I took the bus and was lucky. After cruising up and down for what seemed an age, my patience was rewarded and my heart gave a lurch as I saw her lovely, long legs approaching from the Piccadilly direction. She was with a distinguished-looking, grey-haired man in a dinner jacket. He wore an opera hat and was smoking a cigar – obviously her father. Together they went into the house in Cork Street and, deliriously happy that I had found out where my dream lived, I took myself off to bed.

It took three days or rather nights of patient toil and careful sleuthing before I finally met Nessie.

I was following her at what I imagined to be a discreet distance, my eyes glued to her wondrous underpinnings, when she stopped and turned so suddenly and so unexpectedly, that I nearly bumped into her.

'Wot the 'ell are you followin' me for?' she demanded.

I went purple.

'I wasn't following you,' I lied. 'I was just on my way to bed.'

'Well, for Gawd's sake go on 'ome, mate. For the last four nights you've been stuck to me like my bleedin' shadow. Wot d'yer want anyway?'

I stammered and looked wildly to right and left. Suddenly she softened and smiled.

'All right, it's still early and you're a bit young but come on home and I'll give yer a good time.'

Soon she turned into her doorway and in a daze I followed, unable to believe my good fortune.

'A good time' she had said – it had to be at least a ginger beer and listening to the gramophone ... Eileen Stanley singing 'When it's moonlight in Kaluha' perhaps. In a high state of expectancy, I mounted to the second floor behind my glorious new friend.

The flat, above a tailor's shop, was small and smelled of cabbage. In the living-room there was a large divan with a lot of satin cushions and some dolls on it and nearby a small lamp with a red shade. A small kitchen stove was behind a screen. The other room was a bedroom, also rather poorly lit: a tiny bathroom was just discernible in the gloom beyond the huge bed that seemed to sag quite a lot in the middle.

'Three quid,' she said, as she took off her coat.

I didn't quite get the message so she came very close to me and peered into my eyes.

41

'Three quid,' she repeated, 'that too much?'

I gulped and floundered –

'For what?'

'For the best yer've ever 'ad, mate, but then you 'aven't 'ad a lot 'av yer? 'Ow old are yer anyway?'

I was still unsure as to exactly what ground I was on and I kept wondering if her father lived downstairs but I managed to mumble the truth.

'*Fourteen*!!' she practically shrieked. 'Wot the 'ell d'yer think I am – a bleeding' nannie?'

Then she started giggling, 'Oh my Gawd, wot a larf. 'Ow old d'yer think I am anyway?'

'Twenty,' I suggested tentatively.

'Three years yet before that 'appens,' she said. 'Well, come on, let's get on wiv it, *fourteen* ... Gawd, you are a one aren't yer?'

I watched half in fascination, half in apprehension as she walked about the living-room, taking off her little hat and blouse and unhooking her skirt.

''ere, take a look at these in case you need any 'elp.' With that she sat me down on the divan and left me to look at a large album of photographs.

'I'll be ready in a jiffy, dear.' She disappeared into the bedroom.

I had not so far been exposed to any pornography so the contents of that album very nearly finished off my sex life before it got under way. Hideous over-weight ladies, clad only in shoes and stockings, being mounted from every angle by skinny little men with enormous 'prongs': combinations of every sort in threes and twos, all with expressions of the greatest sincerity – and all apparently in advanced middle age.

The awful truth began to filter through my brain.

When Nessie appeared in the bedroom door dressed in the same uniform as the buxom ladies in the album – naked except for black stockings, held above the knees by pink garters with blue roses on them and pink high-heeled shoes – she had a small towel in her hand.

'Come along, ducks, let's see 'ow good you are ... you can wash in 'ere ... I've put in permanganate,' she added. In a daze, I followed here into the dark little bedroom ... another red shaded lamp was beside the bed ... 'over there, dear,' she said, indicating a kidney shaped enamel bowl on a collapsible knee-high stand. She threw me the towel, lay on the bed and put a record on a portable gramophone. The tune has, rather naturally, haunted me ever since. 'Yes ... we have no bananas.' As I was to discover later, Nessie had a wonderful native wit but I still believe her selection at that particular moment was a random one.

'Get a move on, ducks, you don't get all night for three quid, yer know. Get your shirt off for a start.'

I took off my coat and my shirt and started to wash my hands in the bowl.

'Christ!' she yelled, sitting bolt upright, 'not your bleedin' 'ands yer dickie bird! Just a minute,' she went on more gently, 'come 'ere, come and sit on me bed, I want to talk to you ... Now look me in the eye, straight ... is this the first ... 'ave yer ever done it before? ... ever done any fuckin'?'

Miserably, I shook my head.

'And you 'aven't got three quid either I'll bet?'

Again I shook my head and mumbled some inane explanation.

'Aw you poor little bastard,' she said, 'you must be scared out of yer fuckin' wits.' She looked at me reflectively, 'Ever seen a naked woman before?'

'No,' I confessed.

'Well, this is wot it looks like — 'ow d'yer like it?' I smiled weakly and tried not to lower my eyes. Nessie snuggled down and started to giggle again, a deliciously infectious sound.

'Well, you've got this far — why don't you take the rest of your clobber off and pop into bed?'

'What about the ...' I began.

'Oh, you owe me three quid,' she interrupted. 'Christ, I never thought I'd be seducing children ... FOURTEEN ... come on, jump in then.'

'Yes ... we have no bananas' was substituted for something a little more encouraging — the bedside lamp with the red shade was left on and Nessie with her wondrous skin became a most understanding teacher. 'There we are, dear, that's it now — take a little weight on your elbows like a gentleman. Slowly, dear, more slowly — whoa! yer not a fuckin' woodpecker, yer know ... slowly ... *that's* it, enjoy

yerself ... there, that's nice isn't it, dear ... are yer 'appy? ...
'appy now?'

By the time the Easter holidays ended, Nessie had become
the most important thing in my life: my education at her
hands, and in a way at her expense, had continued. She
'worked' at night and slept late but on many afternoons we
met, usually at the entrance to a small movie house – she
loved W. S. Hart – or we went to the music halls, the
Coliseum, the Alhambra or the Palladium, to see Herbert
Mundin, Lily Morris, Rebla, the juggler, or a marvellous
pair of young acrobats – Nervo and Knox. The seats cost one
shilling and threepence and after the shows we had a cup of
tea and a bun in a little tea shop, or we skipped the tea and
the bun and went directly back to her flat. Afterwards, I
would walk down to Sloane Street for a dreary family dinner
during which Tommy would rattle those damn cuff-links in
his starched shirt to draw attention to the fact that I had my
elbows on the table.

Quite early in my relationship with Nessie, I made the
elementary mistake of asking her why she did it ... 'a sweet
girl like you'. She rounded on me like a tigress: 'Now don't
you start trying to reform me. About three times a week some
silly bugger asks the same friggin' question.'

'Look, I'm three years older than you and I'm doing it
because I want to do it ... why I want to do it is none of your
fuckin' bizness so if you don't like it – piss off back to
school.'

Back at school for the summer term, I found that my life
had changed fundamentally. Nessie or the thoughts of Nessie
became the focal point of my existence. What I saw in her
was fairly obvious but there were other things too; quite
apart from the normal and very special physical attachment
to 'the first', she gave me something that so far had been in
rather short supply – call it love, understanding, warmth,
female companionship or just 'ingredient X' – whatever it
was, it was all over me like a tent.

I can't believe that I contributed very much to Nessie's
well-being or peace of mind during this period – a fat fourteen
and a half with no money and less experience – but apart
from the 'hurly burly of the chaise longue', as Mrs. Patrick
Campbell once described a splendid activity, there also grew

up between us a brother-sister relationship that was to last for many years.

Thanks to Nessie's insistence, I lost weight, a lot of extra padding turned to muscle and I became quite a proficient athlete of the second rank ... house colours for practically everything and a frequent performer before I left Stowe in the 1st XI cricket, the 1st XV Rugby Football and in the fencing and boxing teams.

Nessie came down to Stowe to see me in summer and brought a picnic basket and a tartan rug. Together we took full advantage of the beauties of the school grounds. She had never been out of London before and these trips to the country, she told me later, gave her a peace she never knew existed. She took a great interest in my progress at the school and became so intrigued by my hero worship of Roxburgh, that she insisted on meeting him. Basely, I tried to avoid this confrontation but Nessie was not easily put off.

'Look, dear, 'e'll never know I'm an 'ore. 'E'll think I'm yer bleedin' aunt or somefing ... Do I look like an 'ore?'

I told her she looked beautiful and like a duchess — not that looking like a duchess was much of a compliment but she was as easily flattered as she was hard to dissuade.

'That's 'im, innit?' she cried one Saturday afternoon, looking across towards the cricket pavilion. Roxburgh was approaching our tartan rug, resplendent in a pale grey suit topped by the inevitable spotted bow tie.

Nessie stood up, bathed in sunlight. She was wearing a short white silk summer dress that clung lovingly to her beautiful body; her honey coloured hair was cut in the fashion of the time — the shingle; she had a small upturned nose; she looked wonderfully young and fresh.

Roxburgh came over smiling his famous smile, 'May I join you?'

I introduced him.

''e's just like you told me,' said Nessie in a stage whisper.

''e's beautiful,' and then to Roxburgh. 'Don't look a bit like a schoolmaster dew yew, dear?'

J.F. settling himself on the rug missed a tiny beat but thereafter never gave any indication that he was not talking to a beautiful duchess.

He stayed about ten minutes, extolling the glories of Stowe

House and its history, and Nessie bathed in the full glow of his charm. Never once did he ask any loaded questions and when he got up to leave, he said, 'David is very lucky to have such a charming visitor.' The charming visitor nearly got me expelled a year later but it was certainly not her fault.

In the summer of 1926, by now a robust sixteen-year-old and appreciably ahead of my time in worldly experience, Roxburgh must have sensed a change in me. He sent for me and told me that I was one of four boys he had selected to become 'monitors' in a new house – Grafton, which was to open the following term.

The housemaster was coming from Fettes, Mr. Freeman, and the boy chosen as prefect or head of the house was Bernard Gadney.* It was a huge compliment for any boy, but for me to feel that J.F. had this faith in me was an enormous boost. However, before I could bask in the glories of my new responsibilities. I had to overcome a slight hazard – the School Certificate. I was to sit for the exam in two weeks' time. It was a sort of long shot really . . . if I failed this time, I would still have three more chances but I had to obtain the certificate soon in order to qualify to sit for the entrance exam to the Royal Military College, Sandhurst, eighteen months hence.

Apart from the dreaded mathematics, I was quite confident that I could pull it off this first time. My prospects in the new house were very exciting, my fat had disappeared, I had many friends at school and at Bembridge, I had Nessie in the background and I was at last beginning to get to know and to love my mother. In fact, everything was 'roses' for me. Then that damn wind started puffing those weeds in my direction once more.

I sat for the exam in the big school gymnasium and made mincemeat of the first two papers, French and history, and after the science, geography and English papers, I remained supremely confident. The last two tests were mathematics and Latin translation. In mathematics, as already explained, a 'credit' (about 80 per cent) was obligatory; without it, I would fail in the whole exam. When the questions were put on my desk, and all over the country at that particular

* B. C. Gadney was later to captain the English XV in many Rugby Internationals.

moment identical papers were being put in front of thousands of nervous boys, I took a deep breath and started to read.

One glance was enough. It was hopeless. I knew that I just couldn't cope and there is no more suffocating feeling when sitting for a public examination.

I made a few vague stabs at the geometry questions and a token effort at the algebra but there was no point in my even trying to tackle the arithmetic.

I was the first boy to hand in his answers and leave the gymnasium. I went out to the cricket nets and faced the fact that the School Certificate was certainly not going to be mine this time.

Nessie was coming to see me the next day – a Saturday – and her train was due at Buckingham Station at midday. The Latin exam was scheduled from ten o'clock till eleven-thirty, so I decided to get through this now useless and unprofitable period as quickly as possible, pedal down to the station and surprise her there instead of meeting her as planned near the Corinthian arch at twelve-thirty.

It so happened that my Latin teacher was the supervisor of the candidates on that Saturday morning, which meant that it was he who would hand out the questions at the start, collect the answers at the end and in between, wander about the rows of desks making sure that there was no talking, or, perish the thought, any use of notes.

He knew that I could easily pass the Latin exam but only I knew that it was now useless to try.

The trick then was to complete the whole paper in half the time and be on my way to Buckingham Station. Archie Montgomery-Campbell was a good and outstanding friend who occupied the desk on my right during the whole week of exams. He was also an excellent Latin scholar, so I enlisted his help.

The Latin paper was in two parts, prose and verse. It was agreed that I would quickly dispose of the prose while Archie coped first with the verse. Then, after making his fair copy, he would crumple up his first draft and drop it on the floor between the two desks. It was clearly understood between us that if anything went wrong, Archie would merely say that he had thrown away his first translation after he had made

47

his fair copy and if somebody picked it up it was none of his business. The dirty work was to be done by me alone; he was to be blameless.

It all went beautifully according to plan. I copied out Archie's verse translation beneath my own effort at the prose, handed in my paper, and bicycled happily off in plenty of time to surprise Nessie.

We spent a blissful day together, eating shrimp paste sandwiches and sausage rolls, drinking shady-gaff* and rolling around on the tartan rug. Nessie had begun to tell me a little more about herself and I listened adoringly that afternoon to her descriptions of her childhood in a Hoxton slum; six children in a tiny room, the three youngest in the bed, the others sleeping on the floor and all cowering away from the drunken Friday night battles between the parents.

At fifteen she and her sister of a year older had run away. For a while, they found work as waitresses in dingy tea shops and restaurants in Battersea and Pimlico. A few months later they were engaged as hostesses in a sleazy 'club' in Wardour Street. Then the sister started taking drugs and one night told Nessie she was going North with a boy friend to avoid the police. Nessie didn't miss her much and soon was employed by Mrs. Kate Meyrick at the 43 Club. She had to be on hand in evening dress as a 'dancing partner', making a fuss of 'Ma' Meyrick's rather high class clientele and persuading them to buy champagne at exorbitant prices.

She was not allowed to solicit on the premises – a rule that was strictly enforced because 'Ma' Meyrick's establishment was often infiltrated by police officers in evening clothes, posing as the tipsy aftermath of regimental dinners or bachelor parties, but, in fact, contacts were easily enough made and Nessie soon built up the basis of an enthusiastic clientele.

'I'm not an 'ore wiv an 'eart of bleedin gold, you know, dear, I'm out for everything I can get out of this game for another couple of years – then I'm going to marry some nice Yank or Canadian and fuck off abroad and 'ave kids.

'The only reasons I work the streets is that I'm on me own. I don't 'ave to sit in a Club all bleedin' night talkin' to a lot

* A mixture of beer and ginger beer.

48

of drunks. When I git tired, I can go 'ome and lock me fuckin' door ... I make much more money too, and the best bit, it's not like bein' one of those wotsits on the end of a phone. I can see wot I'm gettin'. If I don't like the look of a bloke, I don't ask 'em up, see.'

Watching Nessie while she talked, it seemed incredible that she could be leading this sort of existence – her very youth and yes, her very freshness were in complete contradiction to everything she was describing – 'A lot of blokes want to 'ave me all to themselves ... you know, set me up in a bleedin' flat in Maida Vale with a maid an' a fuckin' puppy but when the time comes – I'll set meself up. I've got to move out of Cork Street tho', it's gettin' so fuckin' noisy, dear, with that big ginger who's moved in above. An army officer by all accounts. 'E goes round the coffee stalls at Hyde Park Corner and picks up them corporals in their red tunics an' all, then he brings 'em 'ome and dresses himself up as a fuckin' bride, make-up, white satin, 'igh 'eels, a bleedin' veil, orange blossom – the lot. Then 'e chooses one of these blokes – 'e always 'as about 'arf a dozen of 'em up there at the same time – and 'e fuckin' *marries* him! Goes through a sort of service, then, arm in arm wiv 'is 'usband, 'e walks under a fuckin' archway of swords 'eld up by the other blokes. I've talked to a coupla soldiers – they're not gingers, mark you, far from it, but they pick up a coupla quid apiece for the job and a fiver for the 'usband.

''E doesn't lay an 'and on any of them, just plays the Weddin' March on 'Is Master's Voice an' shoots 'is wad walking under them fuckin' swords. But the noise, dear – Christ! I can't stand it! Everythink is very military, 'im being an ex-officer an' all, and when it's all over 'e gets back into 'is nice blue suit, sits down be'ind a table with a fuckin' army blanket on it and they all form up like a bleedin' Pay Parade. "Guardsman So-and-So." "Sir!" one pace forward march ... crash! Forty shillings ... SIR! about turn ... crash! NEXT MAN ... CRASH! SIR!! CRASH! CHRIST! ... those fuckin' army boots, dear. I'm going to 'ave to move.' ... She shook with delicious laughter.

'Of course, I don't get mixed up with no funny business myself ... it's just me and a bloke that's all ... No exhibitions, none of that stuff. Of course. I'm not saying I don't occasion-

49

ally pick up a little fancy money – watchin' 'em sit in cakes sometimes an' there's this little Aussie millionaire, dear, about fifty, who gets about eight of us up to 'is 'otel, then we all strip down to the stockin's and 'igh 'eels and 'e takes off everything! Then he gives us each an 'en pheasant's tail feather to stuff up the arse – 'ell of a job keepin' it in there it is because we 'ave to walk round in a circle – then, would you believe it, dear, 'e stands there in the middle with a cock pheasant's feather up 'is own arse and sprinkles corn on the fuckin' carpet. Of course we 'ave a terrible time not larfin' but if we do larf, we don't get paid and it's a tenner each too . . . Well, there he stands, kind of crowin' or whatever the 'ell cock pheasants do, and we all 'ave to kinda peck at the fuckin' corn . . . it's amazin' really, he shoots off right there all by 'isself in the middle of the circle. We never 'ave to touch 'im . . . pathetic really when you think.'

When Nessie went back to London after these outings, I always felt terribly lonely. I loved walking about the fields and woods with her. I've never seen anyone get such real pleasure out of trees and flowers and birds and it gave me a feeling of importance to be able to point out different animals and to tell her about life in the country.

Sadly, I waved her away at Buckingham station and pedalled up the long avenue in time for evening chapel.

The whole school attended chapel twice a day and, after the evening service, announcements of special importance were made by the Headmaster.

In chapel about three weeks after Nessie's visit, J.F. motioned the boys to remain in their places. An expectant murmur arose.

'All over the country,' J.F. began, 'overworked examiners have been correcting several thousand papers sent in for this year's School Certificate examinations.

'Stowe is a new school and these same examiners have been looking at the papers sent in by us with special interest.

'Boys who sit for a public examination are representing their schools in public and they, therefore, have a very great responsibility. Schools are judged by the boys who represent them.

'It is, therefore, with grief and great disappointment that I have to tell you that two boys representing Stowe in the

School Certificate have been caught cheating. I shall question the two concerned this evening and I shall deal with them as I see fit.'

Only when I saw Archie Montgomery-Campbell's ashen face did the horrible truth sink in. As the school rose to leave the chapel, my legs turned to water.

CHAPTER FOUR

RATINGS of the Royal Navy have always prided themselves on the fact that without any official signals being made, news and gossip passes between ships at anchor with a rapidity that makes African tribesmen blush over their tom-toms. The ratings themselves would have blushed that day: ten minutes after chapel, the whole school knew who were the two culprits. Perhaps like people being attacked by dogs or run away with on horses, Archie and I smelled of fear.

Poor Archie was the first to be summoned to the Headmaster's study – he went off like Sydney Carton at the end of *A Tale of Two Cities*. A quarter of an hour later, I was located near the lavatories where I had been spending the interim.

No smile on J.F.'s face this time, just a single terse question, 'Have you anything to say for yourself?'

For the lack of any flash of genius that might have saved me, I told him the truth – that I had failed the exam anyway and wanted to get out early. I also added that Archie was completely guiltless and stood to gain nothing by helping me.

J.F. stared at me in silence for a long time, then he crossed the quiet, beautifully furnished room and stood looking out of the open french windows into the flower garden where he had first interviewed me. Cheating in a public examination is a heinous crime and it seemed inevitable that I would be expelled. I braced myself for the news as he turned towards me.

'Montgomery-Campbell made a stupid mistake in helping you with your Latin translation and I have given him six strokes of the cane. Until you stood there and told me the truth, I had every intention of expelling you from the school. However, in spite of your very gross misbehaviour, I still have faith in you and I shall keep you at Stowe. Now, I propose to give you twelve strokes of the cane.'

My joy at not being thrown out was quickly erased by the thought of my short-term prospect ... Twelve! that was terrifying! J.F. was a powerfully built man and his beatings, though rare, were legendary.

'Go next door into the Gothic Library. Lift your coat,

bend over and hold on to the bookcase by the door. It will hurt you very much indeed. When it is over, and I expect you to make no noise, go through the door as quickly as you wish. When you feel like it, go back to your house.'

The first three or four strokes hurt so much that the shock somehow cushioned the next three or four, but the last strokes of my punishment were unforgettable. I don't believe I did make any noise, not because I was told to avoid doing so, or because I was brave or anything like that – it hurt so much. I just couldn't get my breath.

When the bombardment finally stopped, I flung open the door and shot out into the passage. Holding my behind and trumpeting like a rogue elephant, down the stone passage, past the boiler rooms I went, out into the summer evening and headed for the woods.

After the pain subsided, the mortification set in. How was I going to face the other boys – a cheat? Obviously, my promised promotion to monitor would be cancelled and my remaining time at Stowe would be spent as an outcast.

Eventually, about bedtime, I crept up to my dormitory. It was a large room that accommodated twenty-five boys. The usual pillow fights and shouting and larking about were in full swing. They died away to an embarrassed silence as I came in. I took off my clothes, watched by the entire room. My underpants stuck to me and reminded me of my physical pain. Carrying my pyjamas I slunk off to the bathroom next door. An ominous murmur followed my exit.

In the bathroom mirror, I inspected the damage. It was heavy to say the least. Suddenly, Major Haworth's cheery voice made me turn, 'Pretty good shooting I'd call that . . . looks like a two-inch group.' He was his usual smiling, kindly self. 'When you've finished in here, get into bed. I'm going to read out a message the Headmaster has sent round the School . . . nothing to worry about.'

When everyone was in bed and quiet, the Major stood by the dormitory door and read from a piece of paper.

'I have interviewed the two boys connected with the School Certificate irregularities. Their explanations have been accepted by me and the boys have been punished. The incident is now closed and will not be referred to again by anyone.'

53

'Good night, everybody,' said the Major, and then with a wink at me – 'When that sort of thing happened to me I used to sleep on my stomach and have my breakfast off the mantelshelf.'

In the darkness, the whispers started – 'How many did you get?' ... 'Did you blub' ... 'What sort of cane is it?' ... 'Promise to show us in the morning'. All friendly whispers. In the darkness, I buried my face in my pillow.

I determined there and then that, somehow, I would repay J.F. I never could, of course, but I became, I think, a good and responsible monitor the next term and, in due course, after squeaking past a mathematical barrier, I passed into the Royal Military College, Sandhurst, and became one of the first three Stowe boys to gain commissions in the Regular Army.

Summer holiday at Bembridge followed immediately after ten days of Officers' Training Corps camp on Salisbury Plain. It was at one such camp that I first smelled success in front of an audience. Several hundred boys from many different schools were attending the camp concert in a huge circus tent. Someone had told Major Haworth that as Stowe was a new school, it would be a good thing if we were part of the programme and he had asked me to do something about it.

There was at that time in England a monologuist named Milton Hayes. I had one of his records at school and had memorised some of his stuff for the benefit of my friends. I must now belatedly apologise to Milton Hayes for stealing from his material, which is what in part I did, adding topical touches of my own to fit the situation at the camp.

His monologue was a take-off of a half-witted politician electioneering. I made mine a half-witted General, inspecting the camp. On the night of the concert, I sat outside the tent, waiting for my turn to go on. The boys were a rowdy audience and the noise from inside was deafening. There were a lot of boos. I experienced, for the first time, that delicious terror that has never left me – stage fright, and with rubbery knees, dry lips and sweating palms, I fought against the urge to dash madly away, grow a beard and emigrate to the Seychelles. At last I was called and I heard the Master of Ceremonies announce – 'Niven of Stowe'.

Miserably, I mounted the steps on to the stage, wearing the baggy General's uniform which Major Haworth had concocted for me. In my eye was a monocle and on my upper lip, a huge grey moustache.

Scattered applause and some laughter greeted my appearance.

The M.C. put up his hand — 'Major General Sir Useless Eunuch!' More laughter.

I gulped and prayed that the stage would open and swallow me up. Hundreds of boys in khaki filled the benches. The first three rows were occupied by officers in red Mess kit. I screwed my monocle into my eye and gazed at the officers . . .

'Sergeant-Major, why is it that these members of the band have no instruments?' I asked. A roar of delighted laughter filled the tent and suddenly, it was easy. Then lapsing into pilfered Milton Hayes —

'What we must do with this camp, Sergeant-Major, is find out where we stand, then get behind ourselves and push ourselves forward. We must get right down to the very roots, right down to rock bottom, then bring the whole thing up into one common pool . . . and looking around here at Salisbury Plain — and how very plain it looks — we should keep the ships at sea . . . the harbours will be much cleaner for one thing . . .' and so on for about ten minutes.

Milton Hayes and I were a riotous success that night and the harpoon of craving success as a performer was planted deep inside me.

Sailing entered my life about this time. My mother bought Grizel and me a twenty-five-year-old 14ft. sailing dinghy for £12. She was called *Merlin* and is still being sailed by children at Bembridge.

I became a good 'hand' and the pinnacle of my sailing career came late while I was still at Sandhurst and was chosen as a member of Great Britain's International Crew in the Cumberland Cup, a race for 8-metre yachts, during Ryde Week. With Sir Ralph Gore, the famous helmsman, in command, we in *Severn* easily defeated the French challenger *L'Etoile* in a best of three final.

First, however, Brian Franks and I formed the Bembridge Sailing Dinghy Club for children between twelve and eighteen. I was the first Secretary, Brian the first Captain. At the end of the first year, the Club showed a profit of £2 12s. 6d. which Brian and I transferred into liqueur brandy. We were both found next morning, face down in some nettles.

When you are a senior boy in an English Public School, you perhaps reach the pinnacle of your self-importance. Given hitherto undreamed of responsibilities and privileges, often receiving the acclaim, even the adulation of your juniors and sometimes served by 'fags',* it is very easy to get carried away.

The Royal Military College, Sandhurst, soon took care of that ... it is never pleasant to be treated like mud but Sandhurst, at least, did it with style and no malice afore-thought: it just came naturally.

We were called 'Gentlemen Cadets'. The officers and non-commissioned officer instructors were the pick of the whole British Army and the drill instructors were exclusively, the pick of the Brigade of Guards. Knowing you were due to become an officer in eighteen months' time, the N.C.O.'s could call you anything they liked provided they prefaced it with a 'Mr. So-and-So, Sir.'

There were about one thousand cadets at Sandhurst divided into Seniors, Intermediates and Juniors. The course was eighteen months so one spent six months in each category.

The Commandant was Major-General Sir Eric Girdwood, D.S.O., etc., etc.; the Adjutant was the famous Major 'Boy' Browning, Grenadier Guards, D.S.O. etc., later to command all British Airborne troops in World War II.

In No. I Company, my Company Commander was Major Godwin Austen, South Wales Borderers, M.C.; my Chief Instructor was Major 'Babe' Alexander,† Irish Guards, D.S.O., and the Company Sergeant Major was 'Robbo' Robinson, Grenadier Guards.

All these were completely splendid soldiers, with im-

---

* American friends are often appalled by this description of younger boys who clean the rooms and run messages for their seniors ... they need not be ... it is not an abbreviation of faggot.

† Brother of the famous wartime 'Alex'.

peccable and gallant records, and however tough they may sometimes have been, they always had a deep understanding and sympathy for the cadets under their command.

The Cadet under-officer* in charge of the Junior platoon to which I was assigned, was a shifty-looking customer with a broken nose named Wright – a singularly, unattractive piece of work. It was small wonder to any of us who knew him at Sandhurst that later, after changing his name to Baillie-Stewart and joining the Seaforth Highlanders he was caught selling military secrets to the Germans, court- martialled and imprisoned in the Tower of London.

The 'mud treatment' started on the first day of our ten weeks of concentrated drill 'on the square'. We were paraded in the civilian clothes in which we had arrived the day before. A strange assortment wearing suits, tweed jackets, plus-fours, hats, caps, boots, shoes and some with umbrellas, we smiled nervously at each other as we awaited the mini-strations of 'Robbo'.

Rapidly and with the minimum of trimmings, Robbo explained that although it looked unlikely at the moment, we were supposed to be officer material and it had fallen to his unfortunate lot to try, within eighteen months, to transform this ''orrible shower' into being worthy of the King's commission.

'I shall address you as "Sir" because that's the orders but when you speak to me you'll stand at attention, look me right in the eye and call me Staff . . . got it?'

Scattered murmurs of 'yes', 'right-ho' and 'jolly good' were silenced by one of the mightiest roars in the British Army.

'GOT IT !!! ??? Now let me hear the answer, Gentlemen . . . ONE, TWO, THREE' . . . 'GOT IT STAFF.' we roared back.

Quickly and efficiently we were stripped of umbrellas and walking sticks and shown how to come to attention, how to march and how to halt. Then, at a hair-raising speed we were marched one and a half miles to be issued with boots and canvas uniforms. Round and round the College we whizzed, sweating and apprehensive beneath the patronising

* In each Company, the five top cadets from Senior term became 'under officers'. They were the élite and wore Sam Browne belts.

glances of beautifully turned out older cadets to the barbers to be shorn like sheep, to the gym to be fitted with physical training outfits, to the stables for breeches, brown boots and leggings, to the laundry 'because I don't want to see a speck of dirt for the next year an' 'arf mind' and finally to the Chapel 'because 'ere, gentlemen, you can thank Almighty Gawd at the end of each week if you are still breathin'. Got it?' 'GOT IT STAFF!'

It was very hard and very exhausting – for the ten weeks on the square, we never stopped running, saluting, marching, drilling, climbing ropes, riding unmanageable chargers and polishing and burnishing everything in sight ... boots, belts, chinstraps, buttons, bayonets and above all our rifles ... 'the soldiers' best friend, mind.'

Normally, there were fifteen minutes between being dismissed from one parade and being inspected for the next in a totally different and spotless outfit. The slightest lapse, a finger mark on a brass button, a cap at the wrong angle or hair not mown like a convict was rewarded with the 'Defaulters' – a particularly gruelling extra drill in full battle order at the end of the day when everyone else was resting.

A rifle barrel imperfectly cleaned invariably meant 'Pack Drill' at the hands of the dreaded Wright – full battle order but with a difference: the pack was filled with sand and in place of normal drill movements, it was a case of being forced after supper to run up and down several flights of stairs with the offending rifle at arms length above the head, shouting at the top of our lungs 'Parade, Parade.'

The cadets incarcerated in their rooms, cleaning their equipment, made bets on how long each individual could stand punishment. Many defaulters found it a matter of honour to prolong their agony in order to impress their listening friends. I was a firm supporter of the doctrine of another group which sought kudos by pretending to pass out long before they would normally have collapsed.

In the riding school, the rough riding Sergeant Majors were particularly heartless. We had a beauty, an Irishman from the Inniskilling Dragoons called McMyn. At 6.30 on a Monday morning, winter and summer, he would be waiting for us with the same grisly joke ... 'Now then, gentlemen, I'm supposed to make mounted officers of all of you so let's see how many dismounted showers we can have here on this lovely morning ... Knot your reins. Cross your stirrups. Fold your bleedin' arms and split ass over the jumps ... go!' Carnage, of course, but in those strange days all officers, even in infantry regiments, had to know how to ride, and ride well.

The great thing about those first ten weeks was that although one was being treated like mud, it was at least grown-up mud. We were treated like men for the first time in our lives and as men we were expected to react.

Those weeks 'on the square' were sheer, undiluted hell. At weekends we were allowed no dining-out passes but by Saturday night we were so exhausted anyway that all we wanted to do was to fall into bed, underneath which was a dreadful receptacle described in Military Stores as 'one pot, chamber, china with handle, Gentlemen Cadets for the use of'.

At the end of the purgatory, we 'passed off the square' and settled down to learning other things in addition to physical training, drill, riding, bayonet fighting and more drill. Instruction was given us in organization and administration, in the manual of military law and of course in tactics and man management.

Of the two hundred and fifty 'Juniors' who passed off the square and still remained in one piece, four in each Company were promoted to Lance-Corporal. I was one of the lucky four in No. 1 Company and as there was now a little more time for leisure, I managed also to get a Rugger 'Blue' and played regularly for two seasons with the 1st XV.

I furthermore performed in a couple of College concerts, writing my own sketches, and played the lead opposite Mrs. Barcus, the wife of one of our Company officers, in *It Pays to Advertise*.

Nessie came down one Saturday to see the show which opened after a particularly gruelling afternoon's rugger battle against the R.A.F. College, Cranwell.

'Yew looked ever so nice up there on that stage, dear, but the sport's better for yew isn't it? – more balls, if yew know what I mean.'

My liaison with Nessie continued more or less full time all through my year and a half at Sandhurst. She still insisted that 'pretty soon I'm goin' to find that nice feller and fuck off to the Fiji Islands'. In the summer term, she came down for the June Ball, the big social event of the year. For the occasion she borrowed a magenta-coloured taffeta ball gown from a friend who danced in competitions on the outer London circuit. Her very great beauty and again, I say, her freshness overcame this extraordinary garment and I basked in her success as we waltzed and fox-trotted round the dusty gymnasium to the fluctuating rhythms of the Royal Military College Band.

Nessie was very specific about my seeing other girls – 'We're just together for the larfs and the fuckin', dear, so don't go gettin' serious wiv me or yew'll spoil it.'

In her wisdom she encouraged my friendships and listened apparently with enthusiasm when I told her I had met a beautiful young actress playing in a naval comedy in London by Ian Hay and Stephen King-Hall – *The Middle Watch* – Ann Todd.

Ann had a tiny part and was infinitely glamorous. I had never been backstage in my life before and she was single-handedly responsible for my becoming incurably stage-struck. I had an allowance of five pounds a month so I was not exactly a well-heeled 'stage door Johnny' but Ann was often sent free tickets for the opening of restaurants or night clubs which helped enormously.

Cadets in their Intermediate and Senior terms were allowed cars. Obviously, I did not own one but the wheels of friends were always available and Saturday night in London on a late pass became the focal point of the week.

In the Intermediate Term, I was promoted to full Corporal and received the ultimate accolade for that rank. Along with one other Corporal, Dick Hobson of No. 3 Company, I was appointed Commandant's Orderly for six months. This post was highly coveted and besides announcing to all and sundry that the holder of it was practically bound to become an Under Officer in his senior term, it also carried various 'perks'. One was excused Saturday morning Drill Parade, which meant early to London, and on Sunday, came the big moment . . . breakfast with the General, Sir Eric Girdwood.

Those breakfasts must have been pure hell for this splendid officer but week after week, he toyed with toast and coffee while Dick and I ploughed through acres of scrambled eggs and miles of sausages. Afterwards, while the General was being dressed in highly polished riding boots, Sam Browne belt and sword, Dick and I waited in the garden proudly holding silver sticks, on which were engraved the names of a hundred years of Commandants' Orderlies. Across our chests were white pipe-clayed belts to which, between our shoulder blades, very beautiful and heavily embossed silver Victorian message boxes were attached. Upon the appearance of the General, we formed up on either side of him and escorted him on to the parade, slow marching together ahead of him up the front rank and down the rear as he inspected his battalion of one thousand spotless cadets: then into chapel, trying not to skate with our hob-nailed boots on the black marble of the nave and, afterwards, leading his Sunday morning inspection of the College buildings, gymnasium, hospital, stables and so on.

The General was a most imposing and awe-inspiring figure with his chest full of medals and his bristling white moustache. He was also a God. A creature so far above the lowly cadet as to make his every word and gesture seem, to us, divine. Of the thousand at that moment under his command, perhaps one would ultimately attain his exalted position.

The silver message box nearly proved to be my undoing. So many cadets asked me what was in it that I decided to give them a little food for thought and I filled it with various commodities. Thereafter upon being asked the usual question I would reply, 'Commandant's personal supplies – take a look.' Inside they were delighted to find a packet of Woodbines, a box of Swan Vestas matches, a roll of toilet paper and a dozen French letters. I believe my purchases went a long way towards relieving the tedium of those Sunday mornings, and cadets, kept standing to attention far too long in all weathers, were deeply appreciative of the fact that visiting dignitaries, Kings, Presidents, Prime Ministers and Archbishops were invariably preceded in their inspection of the ranks by the pompous passing of this curious cargo.

One cloudless Sunday morning after breakfast, Dick Hobson and I were waiting for the General amidst the

61

rhododendrons of his garden when he suddenly changed his routine. Normally, he would issue from the house, booted, spurred, shining like a new pin and we would fall into step on either side of him, listening to his extremely engaging and relaxed small talk as he headed towards the barrack square where the battalion would be drawn up ready for inspection by him and on occasion by his V.I.P. guests.

Some five hundred yards from his house and just out of sight of the parade it was taken for granted that all informality would melt away and Dick and I would put our silver-headed orderly sticks under our left armpits and start our slow march for the tour of the ranks.

This beautiful June morning, however, he came out of the garden door and stopped in front of us.

'I think I'd better inspect you two fellers today,' he said.

We immediately sprang to attention secure and relaxed in the knowledge that we, too, were faultlessly turned out. I was on Dick's right, so the General looked first at my cap, chin, my buttons, my belt, my creases and my boots. Then, with a pace to the side and in the usual army fashion, he started on Dick from his boots to his cap. Round the back he went, inspecting Dick from the rear when Christ! I heard a little click as he opened Dick's Message Box.

The joke of what mine contained had long since been over, hardly anybody bothered to ask me any more what was in it – everyone knew – in fact I had forgotten all about it myself. The few seconds that it took the Commander to inspect Dick's rear view seemed to me to take until autumn. Finally, I heard his breathing directly behind me. I prayed he would move round to the front again without looking into my box. I promised God all sorts of rash things if he would arrange this for me, but he failed me. I felt rather than heard the General open my Box and I sensed him rustling about among its horrible contents – Woodbines, matches, lavatory paper and French letters! My military career was obviously over before it had even started and I toyed with the idea of falling on my bayonet among the rhododendron petals. Dick too had realised the full possibilities of the situation and started to vibrate like a harp string on my left, a condition brought about by a mixture of concern for his partner, suppressed laughter and keen anticipation of impending doom.

After an eternity, Major-General Sir Eric Girdwood stood before me. He looked for a long time at my sea-green face without saying a word. Staring blankly ahead, I waited for the axe to fall.

'Niven,' he said, 'I had heard about that ... thank you very much ... you are very considerate ...'

It was never referred to again, but immediately after Church Parade that day I cleared out my Message Box.

Life at Sandhurst was tough but it was exhilarating and the cadets were a dedicated corps d'élite. Some went on to command Divisions and even armies. Several among the dignified Sikhs and Pathans became leaders in their countries but a heartbreakingly high percentage were destined in little more than ten years' time to meet death on the beaches, deserts and hillsides of World War II, for this was the vintage of soldiers that suffered most heavily when the holocaust came.

Led by Major Godwin Austen and goaded almost beyond endurance by the much loved Robb Robinson No. 1 Company became champion Company and for the eighteen months I was at Sandhurst, I was one of the privileged, proudly wearing the red lanyard of the Champions.

If the work was hard, so was the play. Cadets in their senior term were allowed motor cars and a few well-heeled young men could be seen whizzing up the Great West Road, London-bound for weekends in an assortment of jalopies. Jimmy Gresham in my platoon, owned a Hillman Huskie and was most generous about giving his friends lifts. A very bright fellow destined for the Welsh Guards, he was highly resilient when it came to contretemps. For some mis-demeanour he was not allowed to use his car for several weeks but he solved this temporary inconvenience by keeping a chauffeur's uniform and a false moustache at White's Garage in Camberley and our weekly forays, to the capital continued without missing a beat.

Reggie Hodgkinson, an old Bembridge friend, also headed for the Welsh Guards, was a member of No. 3 Company housed across the Barrack Square in the new buildings. One night, having persuaded some kind friend to sign in for him before midnight, he was almost caught by the watchful

Robbo crossing our Parade Ground at 3 a.m. wearing a dinner jacket. Reggie arrived beating at my door, breathless – 'Give me a pair of pyjamas for Christ's sake, that bloody Robbo nearly nabbed me.' He quickly donned the pyjamas over his dinner jacket and dashed outside again.

From the window, I watched, fascinated, as Reggie, with closed eyes, gave it the full 'I come from haunts of coot and hern' treatment; arms stretched out before him, he ambled in the bright moonlight, straight across the Barrack Square towards No. 3 Company.

He soon realised that Robbo was walking beside him.

'Wod d'you think you're doin', Mr. 'Odgkinson, Sir?'

'Sleep walking, Staff.'

'Then sleep walk into the bleedin' Guard Room. Lef rite, lef rite . . . smartly now, swing the arms, Sir,' and my pyjamas disappeared at high speed in the direction of 'the cooler'.

It had long been decided that no stone would be left un-turned for me to be commissioned in the Argyll and Sutherland Highlanders once I had successfully passed out of Sandhurst. When I say it had been decided, I really mean that my mother had gone to a great deal of trouble to raise old influential friends of my father's from the days when we had lived in Argyllshire. For my part I was delighted at the prospect of joining such a glamorous regiment and revelled in the meetings that were arranged by one of my mother's advisers, the Colonel of the Regiment. The McClean of Loch Buie.

The McClean, three times during my days at Sandhurst, took me, all spruced up, to visit Princess Louise, sister of King George V, who was the honorary Colonel of the Regiment and who took a great interest in all things pertain-ing to that famous outfit.

The first time I was taken to visit her, I was instructed to meet the McClean at his London club so that he could check me over and among other things, teach me how to bow properly to Royalty – never, but never, any arching of the back or movement from the waist – that he informed me was strictly for head-waiters.

'Stand upright, my boy, look 'em right in the eye, then,

with a completely stiff back, a sharp, very definite inclination of the head, bringing the chin almost to the chest.'

I tried this rather painful manoeuvre several times and each time a peculiar squeaking sound issued from my undergarments. A minute inspection disclosed the fact that the new braces which I had purchased for the occasion, complete with a very complicated gadget – a sort of pulley effect ... little wheels over which passed elastic straps – had been delivered with a faulty wheel and this was complaining bitterly at the unusual strain that was being placed upon it. The McClean solved the problem by oiling the offending part with a dab of hair lotion.

The elderly Princess became a great ally and it was at her suggestion that I was invited to spend the day with the officers of the Regiment just before they embarked for service in the West Indies where I hoped to be joining them later. They were a gay and friendly group and Colonel and subalterns alike all made me feel confident of a warm welcome in about one year's time. All I had to do, they assured me, was to pass the final Sandhurst exams and I would be with them for sure.

Before I returned to Sandhurst for my last term and final exams, I spent what was to be my last holiday at Bembridge. The whole family, minus Tommy, was there. My mother, whom I had finally grown to love and to appreciate, presided over the gathering. 'Max' was back from India, having become disenchanted with soldiering. He had resigned his commission and gone to work as the Starter on the Bombay Race Course. This, too, had palled and his adventurous spirit had taken him to Australia, where for the past five years he had been working as a jackaroo (cowboy) on a cattle station new Yarra Weir. Now he was having a last long look at England before sailing away to take a job as manager of a banana plantation on Norfolk Island in the South Pacific.

Looking back on that period, I now realise that at eighteen I must, by today's standards, have been a very square member of a very square group. There seems to have been the minimum of rebellion against the Establishment. There was mass unemployment; conditions in the mines and shipyards were appalling. There were hunger marches and general strikes but my generation of students remained shamefully aloof. We did little or nothing in protest. Perhaps we were still very much in shock from realising that the cream of the generation immediately before ours had been wiped out. Perhaps there was no one left worth rebelling against and in my case, discipline was being pumped and bashed into me to such an extent that any sort of organised student revolt against authority, such as has now become the norm, was unthinkable. We drank a great deal, it is true, but we were immensely physically fit. Pot, speed, hashish and L.S.D. were as yet unheard of so instead of sitting around looking inwards, we rushed about noisily and happily extroverted.

My final term at Sandhurst was a breeze. I had never had it so good. By now promoted to Under-Officer, I was also for the second season running a rugger blue and even found time to produce a couple of concerts and to play the juvenile lead in *The Speckled Band*. I had also discovered girls in a big way and although Nessie might with certain justification have been called 'the head mistress', I had a heart like a hotel with every room booked.

Nessie, as always describing herself as 'an 'ore wiv an 'eart of fuckin' gold', was staying with a gentleman friend on a yacht for Cowes week but managed a few clandestine meetings with me in Seaview. She was still the same, as funny and forthright and as beautiful as ever and, as always, most solicitous as to my sexual wellbeing. 'Gettin' plenty, dear?'

When I sat for the final exams I discovered with pleasure mixed with surprise that they came quite easily to me and as I had also accumulated a very nice bonus of marks for being an Under-Officer, my entry into the Argylls seemed purely a formality. Everything in the garden was beautiful – a fatal situation for me.

Just before the end of term, all cadets who were graduating were given a War Office form to fill in:

'Name in order of preference three regiments into which you desire to be commissioned.'

I wrote as follows:

1. The Argyll and Sutherland Highlanders
2. The Black Watch

and then for some reason which I never fully understood, possibly because it was the only one of the six Highland Regiments that wore trews instead of the kilt, I wrote.

3. Anything but the Highland Light Infantry.

Somebody at the War Office was funnier than I was and I was promptly commissioned into the Highland Light Infantry.

CHAPTER FIVE

I CUSHIONED my mother from the blow of my not being commissioned into the Argylls by a lot of military double-talk about vacancies and people with short service commissions coming from the universities and I told her, with truth, that anyway the H.L.I. was a much older Highland regiment than the Argylls and persuaded her with a big, black lie that, also, I much preferred being sent to Malta instead of to Bermuda.

I had, however, a sizeable problem explaining to her, when I displayed my uniform, why I was wearing 'those funny striped trousers instead of a kilt'. After reading up the regimental history of the Argylls for eighteen months I was woefully short of material about the H.L.I., but I did remember hearing that this, the second oldest Highland regiment, had so distinguished itself at some point in its history that the men of the regiment were paid the supreme compliment of being allowed to dress like the officers in the other Highland regiments – in trews – the kilt being, they were told, the symbol of serfdom. An unlikely story, I always felt, particularly since the H.L.I. insisted in wearing white spats with their trews to make quite sure that nobody confused them with the Lowland regiments, and a campaign to be allowed to wear the kilt was always simmering on the regimental hob. It finally came to the boil soon after I joined and the kilt was restored to us.

Nessie accompanied me to various pompous tailors and bootmakers in London while I was being outfitted and eyebrows flew up and down like lifts at some of her observations.

'Don't like that fuckin' black bonnet at all, dear. Makes you look like a bleedin' judge 'andin' out the death sentence.'

'Better not sit down in them tight trousers, dear, or you'll be singin' alto in the fuckin' choir.'

When one considers that the most expensive tailors in London at that time charged only fourteen guineas for a suit, it must have come as a body-blow to my mother to receive bills for £250 for tropical clothes all 'suggested' in a list provided by the Adjutant. Salt was doubtless rubbed into my poor mother's financial wound when I handed over my 'clothing grant' from a grateful Government – £50.

Nessie took me in uniform to a photographer in Piccadilly called 'Cannons of Hollywood' and had me preserved for posterity. She also insisted on coming to see me off at Tilbury Docks on a bleak, January morning when I embarked in the *Kaisar-i-Hind* for Malta, two months before my nineteenth birthday. At the last moment, my mother, who had been suffering one of her increasingly frequent bouts of what the family called 'Mum's pain', decided to get out of bed and come too.

'Don't worry about me, dear,' said Nessie when I told her, 'I won't embarrass your mum, I'll hide behind a fuckin' packin' case or somefink, I just want to wave goodbye, that's all.'

In the event it was my spats that brought them together. I put on my outfit, Glengarry, cut-away short khaki jacket with one 'pip' on the shoulders, McKenzie tartan trews and my mother took me, with a mound of tin mothproof uniform cases, in a taxi to the docks. Far from hiding behind a packing case, Nessie was very much in evidence standing by the barrier wearing a little beret over her fair hair and a very short white tightly belted raincoat that took nothing away from her fabulous figure and long slim legs. She was doing a very poor job of pretending not to look in my direction; she looked ravishing and I realised with a lurch of the heart just how much I was going to miss her. As my mother and I walked towards the barrier, a noise like castanets came from the region of my shoes. A few heads turned in our direction and suddenly Nessie doubled up with laughter. 'Christ, yer fuckin' spats are on the wrong feet.' My mother caught Nessie's laughter and I caught hers and in the ensuing hysteria, I introduced one to the other. My mother's famous disdain for punctuality had already brought our arrival at the docks perilously close to sailing time so with Nessie in tow we barely had time to inspect the cabin which the aforesaid grateful Government had arranged that I share with three others before the booming gong and a cry of 'all visitors ashore please' sent them both scurrying back down the gangplank. I have always been embarrassed by long drawn out farewells: once I have got to the point of departure – like an operation – I want to get the damn thing over. We had all agreed that there would be none of that business of smiling bravely and waving while swearing dock-hands wrestled with gangplanks so the last I saw of them was walking away through the damp, dreary Customs Shed. Nessie was holding my mother's arm.

The ship was filled mostly with Service families heading for Egypt, India and the Far East.

'Posh' – I soon learned the origin of the word: Port Out Starboard Home, and it summed up the suburban snobbery of my shipmates whose supreme status symbol was a cabin on the shady side of the ship. Although civilian clothes were worn aboard, rank was still strictly observed, and if the Navy tended to feel superior to the Army both turned up their noses at the Air Force and all combined to ignore the few civilians. The wives were the worst and in the prevailing atmosphere I clung like a drowning man to a very attractive Jewish couple who nobody spoke to and who had misguidedly booked passage to Alexandria.

One wonders what sort of welcome they would receive there today but at that time Mr. and Mrs. Marks were a boon and a blessing. On the voyage they invited me to sit at their table and took me with them when we went ashore at Marseilles. We spent the day at Arles where I was initiated into the glories of the art galleries and the Roman amphitheatre.

There was one other officer on board from my own regiment. I had spotted him from his uniform on the dock and I knew that he had also identified me for the same reason, but he chose not to speak to me until the day we arrived at Malta. It was a pretty ridiculous situation because between us we represented fifteen per cent of the total complement of officers in the 1st Battalion, the Highland Light Infantry, and would presumably be living cheek by jowl for the forseeable future – but for ten days on a smallish ship he preferred to avoid me. This behaviour later turned out to be typical of a large percentage of my brother officers but I was in no position to argue about it and I had a nasty cold feeling that the comedian at the War Office might have passed on the happy news of my three choices of regiment.

The *Kaisar-i-Hind* dropped anchor in the deep blue Grand Harbour of Valletta just as the sun was setting and it was an unforgettable sight, tier upon tier of honey-coloured houses rising on one side and Fort Ricasoli, built in 1400 by the Knights of Malta, brooding benevolently on the other. In between lay the leviathans of the greatest navy in the world. 'Retreat' was being sounded by the massed bands of the Royal Marines on the Flight Deck of the giant carrier *Eagle* whilst astern of her lay three more – *Furious*, *Argus* and *Ark Royal*.

Ahead there was a line of huge battleships and beyond them again, the tall rather old-fashioned looking county class cruisers. The harbour was filled with three giants and their escorts, the light cruiser squadrons, the destroyer and submarine flotillas, with their mother ships and oilers and the battered old target ship *Centurion*. Pinnaces, Admirals' barges and shore boats slashed the blue water with white as they fussily dashed about on their errands leaving hordes of gaily coloured local dghajjes with their lowly civilian passengers humbly bobbing about in their wake.

As the final plaintive notes of the Retreat floated out from *Eagle*, the sinking sun kissed the topmost houses and churches of Valletta with gold and all over the Grand Harbour as the signal lights winked from a hundred mastheads, the White Ensign and Union Jacks of the Royal Navy were lowered, rolled up and put reverently away for the night. If my vintage at Sandhurst was to be decimated in the war that the Germans were to unleash ten years later, it is even more horrifying to speculate on the fate of those magnificent ships and their ships' companies that I glimpsed for the first time on that balmy evening.

Captain Henry Hawkins had been a trooper in the Life Guards but through a combination of bravery and efficiency, he had been commissioned from the ranks and was now Adjutant of my regiment. Tall, almost Phoenician-looking with his swarthy features and black moustache, resplendent in Glengarry, blue patrols and strapped evening tartan trews, he came aboard the liner to meet me. Flashing white teeth and a hearty hand-shake did much to de-congeal me from the chilling apprehension that had descended upon me when I had put on my new uniform for the first time since I had left Tilbury Docks.

'Of course you have been with Jimmy for the whole voyage so at least you know somebody in the Battalion.'

'Jimmy, sir?'

'Don't call me "Sir" except on Parade. Colonel and Majors you address as "Sir", always; everybody else by their Christian names once you get to know them. Jimmy McDonald – he's on board isn't he? Ah, here he is now.'

Henry Hawkins then gave a rather restrained welcome to my shipmate and snorted when he learned that we had so far not met.

'How bloody silly,' he said and introduced us.

Jimmy McDonald was a fairly senior subaltern with rather shifty eyes, the complexion of a hotel night porter and a blonde straggly moustache. I was relieved to learn from Hawkins that I was to be in 'C' Company while McDonald was to join the Headquarters wing.

Hawkins brought McDonald up to date on various regimental news while we were gathering our hand baggage together and being ferried ashore by Carlo, the regimental boatman. The Markses pressed an antique Hebrew silver amulet into my hand for good luck and waved from the upper deck till I could no longer see them.

On the dock were several tough-looking 'Jocks' from the regiment working under the supervision of a sergeant. They were busy loading our heavy baggage and a mound of regimental stores on to mule-drawn drays. Only a few years before the German blitzkrieg would shatter the British Army, mechanisation had still not come to our infantry regiments.

'Just room for two comfortably in the gharry', said Henry Hawkins, 'so you and I'll go ahead to the Mess. Jimmy knows the way so he can follow.' Actually there was room for four in the rickety horse carriage that now transported us up from the landing-stage down the main street of Valletta and out across the vast underground granaries to Floriana Barracks.

'Watch the driver,' said Henry Hawkins, 'they are so superstitious here that, now the sun has gone down, he'll keep changing his position so that the devil can't come and sit beside him.'

We clip-clopped along at a good pace but I had a chance to notice the ornate sandstone buildings on either side and the Sunday evening promenade in the streets, the men walking up and down on one side, the women on the other. All the men in dark suits and clean white shirts; the women in black and a large percentage wearing the *faldetta* – a large black cresent-shaped hood.

'Yells, bells and smells – that's how the Jocks describe Malta,' chuckled Hawkins. 'Just listen to their bloody bells now, Sunday evening is the worst. They all have a go but you'll get used to them. You may get used to the yelling too. Most of that is the poor sods trying to sell goat's milk, hot from the udder, but I don't think you'll ever get over the smells – I haven't.

'Now let me tell you a few things and ask me any questions you like. When we get to the Mess, you'll meet Jackie Coulson – he's orderly officer today. He's about a year senior to you and he's going to look after you and give you a shove in the right direction. Being Sunday evening, there probably won't be anybody else about. Incidentally, people in this regiment make it a point to take a long time to get to know newly joined officers. They reckon that they don't have to rush things because joining a regiment is for a lifetime. So don't worry if some of them, specially the more senior ones, are not very forthcoming for a little while. I had a hell of a time.'

He smiled to himself and tickled the back of his neck with his swagger cane.

Mine was a rather daunting prospect; being abroad for the first time in my life; joining a regiment in which I did not know one single soul; taking command of a platoon of hardened professionals, many of whom had been soldiering abroad for a dozen years or more, all under the watchful eyes of brother officers who, I gathered, were not going to be very helpful – and my nineteenth birthday still some way off.

To say that I was relaxed during our half-hour to Floriana would be a slight exaggeration. I was damp with apprehension which was not eased when H.H. told me that we

73

would probably go on an Active Service 'Stand to' the following week.

'The whole Mediterranean Fleet is pulling out for two months for their Spring exercises and we are expecting serious trouble – riots and sabotage at the Dockyard – that sort of thing. The Italians have been stirring up the Maltese for a long time and getting them all excited about kicking out the British and becoming part of Italy. When the Navy leaves we'll be on our own – just one miserable battalion to control this whole bloody island.'

The officers' mess of Floriana Barracks was glued to the side of a huge church which housed the biggest and busiest and noisiest bells in Malta. They were banging away as we arrived.

Jackie Coulson met us at the door and Hawkins effected our introductions with sign language then, roaring above the din, explained that his wife and his dinner were waiting for him; he was driven off in the evil-smelling gharry.

Coulson signed to me to drop my two pieces of hand luggage inside the courtyard and to follow him. We passed through a door in a far corner and I found myself in a monstrosity, typical of the living quarters of British Army officers at home and abroad ... brown leather sofas and chairs, a few functional writing desks, a large round table in the middle of the room covered with elderly copies of English daily and weekly papers; a large fireplace and mantelshelf with, above it, two signed sepia reproductions of pictures of King George V and Queen Mary and below it a large bum-warmer. Two morose and to my eyes middle-aged officers in mufti were seated on this piece of furniture with drinks in their hands. The bells were a little fainter in here but the room had a gloom all of its own and was covered entirely with a thin layer of dust.

'This is Niven,' said Coulson, jerking a thumb in my direction. Like the guns of a battleship, two pairs of cold eyes swivelled towards me. There was a long silence. The elder and more mauve coloured of the two finally spoke. 'Oh,' he said.

They both continued to stare at me.

Coulson pressed a bell on the right hand side of the fireplace and a Corporal appeared in a white mess jacket with two gold stripes on his arm. 'Sir?'

74

'Double whisky,' said Coulson.

'Same,' said the most mauve man draining his.

'Same,' reiterated the less mauve man draining his.

'If you want something,' said Coulson to me, 'order it yourself. We don't stand drinks in the Mess.'

'Same, please,' I said faintly.

Nothing much happened till the drinks arrived, the two mauve men returning to their interrupted conversation about Maltese priests.

'Not a bad job, really,' said the most mauve man, 'if some woman can't have a baby, she sends for the priest and he has a go to help things along in the name of the Church.'

'Always remembering to hang his umbrella on the doorknob to warn the husband to stay away till he's finished,' said the least mauve man. Knowing winks and chuckles followed this exchange.

Coulson led me to a far corner of the anteroom and in subdued whispers, or at least in subdued shouts against the clamour of the Sunday evening bells, proceeded to bring me up to date. No one could have described Coulson as a warm and friendly man but he was better at first sight than the two highly coloured gentlemen on the bum-warmer. He was thin, sandy and weedy. He exuded an aura of defeat.

'Malta is a sod of a place,' he said, 'you'll hate it. Nobody knows how long we'll be here. The second battalion is in India and we were supposed to be on home service for the next ten years but they suddenly winkled us out of Aldershot and shipped us out here a couple of years ago. It's a bloody mess being a home battalion on service abroad, they don't even give us tropical kit. Just wait till you have to wear full mess kit with a stiff shirt and waistcoat in August when the sirocco is blowing ... Christ, you'll melt!'

'Who are those officers?' I asked, nodding at the other occupants of the room.

'McDougall and Galt,' said Coulson. 'Subalterns both in D Company.'

'Subalterns' – I was amazed.

'Both subalterns,' said Coulson, divining my thoughts, 'about halfway up the list. Nobody ever gets promoted in the regiment. It takes at least ten or twelve years to become a captain.'

'Twelve years!' I gasped – my dream of becoming a general fading rapidly.

'At least,' said Coulson, 'and then it will be another seven or eight till you have a chance of commanding a company and if you ever get that and become a major, it will be four to one against you ever commanding a battalion. So the chances are that at the age of forty-five you'll be out on your arse with a pension of a hundred and eighty pounds a year, after twenty-five years' service!'

I must have looked fairly shaken because he added almost kindly, 'Well, we're all in the same boat, aren't we? Anyway if some silly bugger starts another war, we'll get plenty of promotion tho' it seems pretty quiet at the moment. In the meanwhile, you get two months' leave a year; after you've completed a year's service, you get about ten shillings a day pay and messing allowance but whisky we get in bond so that's only six shillings a bottle.'

Coulson morosely painted thumb-nail portraits of some of the senior officers and ended by giving the following advice – 'The only people you have to look out for are the Colonel, the Adjutant, your Company Commander and, of course, Trubshawe.'

'Trubshawe?'

'Trubshawe, look out for him – he's nothing but trouble. If it hadn't been for Henry Hawkins covering up for him, he would have been flung out months ago ... he's a disaster!'

'Which company is Trubshawe in?'

'"B" Company, thank God, and they're over there on the other side of Grand Harbour in Fort Ricasoli. He's confined to barracks anyway at the moment so he's practically locked up and a good job, too!'

Just as I was about to ask a few pertinent questions about this intriguing character my erstwhile shipmate, Jimmy McDonald, stormed in.

'These fucking Malts!' he said, addressing the bum-warmer, 'they think they own the bloody island – said I had to go through Customs. Told 'em where to get off, of course, but the head grease ball got quite offensive till I threatened to put him under close arrest.' He jabbed the bell with his finger and ordered a double whisky.

'Have a good leave, Jimmy?' asked one of the mauve men.

'Not bad, spent most of it at home. Nearly got married but managed to talk my way out of it. Any supper left?' The three of them disappeared into the dining-room carrying their glasses.

'Cold food on Sunday nights,' said Coulson, 'go on if you want anything . . . I've eaten.'

I was very hungry but the thought of sitting alone with the three who had just gone in there filled me with alarm.

'So have I,' I said. 'I think I'll go and unpack.'

Coulson showed me my room. 'Your batman is McEwan. He looks like a decent sort of Jock. I'll tell the Mess Corporal to send him over.' He turned to go and then paused at the door.

'Oh, you'll need a mosquito net, did you bring one?'

'No, nobody told me.'

'Well, I have a spare one you can have. It's never been used so you can have it for what I paid for it.'

'Very good of you, thanks!'

I've forgotten what I paid Coulson for his net but it was about double, I subsequently discovered, the going rate in Valletta.

I looked around the room. It was on the ground floor, large, stone-floored and almost bare. The smell of horse, donkey, mule and goat dung which came through the window was very strong indeed. I was very depressed.

'Private McEwan, sorr,' said a voice behind me.

I turned to find a stocky, fresh complexioned soldier of about my own age.

'Corporal Deans sent me over tae help ye unpack.'

My boxes and bags were in a corner and in silence we bent to the task.

'I've no done this sort o' work before, sorr – ye'll have tae tell me what ye want me tae do.'

'What are you supposed to do, McEwan?'

The square bandy-legged figure stood up very straight. 'Sorr, in time o' war I'm yer runner. I carry yer messages tae the Platoon and see that ye have food and a place tae sleep . . . in time o' peace, sorr, I look after ye as best I can.' He paused and then added, 'That's what the Company Sarnt Major told me this morning.'

When the recitation ended, we continued the unpacking and I learnt a little more about Private McEwan.

Like many others he had joined the Army because he was sick of being unemployed. A day labourer from the Glasgow slums, he had grown weary of standing in line in drizzling rain, week after week, waiting to collect the dole. A man of fierce pride and stainless steel integrity, as I was to learn during the four years he remained with me, for him it must have been a degrading experience. So one day, he and five cronies sauntered in to Maryhill Barracks and announced that they were joining the Highland Light Infantry.

As was the custom, they were deloused, given a bath, a hot meal and a bed for the night. Next day four of the cronies disappeared before breakfast but McEwan signed on for five years with the Colours and two with the Reserve. His remaining chum opted for seven and five because he was wanted by the Glasgow police for housebreaking, assault and battery. Like many others in that tough town he had decided that the best way to avoid civil justice was to change his name, join the Army and disappear abroad.

'Have ye no had yer supper, sorr?' McEwan asked when we had got everything stowed away as best we could.

Before I had time to answer he went on,

'Corporal Deans said that maybe as this is yer first night in the Mess, yer'd like tae eat in yer room and he said tae tell ye that he has some cold grub and a bottle o' beer for ye ... I'll go an' get it the noo.'

When McEwan came back with this most welcome repast he also brought me the news that I was to report to my Company Commander at the Company Office at 0800 hours the following morning.

'I'll wake ye at seven o'clock, sorr, wi a cup o' gunfire and then I can show ye the way to t'Office.'

I slept fitfully and during the long periods I was awake, I became increasingly excited at the prospect of taking over my Platoon. In the morning I avoided the Mess as I was extremely apprehensive of meeting brother officers on an empty stomach and, fortified by 'gunfire',* I was escorted across the granaries by McEwan, past the guardroom, across the Barrack Square and deposited outside the door marked 'C' Company Office.

Company Sergeant Major 'Sixty' Smith was the sole occu-

* The very strong, very sweet tea the Jocks made.

pant, arranging papers on a trestle table covered with a grey Army blanket. He sprang to attention as I came in and I caught a glimpse of the medal ribbons of the D.C.M. and M.M. on his chest. A rather portly figure with a friendly and revealing smile – revealing the absence of four front teeth. He had spent his whole life in the regiment, having joined as a band boy aged fourteen.

'You'll be Mister Niven, sorr? The Company Commander will be here in a wee while. Welcome to "C" Company, sorr.'

'Sixty' Smith was a regimental character recommended for the Victoria Cross in 1917. He was renowned for his toughness and the fact that his Company Commander was hardly ever called upon to deal with small 'offences' was not so much a measure of the high standard of discipline in 'C' Company, as a tribute to the strong right arm of 'Sixty' meting out his own brand of punishment behind the latrines with a big leather belt.

'Company Commander crossing the Barrack Square, sorr.'

I looked out of the window with interest well mixed with apprehension. For the foreseeable future the officer approaching would be both my boss and my judge; answerable only to the Commanding Officer, it would be in his hands alone to make my life pleasant or very unpleasant, interesting or deadly dull. I saw a long sleek Lagonda swing up to a stop outside the Company office. The morning sun was beginning to beat down and the glare from the parade ground hurt my eyes. Dust from the sudden stop billowed up around the car. From the driver's seat a tall and powerfully built figure emerged. Major Harry Ross-Skinner was a man of about forty-five – on his chest his bravery, D.S.O. and M.C., in his hand, a battered briefcase, on his head, nothing.

He unhurriedly addressed a well-turned out soldier who was sliding over behind the controls – 'Wash the car, then pick up my wife at 11 o'clock, and take her shopping. At noon be back here for me and don't forget to tell them at the stables that I'll be playing six chukkas this afternoon.' He picked up Glengarry, Sam Browne belt and swagger cane from the back seat, and ambled towards the door. As he entered, silhouetted against the fierce glare from outside, he was even larger than I had first thought. His complexion was florid; his eyes, bright blue; his hair and rather large moustache sand and salt. He gazed at me with vague alarm as I snapped off my best Sandhurst salute.

'Oh hullo,' he said amicably, 'what can we do for you?'

'Niven, sir ... posted to "C" Company!'

'Well, that's nice,' he said, 'who told you so?'

'The orderly officer, sir, Coulson.'

'I wonder why nobody told me.' He raised his voice very slightly, 'Sixty!'

The Company Sergeant Major could only have been out of sight by a couple of feet. He shot round the door and stood to attention. 'SORR?'

'Do we know anything about this?'

'Yessir, it was in Battalion Orders last week and the Adjutant sent you a personal memo two days ago.'

'Oh, I see ... well splendid ... do you play polo?'

'I'm afraid not, sir.'

'Why not?'

'I don't think I could afford it, sir.'

It seemed to take an appreciable time for this to sink in.

'Which platoon have we given him?'

'Yer said No. 3, sorr,' said 'Sixty' Smith gently.

'Ah, yes ... well he can have that or No. 2 or No. 4 whichever he likes ...'

He brushed up his moustache between the forefinger and thumb of his left hand and looked down on me ... 'Any preference?'

'Er ... no, sir ... er, anything will do.'

'All right then, No. 3 ... let's see, "Sixty", who's the Platoon Sergeant of No. 3?'

'Sarnt Innes, sorr.'

'Oh yes, of course.' Ross-Skinner was putting on his belt and cap during this conversation.

'Anybody for Company Office?' he asked.

'No charges today, sorr, but the storeman has reported the loss of seven blankets and a pickaxe. He thinks he can make them up before the next Quartermaster's Inspection.'

'How's he going to do that d'you suppose?'

Sixty chuckled. 'Best not ask, sorr.'

Ross-Skinner took off his belt and bonnet again and sat down behind the table with a sigh. Then he opened his briefcase and spread out on the grey blanket some saddlery catalogues. A solidly built old soldier appeared in the doorway with a great stamping of feet.

'Adjutant's compliments, sorr,' he bellowed towards the ceiling. 'Commanding Officer wants to see Mister Newton.' He made this statement with such tremendous authority that it was a moment before I realised that he was referring to me.

'You'd better cut along then,' said Ross-Skinner. 'Pity about the polo,' he added.

Across the barrack square, the old soldier set a rapid pace and between keeping up with him and proudly answering meticulously the first salutes ever thrown in my direction, I was bathed in perspiration by the time I arrived at Battalion H.Q. I was shown in to the Adjutant's Office.

Henry Hawkins smiled up from behind his desk – 'Shaking down all right? It's very strange at first I know. Just let me finish signing all this bumph and I'll take you in to meet the C.O.' For a few minutes the scratching of his pen was the only sound in the warm office, then he spoke again.

'Incidentally, when you were posted to us, some joker at the War Office sent us a memo about you, something about your preference for Regiment.'

My sweating increased a hundredfold. Hawkins never looked up, he continued signing documents.

'It came directly to me and it is now locked up in the Adjutant's confidential file. Nobody else can see it.'

He looked up, put down his pen and smiled again.

'Now ... let's go and see the Colonel.'

This was an awesome moment. The Commanding Officer was seated behind his desk, that is to say like Ross-Skinner, Henry Hawkins and everyone else in Floriana Barracks who was seated behind anything, he was seated behind a trestle table on which was spread a grey army blanket.

'Mr. Niven, Colonel,' announced Henry Hawkins, loosing off a salute. I did the same.

It took weeks for my Commanding Officer to address a word to me directly. I never discovered whether he thought it was impressive or whether he was shy or whether he just didn't know what the hell to say, but for whatever reason, he preferred to address the junior officers of his battalion through an intermediary. Nobody had warned me of this and it came as something of a shock when he turned to the Adjutant and said,

'Did he have a good trip?'

'Yes, sir, very good,' said Hawkins firmly.

'I hate those bloody P. and O.s. They always smell of sick,' said the Colonel ... 'What sport does he play?'

Henry consulted with a file he had in his hand, 'School Rugby XV and Cricket XI, School teams for Boxing and Swimming. Rugby Blue at Sandhurst, good horseman and passed for Hunting.'

'Is he going to play polo?'

Hawkins made a question-mark face in my direction.

'I may not be able to, sir,' I said now addressing Hawkins, 'it might be a bit ... er ... too much for me.'

'Well, tell him about the fifteen bobbers, Henry,' said the Colonel, 'and explain that people in the Navy always have ponies they want exercised ... I think we can expect him down at the Marsa.'

To show that the interview was now concluded, the Colonel rose from behind the desk. Unfortunately, he was so short that his head remained almost exactly the same distance from the floor. Sitting down in the darkened office he had seemed quite impressive – large brown eyes set in a deeply tanned face, dark hair, grey at the temples and at least three rows of medal ribbons – but when he walked to the window and displayed tartan trews that somehow managed to look both skimpy and baggy at the same time, he looked like a little bird, a similarity that to my astonished eyes became more pronounced when, with his back to the room, he raised both arms high above his head with the palms flat and fingers extended ... he reminded me instantly of a cormorant drying its wings.

'Wait behind, will you, Henry,' said the Commanding Officer over his shoulder. I saluted his strange back view and went out into the hot sunlight.

Back at the Company Office, Sergeant Innes was waiting for me and a splendidly reassuring sight he was too. Strong as an ox, he was also comparatively tall, about five feet ten. Most of the men in the Regiment were much more stocky. He had bright red hair, very close cropped and a deep scar under his cheek bone which raised one corner of his mouth in a permanent grin. It was probably a razor slash. The Jocks had a great partiality for the razor as an offensive weapon and invariably had a couple of safety blades sewn just inside the peak of their Glengarrys. In a brawl, an adversary was well advised to stay out of range because with one quick movement, the bonnet was off and swinging in a wide arc held by the ribbons at the back.

'Ginger' Innes saluted. 'I'll take ye tae the Barrick Room, sorr, so ye can see yer platoon.'

So this was it – the moment of truth! At last I was about to come face to face with the forty-odd professionals who would be under my command. This was the crunch. In a strange mood of exaltation, I marched confidently alongside Sergeant Innes. Outside a Barrack Room door, excitingly marked 'No. 3 Platoon', Sergeant Innes stopped – then flung it open. A stentorian bellow rent the sultry air.

'STAND TAE YER BEDS!!'

A sound of scuffling feet came from within. After that, silence.

'No. 3 Platoon ready for yer inspection, sorr.'

Proudly, I passed him to confront, for the first time, my long-awaited charges.

Seven rather crestfallen soldiers in various stages of undress stood waiting for me beside their beds.

CHAPTER SIX

ONLY seven stood by their beds but there seemed to be many other beds displaying kits laid out for inspection.

'Why only seven, Sergeant Innes?' I asked.

'Four on Regimental Guard, sorr, six on Palace Guard, three on cookhouse fatigues, three on Regimental fatigues, two on Officers' Mess fatigues, four awa' sick wi' sandfly fever and two doing sixty-eight days detention in Military Prison for attempted desertion, sorr.'

Even my faulty mathematics could work out that my platoon was woefully under strength, but I swallowed my disappointment and inspected my meagre flock.

They were a hard-faced lot and although they stared unblinkingly at some fixed point about two feet above my head, I was pretty sure that within thirty seconds of my having walked through the door they had all thoroughly inspected me.

Foot regiments in the Regular Army consisted of two battalions; one of which was permanently on service abroad in different parts of the Empire, while the other, based in the British Isles, acted as a holding and training battalion for the one overseas which, perforce, had to be kept up to full strength.

Back at 'C' Company office 'Sixty' Smith gently explained that for a young officer still in his teens, trained to the hilt, and pumped full of ambition and enthusiasm to find himself in a Home Service battalion of very diminished strength, trying to fulfil overseas garrison duties while completing its own training programme and at the same time being constantly drained of its best men, the result was almost inevitable – deadening frustration. It didn't descend on me like a cloud that very first day, but slowly like the damp of a disused house it bored its way into me during the next few months. Meanwhile so much was new, so much was exciting and everything was different.

Nothing much else happened that morning. My company commander disappeared in his Lagonda at about eleven-thirty, two other subalterns of the company appeared briefly, peered at me and went about their business. The other subaltern and the second in command were away on leave so I hung about the company office till lunch time, not knowing what to do.

Luncheon in the mess was a hazard. About twenty officers were present including the birdlike Colonel but nobody spoke to me except Mr. Gifford, the civilian steward employed by the officers' mess. A charming Jeeves-like character, Mr. Gifford was responsible for the catering and for keeping the officers' mess bills. At dinner time, in white tie and tails, he acted as a glorified butler and at all times he was the supreme boss of Corporal Deans and two permanent mess orderlies. On guest nights or other highly charged occasions, a roster of officers' batmen was also pressed into service and these too he ruled with a rod of iron.

Mr. Gifford seated me at a long mahogany table, gleaming with hideous pieces of Victorian silver donated by retiring officers, horses and pheasants mostly, but also a profusion of cigar and cigarette boxes, lighters, ash-trays and menu holders.

The menu displayed in the holders was extensive but my nerves were not quite up to it so I settled for something cold off a groaning sideboard, washed it down quickly with some beer, and fled to my room.

Soon Private McEwan appeared. 'Adjutant's compliments, sorr, ye'll be playing cricket fer the Battalion at fifteen hundred hours this afternoon.'

I must have looked a little dazed because he added, 'We've a verra poor team just noo, but the lads all say, ye'll be a big help, an we're playing aginst the Gunners an' they're good.'

'Christ,' I said, 'I haven't played cricket since I left school – I can't possibly play for the Battalion.' McEwan smiled encouragingly, 'Ye'll be one o' the best if ye've played at all, sorr.' He was tactfully explaining that in a regiment recruited from Highland villages and the slums of Glasgow, cricket was almost unknown.

At three o'clock that afternoon, I presented myself at the Marsa cricket ground. The heat was like a blast furnace. A jovial deaf major, the shape of an avocado called with heavy humour 'Roundy' by his contemporaries, greeted me and introduced me to the team, mostly elderly sergeants and young officers. They seemed a friendly and cheerful lot and I began to relax.

Suddenly, an ear-splitting belch rent the air. I spun round and perceived a truly amazing sight. Trubshawe was approaching. Six feet six, with legs that seemed to start at the navel, encased in drain-pipe tight white flannels. He sported a blue blazer with so many brass buttons on it that he shone like a gypsy caravan on Derby Day; on his head a panama hat with M.C.C. ribbon; on his face the biggest moustache I had ever seen: a really huge growth which one could see from the back on a clear day. Part of it was trained to branch off and join the hair above his ears. It was in fact not so much a moustache as an almost total hirsute immersion.

'My dear fellow,' boomed this splendid apparition. 'Welcome! I'm delighted to meet you.' A row of very white teeth blazed out of the foliage as Trubshawe shook my hand. The sergeants, I noticed, were nudging each other and smiling with great affection in his direction but the officers tended to drift away and busy themselves with their cricket gear.

'This, old man,' said Trubshawe, tapping a brief case he was carrying, 'is an invention of mine. It's called the "dipsomaniac's delight".' He flicked the lock and inside, set in green baize slots, I perceived a bottle of whisky, a soda water syphon and two glasses.

'Come, let us drink to your most timely arrival with a glass of Scottish wine.' In the heat of that blazing afternoon I downed what was to be the forerunner of many thousands of toasts in the company of this amazing and wondrous creature.

Never in the history of human conflict has there been a more unlikely officer in a Highland regiment. Just for a start he was English — a felony which he compounded by not being Sandhurst-trained but by arriving via Cambridge University and the supplementary reserve of a smart cavalry regiment. He was also highly eccentric with a wild and woolly sense of the ridiculous, an unabashed romantic who had a grand piano in his room on which for hours he played sixteenth-century folk music and Peter Warlock's haunting melodies. His reading matter was influenced by an old Cambridge chum, T. H. White. He was, in short, an Elizabethan with a hunting horn.

I didn't remember too much about that afternoon's cricket but I believe I acquitted myself adequately. With the shortage of bowlers I was made to trundle down my slow off breaks for hours on end. The Royal Artillery gleefully dispatched these to various boundaries but I managed to take a few wickets – one a glorious catch on the boundary by Trubshawe who was not supposed to be there at all: he was easing his way back to be close to the 'dipsomaniac's delight'.

I made a few runs and for a brief spell was joined at the wicket by Trubshawe. He was a fascinating sight, full of confidence, taking guard before each ball, patting non-existent divots on the matting wicket and inspecting the positions of the fielders with an imperious and disdainful gaze. But something was very wrong with his timing for although each individual stroke was immaculate in style and execution, it was played so late that the ball was well on its way back to the bowler by the time he had completed his shot.

The match was drawn but not because our team was of the same standard as the Gunners. Cook Sergeant Winters, who was extremely portly as befitted his station, had considerable difficulty in bending down while fielding, a shortcoming he gallantly overcame by stopping ground shots with his shins. A hard drive to mid-off had just connected with a horrible 'crack' just below his knee when a dispatch rider roared on to the field and gave 'Roundy' Cavendish a message. 'Roundy' gathered both teams together and sombrely told us to return to our barracks at once. The situation caused by the Italian-inspired troublemakers, which Henry Hawkins had outlined on the day of my arrival, had deteriorated rapidly and we were to stand by for riot duty and for the guarding of important points against a possible 'coup'.

Back at Floriana Barracks, everything was hustle and bustle but I managed to locate Jackie Coulson and ask him what I should do. 'Battle order, I should think, and report to your company office,' he said curtly over his shoulder, hurrying away. Private McEwan, already himself caparisoned like someone during the retreat from Mons, buttoned me into webbing equipment, water bottle, revolver, map case and steel helmet and with, admittedly, a certain number of Cabbage Whites in my stomach, I made my way across the Granaries. At the company office, the other subalterns were already waiting. 'Sixty' Smith was issuing them with revolver ammunition and maps. We all came to attention when Major Ross-Skinner strode in. Gone was the vague and bumbling sportsman and in his place was the fully efficient, calm, professional commander. As we stood in front of him, he quickly and lucidly issued his orders.

I scribbled frantically as he laid down the duties of No. 3 Platoon, the positions to be occupied, the organization of rations and ammunition, the arrangements for communications, evacuation of wounded and numerous other pieces of vitally important information. He even included a brief résumé of the political situation that had just come to a head: according to Ross-Skinner, the Maltese had been British subjects for a hundred and twenty years but somehow during that time, while English had become the official language of the Administration, Italian had remained the legal language used in all disputes. The local Strickland Government had lately fallen out with the island's Church leaders. The Vatican had consequently become involved with the British Foreign Office and now it had mushroomed into a full showdown between Italy and Great Britain.

It sounded complicated to me but when I recited it to my amazed platoon a few minutes later, it resembled one of the more unlikely plots by Gilbert and Sullivan.

The platoon as presented to me that afternoon by Sergeant Innes had grown to more respectable proportions and I was relieved to note that our fighting strength was now about thirty. They were a tough-looking bunch – mostly Glaswegians, and when I first entered the barrack room, they were clustered round a highly nervous middle-aged Maltese in a sweat-soaked singlet. Like a man possessed, he was turning the heavy stone wheel of a giant knife sharpener. One of the Corporals stepped forward proudly. 'He hoppened to be passin', sorr, so I persuaded him tae come in wi' his wee contraption and touch up the laddies' bayonets.'

We soon embarked in two local buses that had been commandeered for the occasion and were driven to the

Customs shed on the St. Elmo side of the Grand Harbour – our responsibility till relieved. I made a quick reconnaissance with 'Ginger' Innes and issued my orders for the disposition of my troops. Later, Ross-Skinner arrived in his Lagonda and had a look round. To my great relief, he altered nothing, just made a few suggestions about drinking water and a better place to be used as a latrine.

For hours nothing happened. Then some confused shouting around midnight heralded a half-hearted attack by a few hooligans, armed with stones and iron bars. A Jock standing next to me was hit on the steel helmet with a loud clang: 'FOOK THAT!' he roared and charged out with his bayonet flashing in the moonlight. That was the last appearance of any opposition and incidentally, the one and only piece of active service I was to take part in during four years with the Highland Light Infantry.

The next morning, the platoon was withdrawn and the general order to 'stand down' was given. The crisis was over. The British Empire was intact.

Trubshawe, always a mine of information on questions political, told me later that it had all been very simply arranged. The British Government had promptly suspended the Maltese Constitution, forbidden Italian as the official legal language and put His Majesty's Governor in sole charge of everything, 'thereby, old man, putting the whole place back at least a hundred and twenty years'.

Once this little flurry of excitement was over, the battalion settled back into its dreary, soporific routine of garrison duties. Training programmes were issued but there were few men available to train.

With the advent of the hot weather, the leave season moved into high gear and many officers headed for England.

Aided by Trubshawe, whose period of incarceration in Fort Ricasoli was now ended and who had, much to my delight, appointed himself my guide and sponsor, my shaking-down period proceeded apace. First I had to make official calls on all the married officers. The routine was simple. First Private McEwan would find out from the batman at the quarters in question just when the people would be out and I would then slip a couple of calling cards on to the silver tray just inside the door. The wives had a nasty habit of testing the surface of these cards with their thumbs to make sure they were engraved: no 'gentleman', of course, would ever have printed cards. I had also to make the rounds and sign my name in various visitors' books, including the Governor's at Government House and certain Admiral's establishments.

After a few weeks, one or two officers in addition to Trubshawe occasionally spoke to me. But it was a great joy when Trubshawe's Company 'B' (Machine Gun) arrived at Floriana Barracks; things perked up a lot. The Major was 'Tank' Ross, a famous Army and Scotland Rugby footballer, the second in command a young Captain, R. E. 'Wallard' Urquhart. A serious soldier of great charm and warmth, he was unfailingly kind and helpful to me and his splendid qualities, from all accounts, were never seen to greater advantage than in 1944, when, as a Major-General, he led the daring air-drop on Arnhem.

The first regimental guest night which I attended was, quite simply, a nightmare. As the newly joined subaltern, in a sort of travesty of welcome, I was ordered to sit at the Colonel's right hand.

About forty officers were present, including a few guests – Greville Stevens, A.D.C. to the Governor, an amusing pink-faced, sandy-haired captain in the 60th Rifles, known locally as 'the amorous prawn'; a brace of Admirals; an Air-Marshal, some assorted soldiers and two naval guests of Trubshawe's, a Lieutenant Anthony Pleydell-Bouverie and a midshipman David Kelburn* – two, incidentally, of the gayest and brightest men ever to put on naval uniform.

Round after round of drinks in the anteroom and finally just as I was headed for a most necessary trip to the lavatory, Mr. Gifford announced dinner. Like a lamb to the slaughter, I was led with bursting bladder to my chair next to my Commanding Officer. As he had still not spoken to me directly during my service, I was in no position to ask him if I might be excused, an unthinkable request as officers and gentlemen never left the table under any circumstances until the end of the meal when the King's health had been drunk. Sweat broke out all over me as I contemplated the hours of agony ahead.

* Now Admiral the Earl of Glasgow.

I've long since forgotten who was on my right. Whoever he was, he too never directed a word in my direction.

So I sat in miserable silence with crossed legs, perspiration trickling down inside my stiff shirt front, my stand-up wing collar wilting with pain.

Cold soup (more strain on the bladder) was followed by other courses, each washed down by a different wine. I drank everything that was placed in front of me in the vague hope that something might act as an anaesthetic and reduce the torture.

By the time we arrived at the cheese, I was desperate, past caring. As far as I was concerned my career could end in a pool right there under the polished mahogany and the regimental silver, but succour was at hand. Mr. Gifford bent over and whispered in my ear, 'With Mr. Trubshawe's compliments, sir, I have just placed an empty magnum underneath your chair.' Relief, when I heard his words, did not flow over me – it spurted out of me. In an apparently endless stream, but thanks to a firm grip on the bottle with my knees, I was able to aim with one hand and leave the other available to crumble, nonchalantly, a water biscuit. This proved just as well because suddenly the Colonel zeroed in on me and spoke to me for the first time. I was so unnerved by this sudden reversal of form that I nearly released my grip on the warm and by now heavy receptacle below the table.

His words were few and his point was made with admirable clarity. 'I have,' he said, 'fucked women of every nationality and most animals, but the one thing I cannot abide is a girl with a Glasgow accent. Pass the port'. He never spoke to me again.

After the port completed its circle, a toast was given to 'The King'. Many of the glasses I noticed were ostentatiously passed over the top of a glass of water on their way to the lips in a rather juvenile gesture to show that Highlanders were still drinking to the exiled Stuarts – 'the King over the water'.

After the toast, the Mess pipers filed in, eight in number. From the top drone of each instrument fluttered a heavily embroidered silken banner – the coats of arms of the senior regimental officers present. The eardrums of the diners,

91

particularly those of the Sassenach guests, were subjected in the confined space of the dining room to a veritable barrage of sound. Round and round the table marched the pipers, and round and round the table went the port, brandy, Kummel and Drambuie.

Finally, after the pipe major had played his solo pibroch, the haunting lovely 'Desperate Battle of the Birds', the Colonel tottered from the room followed by the survivors who then indulged in a monstrous barging march, punctuated by wild cries, which passed for Highland reels. These in turn further deteriorated into a competition to see who, by using the furniture, could make the fastest circuit of the ante room without touching the floor. Trubshawe, Pleydell-Bouverie, Kelburn and I left in some alarm when a visiting air commodore ate a champagne glass whole, stem and all, and the majors decided to have a competition to see which one could pick up a box of matches off the floor with his teeth while balancing a bottle of champagne on his head.

Anthony and David borrowed some civilian clothes and the four of us, now more suitably attired, Trubshawe in a strange green almost knee-length hacking jacket, made a memorable tour of the late bars of the Strada Stretta known to the Jocks as 'the Gut'.

At five in the morning after hoovering down 'prairie oysters', raw egg yolks mixed with equal portions of port and Worcestershire sauce in 'Aunties' – a red plush establishment run by an enchanting elderly ex-whore from Leeds – I was sick at the top of the Marsamacetta Cliffs.

In the months that followed, my military ambitions suffered a certain seepage as, slowly, but surely, it dawned on me that there was very little point in being a keen young officer. The Army list was kept in the Mess and the pages devoted to the Highland Light Infantry were grubby from the probing fingers that had endlessly traced the inevitable promotions that would come in the long, long years ahead.

However, there was so much new, so much to enjoy that it was almost two years before the deadening horror of the whole thing finally descended upon me and enveloped me like a black Bedouin tent. In the meanwhile Trubshawe's guidance continued apace. He explained to me that I could hire polo ponies for fifteen shillings a month and that apart from buying some mallets, I had nothing to worry about financially, the grooms being soldiers and the ponies all being on the regimental strength as officers' chargers. In addition, as I got better at the game, he assured me that many naval officers would be delighted to lend me their ponies just to keep them exercised during the long periods they would be away at sea.

All this was indeed true and I found myself quite soon with as many mounts as I could play and quite a respectable handicap.

The Marsa Polo Club was the smart place to be – smart in the most colonial sense of the word; it was mounted suburbia. It was parasols and fraightfully refained voices. It was 'Boy bring me a stingar', and naval wives who announced with a smirk – 'We're going in to have our bottom scrubbed next week,' but it was still heady stuff compared with what I had been exposed to before and I thrived on it. Girls there were in plenty. Apart from the resident ones, daughters of senior officers and officials, there were also for several months a year hundreds of young and lonely naval officers' wives. There was in addition the 'Fishing Fleet', a motley collection of passed-over debs and pink-cheeked country cousins who annually timed their arrival to coincide with the return, after many months at sea, of several thousand sex-starved mariners. Finally, there were the whores, and Valletta was full of professionals busily catering to the needs of all ranks of the biggest fleet in the world. Many were mid-European or Russians, refugees of impeccable lineage with sisters plying the same desperate trade in Singapore and fathers driving taxis in Paris.

There was a professionally languid Captain in the Head-quarters wing who wore a monocle. His wife was very pretty in a sort of chocolate boxy way and could have been described in polite society as a flirt; anywhere else she would have been called a cock teaser.

I had, it's true, nibbled her ear and snapped her garter a couple of times while watching the polo from her car, but nothing more, so I was all unsuspecting when a runner informed me that the Captain wished to see me immediately in his company office. I entered and saluted. He was busy looking over some ammunition returns with the Quarter-master Sergeant. I fidgeted around for a while but he still did not look up. Finally, head still down, he spoke.

'Niven, are you very much in love with my wife?'

My toes tried to grip the floor through my brogues to stop me from keeling over.

'No, sir ... not at all, sir,' I murmured and then, for no apparent reason, I added,

'Thank you very much, sir.'

'Well, if you're not,' said the Captain, putting some papers in a folder, 'be a good chap, don't go telling her you are ... upsets her you know. Now Quartermaster Sergeant, about the Range Allotment of 303 ...'

I saluted the top of his head and withdrew.

After that I decided to be a good deal more selective in my nibbling and snapping.

The Fleet was sailing for several weeks of exercises off the Greek islands, leaving behind literally hundreds of ladies in different stages of availability. I discussed the situation with the wife of the Signals Officers of a destroyer who had made it very obvious that she had no intention of sitting around twiddling her thumbs during his absence.

It was a nasty little intrigue really but quite exciting especially when the husband gave a party in his cabin before he sailed and said to me, 'Look after Eunice for me till I get back.'

'I certainly will,' I said, avoiding her eye.

When sailing time came, Eunice and I climbed to the top of the cliffs and watched the splendid spectacle of the entire Mediterranean Fleet steaming out of the harbour, Royal Marine bands playing and bunting fluttering.

We used my field glasses and paid particular attention to her husband's destroyer. He was on the bridge. We had told him where we would be watching and with his binoculars he found us. Lots of waving went on and we even staged a big amorous embrace to make him laugh. I wish I could report that I felt a twinge of shame at that moment but I didn't. I had other feelings of a more animal nature to contend with.

The Fleet sailed away into the sunset and disappeared over the horizon bearing the poor cuckold-to-be towards Corfu; never has a safer stage been set for infidelity but Eunice was in no rush and decided to savour the moment. After all, we had at least six weeks ahead of us in which to indulge ourselves so she insisted that I take her to the Sliema Club to a party with some others, escort her home to her house and then ...

So we danced close and drank champagne and toasted each other over the rim of our glasses, all very high powered romantic stuff; finally I found myself in her bed.

Some far from routine thrashing around was going on because Eunice was an expert at prolonging everything when suddenly she went rigid.

'Christ!' she hissed, 'he's back!'

He was too and downstairs in the sitting room.

'Get in that cupboard,' ordered Eunice.

It was pretty ridiculous because my clothes were all over the floor but I did as I was told and stood quaking in a black hole that smelled of mothballs.

I didn't have time to reflect on the old French farce situation that I was in. All I could think of was the certain death that would soon come up those stairs.

Eunice was made of different stuff. She went down naked to meet him.

'Darling, how did you get back?'

'Stripped a bloody turbine thirty miles out ... towed back.'

Somehow she persuaded him to get in the car and go and get a bottle of champagne so they could celebrate.

I dressed in about eleven seconds and with my shoes on the wrong feet shot downstairs and out of the house. I was impotent for days.

So long as the ex-ranker, Henry Hawkins, was Adjutant, my interest in things military remained at least dormant. Somehow, he could revive it after telling me the frustrating news that, after months of training, the twenty best men in my platoon had been posted to the Second Battalion in India. Somehow, he encouraged me when a great favourite of mine, a gigantic piper from the Western Isles, was listed as a deserter and caught trying to stow away on a tanker bound for Cardiff.

'Johnstone will be court-martialled,' said Hawkins, 'he is in cells now and wants you to defend him.' Any man had the right to nominate any officer he wished to defend him before a court-martial. Flattered by this demonstration of respect but alarmed by his poorly developed sense of self-preservation, I hurried off to the military prison where Johnstone was incarcerated.

'Hoo many days d'ye think I'll git, sorr?' demanded the prisoner before I was half way in his cell.

'Well,' I said, 'I'll do everything I can to prove you intended to come back so they might make it "absent without leave" instead of "desertion" but I'm afraid you'll get between sixty days and six months whichever way it goes.'

'Naebody's goin' tae put me awa' in the glass hoos for six months,' said Johnstone slowly and with that he put his left hand round the edge of the great iron door of the cell and with his right hand, slammed it shut. All four fingers of his left hand were smashed and dangling like those of a rag doll.

A few weeks later, when he was back in a cell once more awaiting his court-martial, he asked to see me again. It is incredible that I fell into the trap.

'Hoo mony days will they put me awa' for noo, sorr?' he asked but before I could answer, the door clanged shut and he was grinning triumphantly at the same mangled hand.

He never did go to prison. He was dismissed from the service as an undesirable character. He came to say goodbye before he left and was very depressed that he would never be able to play the pipes again.

One sad day, Henry Hawkins, the subalterns' friend, was promoted to Major, and his place was temporarily taken by 'The Weasel'.

'The Weasel' was a most unsavoury piece of work. Yellow teeth protruded from beneath a small nicotine-stained moustache and a receding chin did nothing much to help a pair of shifty eyes that were pinned together like cuff-links above a beaky nose. On his thin chest there were no medals for valour. He made a bad move early. He called Trubshawe in and informed him that he drank too much. Questioned as to how he could have arrived at such an outlandish conclusion, the Weasel announced that he had carefully checked Trubshawe's mess bill and would check all subalterns' mess bills each month in the future. Trubshawe quickly made arrangements with Mr. Gifford for a sizeable proportion of his future alcoholic intake to be charged as 'C.O.D. packages', but the Weasel's spy system was born that day and from then on none of us felt secure, least of all myself when he said to me, 'I've been looking through your file, Niven – I wouldn't say that the Argylls have missed you very much, would you?'

He was never openly hostile to me till one day when platoon training was at its height. I was given the task of attacking a small hill across a mile and a half of completely barren land. The Colonel, accompanied by the second in command and several other officers, was on top of the hill. He listened uninterestedly while the Weasel gave his orders.

'No. 3 Platoon will attack demonstrating the fullest possible use of cover: road and sea are your boundaries, both inclusive.'

As we marched down the dusty road to our start point out of sight in a dip, 'Ginger' Innes and I held a council of war. At all costs we must try to avoid cutting ourselves to pieces crawling in full view across a mile and a half of razor-sharp volcanic outcrop, but nobody in the platoon could swim unnoticed a mile and a half naked, let alone wearing full equipment. The road, too, was in full view and so dusty that the approach of a goat sent a cloud of tell-tale white puffs billowing into the sky. Salvation, however, in the shape of a half-empty bus stood waiting in the hollow as we descended below the line of vision of the group on the hill. Country women, wearing voluminous black *faldetta* head-dresses, were already seated in the bus clasping on their knees baskets of chickens, fish and other goodies which they were taking to market.

'Road inclusive' had been the Weasel's orders so, blessing my good fortune, I judiciously scattered the platoon about the bus. Some lay on the floor with the goats and shielded from view by the black tent-like confections on the good ladies' heads, the whole platoon motored peacefully past the unsuspecting brass. Half a mile behind them was another dip in the road. There we debussed and with their backs towards us, our quarry were easy to stalk. Thirty yards from the group, while our two Lewis guns happily opened up with their football rattles, the rest of us charged with fixed bayonets and blood-curdling yells. Perhaps I overdid it a little on arrival by saying to a stunned Weasel, 'Bang bang, you're dead!'

Not only did he give me a monumental bollocking in front of my own men, calling me among other things a 'bloody boy scout', but he sent us, at the double, a mile and a half to our original starting point and then made us crawl back across the volcanic razors. Far from holding this purgatory against me, the Jocks said they had enjoyed the whole day hugely and the episode was ever after referred to as 'the Desperate Battle of the Bus'.

Trubshawe was not the Weasel's type of man at all and his wonderful eccentricities were like a red rag to a bull. Trubshawe's steel helmet caused a certain strain on an important parade.

'Can't possibly wear the bloody thing, old man, it's too heavy and red hot to boot so I've had this little number run up for the occasion.'

He then placed on his head a papier-mâché replica that was as light as a feather and from three feet was indistinguishable from the original.

'Can't go wrong, old man, I'll get one for you next time.'

Throughout that increasingly sulphurous mòrning, I watched Trubshawe jealously as he strode about at the head of his platoon as fresh as a daisy with his helmet on at rather a rakish angle like a yachting cap.

Just before the end of the parade, the threatening storm broke and in the torrential downpour, Trubshawe's hat melted and closed over his ears. An uncertain twittering came from the ranks behind him as the soldiers beheld their splendid officer transformed into something resembling a very lanky hirsute pantomime gnome with a bluebell on his head.

The Weasel confined Trubshawe to barracks for that but Trubshawe hired a string quartet to play for him in the evenings in his room. As his quarters happened to be immediately above the Weasel's lair, he was soon released.

I don't believe that Trubshawe was ever a very serious soldier though he was full of compassion for those who were. He was able to indulge this rather aloof, though never patronising attitude towards the military because, like many officers in the regiment, he had a private income which handsomely papered over the bare patches between a subaltern's pay and the financial facts of garrison life. I had no such cushion but Trubshawe's generosity, which was boundless, made it possible for me to be constantly in his company without feeling a sponger.

I was two years on the island before the Weasel gave me an affirmative answer to my many requests for two months' leave and permission to spend them in the United Kingdom.

One night in a dilapidated ferry boat, *The Knight of Malta*, and I was in Tunis whence a freighter took me to Marseilles, followed by a long train journey to Calais, Dover, Portsmouth and Bembridge.

Two years had wrought awful havoc with the beauty of my mother but when Grizel told me that 'Mum's pains' were more and more frequent, so selfishly occupied was I with my immediate pleasures that I only dimly realised how serious her illness had become. She herself was gay and vague and wonderful and pushed it all aside as something boring she had to live with.

Tommy was nowhere to be seen and my brother, who was now busy growing bananas on Norfolk Island, was back from the South Pacific. Bembridge was in full swing and I had an unforgettable home-coming.

Nessie had never been a great correspondent and her last letter had filled me with unease. It had ended ominously ... 'I've a bit put by now, dear, and I've found a bloke who might suit very nicely, so I might say thanks ever so and piss off to America. He knows all about me and says it makes no difference. If I do decide, I hope you get back before I go so I can see you. I'll close now – love – Nessie.'

I never did see her again. When I arrived in London, I gathered from her friends and co-workers that she had left a month before to get married in Seattle. Most unreasonably, I felt jealous and jilted. She never wrote to me again.

CHAPTER SEVEN

AFTER my leave, I pondered deeply about my military and, with increasing pressure, my financial future.

Brian Franks had been at Bembridge and was learning the hotel business. At the moment, he was working his way up through the kitchens of the Dorchester but was filled with enthusiasm and painted a glowing picture of his prospects.

Most of my other friends had, by now, left University, and were launched on glamorous and seemingly profitable careers in business. I felt rather left out of the scheme of things, a feeling that was not helped by meeting two young officers on leave from the Argylls in Bermuda. Their regiment was not only heading soon for China but in every way it sounded a far happier and more human situation than the one in which I had found myself on my return to Malta.

For a start, Trubshawe had fallen in love and much of his time was taken up by a beautiful blonde called Margie Macdougall who was spending a few weeks with Celia Tower, the equally beautiful wife of a lieutenant commander in destroyers. Trubshawe in love was something to behold. He went about looking pale and interesting. I charged him with being off his feed but he refuted this in a dazed way and mumbled that Margie was a Christian Scientist and that although he did not wholeheartedly agree with much of her indoctrination, he was prepared, under certain conditions, to forego a sizeable percentage of his daily ration of bottled goods. Sinister cracks were appearing in the Trubshavian façade. 'We should give up blood sports, old man. No more the chase, be it fox, stag or field mouse. Amateur theatricals – that's something for us.'

In a day or two my bemused friend and I presented ourselves to Captain Hoskins of the Rifle Brigade who was Military Secretary to the Governor and the undisputed leading light of the Malta Amateur Dramatic Society. After reading a few lines from Frederick Lonsdale's *The Last of Mrs. Cheyney*, we would-be amateurs were dusted aside with the

100

classic, professional brush-off – 'Nothing for you at the moment but don't call us – we'll call you!'

We drowned our disappointments in a sea of 'gimlets' in the 'snake pit' – the ladies' annex of the Union Club in Valletta, while Margie looked on with an apprehensive eye and Celia with a twinkle.

'It's a plot, old man. We'd better get our own show together and break the monopoly.'

So, we resuscitated an old regimental concert party called 'The Hornets' and presented an abysmal confection for three consecutive nights at the Coronado Canteen above the Dockyards.

As in all 'amateur dramatics', the performers had a wonderful time and went on far too long in front of a stoic and partisan audience. We regaled ourselves, and spasmodically our friends, with scenes stolen from the Co-Optimists, and the Hulberts, interlarded with Highland dancing and Sauchiehall Street wit.

Trubshawe had designed the posters which announced the forthcoming event in these terms – 'OFF LIKE A FLASH!!! (AS THE NIGHTLIGHT SAID TO THE NIGHTDRESS)'

These posters were sent round to all the wardrooms and gunrooms of the Mediterranean Fleet so the Weasel, in an ugly scene in which he invoked regimental honour, ordered us to visit every ship in turn, to apologise to the Mess President of each one and to retrieve the offending advertisements. Anthony Pleydell-Bouverie and David Kelburn came with us and it was a miracle that we didn't all drown in pink gin during our futile efforts to obtain the surrender of documents which the Royal Navy had no intention of giving up. At least it had the beneficial result of getting Trubshawe further off the wagon – 'Weasel's orders, old man'. Trubshawe and I had by now become the focal point of the Weasel's distaste. Hardly a week went by when we were not saluted by his orderly – 'Report immediately to Battalion Orderly Room, gentlemen, please,' and off we'd trot to collect another raspberry. So many did we collect at one point, that when the whole shooting match marched out of barracks and went under canvas for summer manoeuvres, we decided not to be outdone when it came to the decoration of our tents. The colonel had a little marker stuck in the ground at the entrance to his marked 'C.O.', and there were others denoting the citizens of all the important tepees – '2nd I/C', 'Adj.' 'Q.M.' 'R.S.M.' etcetera so Trubshawe and I persuaded the Armourers' painter to install a couple for us 'Chief Raspberry Picker' and 'Asst. Raspberry Picker'. The Jocks were delighted but the Weasel hammered another nail in our coffin.

The summer manoeuvres were something that Lady Baden-Powell would have been ashamed of if conducted by a group of Brownies and I was still close enough to Sandhurst to be staggered by the fact that a long halt in the proceedings was always called at midday. While the Jocks sat in searing heat among the crickets and lizards devouring their 'stew and duff' and swigging down their 'gunfire', the officers repaired to a huge marquee where Mr. Gifford, in a white tropical suit and white shoes aided by three mess waiters, presided over an Ascot-type meal of gargantuan proportion.

About this time, the Raspberry Pickers received a reinforcement – John Royal, a vast young man of phenomenal physical strength and an anarchist at heart. He appeared one day straight from Sandhurst and I want to introduce him clearly because he will turn up again much later in this dull story and, as he may enliven it, I don't want him, on his reappearance, to pass unnoticed.

His opening line was memorable. Trubshawe and I were sipping something cool on the balcony of the Sliema Club when a voice behind us said 'I've been looking all over Valletta for you two: that twerp in the Orderly Room told me that I should avoid you at all costs!'

John was almost as tall as Trubshawe but built like a heavyweight fighter in his prime. A broken nose did nothing to dispel this impression. He was extremely handsome in a dark, Celtic way and extremely hostile when drunk. Also, as Trubshawe succinctly put it, 'the man puts in some very plucky work with the elbow'. Very soon after his arrival in Malta, John was posted to the Second Battalion and departed for India but during the few weeks he was with us, he made an indelible impression.

He was devoted to animals and could not bear to see the Maltese drivers ill-treating their horses. When he saw one poor emaciated beast, straining uphill with a huge load of sandstone blocks, being belaboured with a heavy stick, he pulled the man off the shafts, put him across his knee and gave him six of the best with his swagger cane.

John also introduced us to green beer.

Trubshawe and I had been ordered by the Weasel to make all the arrangements for the annual Regimental Party at the Marsa Polo Club. Knowing we were given this assignment in the hopes that a normally deadly supper dance might be infused with something perhaps a little unusual, we went to great lengths planning to decorate the place differently and while Trubshawe spent days bashing some sort of rhythm into the regimental band, I busied myself with the catering aided by Mr. Gifford.

Three weeks before the party, John told us about the green beer. It appeared that a brewer in Edinburgh had come up with this novelty and he quickly talked us into ordering it for the occasion. Cables were exchanged and to obtain a decent price per crate, we ordered an enormous amount of the stuff. The shipment arrived at the Docks just in time and the mule teams in the transport lines were hastily pressed into service to cart it to the Polo Club where Trubshawe and John and I were waiting to try it.

It tasted all right but the colour, far from being the joyous sparkling creme de menthe we had anticipated, was that of some loathsome opaque and polluted pond.

On the night of the party, acres of green bottles stood hopefully on the tables while the guests avoided them like the plague and drank everything else in sight.

The next day, the Weasel sent for the Raspberry Pickers and said that it was our responsibility to get rid of the green beer. We thought we might be able to 'con' the sergeants' mess into buying some. So together with John Royal we organised, one Sunday, a sergeants' mess picnic, the idea being that if we gave the sergeants enough of it free and slipped them a lot of whisky to help it down, they might overlook its horrendous colour and relieve the officers' mess of a sizeable portion of the stock.

It didn't work, of course. We took several carloads of sergeants, sandwiches, whisky and crates and crates of beer to a remote bay and for hours a glorious time was had by all – swimming, singing, telling exaggerated regimental anecdotes, boasting and drinking. In an effort to get them hooked on the stuff, the three of us, while carefully leaving the whisky out of our own mugs, dreamed up toast after toast, but as the evening approached, wild highland cries became fewer and the sound of snores and throwing up became the norm.

When finally we delivered our subdued charges back to the sergeants' mess, it was all too plain that we had over-played our hand: to a man they swore they would never touch the stuff again.

I remember the end of that picnic very clearly because the pipe major was so drunk that 'Sixty' Smith and I had to put him to bed and valiantly trying to get his kilt off while he was thrashing around and muttering obscenities in Gaelic, we unveiled an elderly pair of green regimental boxing shorts. There is always speculation about what a true Scot wears under the kilt: here was additional evidence that it is a very personal decision.

John Royal departed for India the same day that Trubshawe became engaged to Margie Macdougall. Neither event ended well but John's problem came to a head first.

Soon after his arrival, the officers of the Second Battalion were invited to a ball given by the local maharajah and John became sleepy, so after dinner he lay down behind some potted palms and stole forty winks. He was awakened by a captain of a cavalry regiment who stirred him, none too gently, with his foot.

'Stand up,' said the Captain. John stood.

'You are drunk,' said the Captain.

'You are right,' said John and flattened him with a left hook. He then composed himself once more behind the potted palms. Pretty soon he was awakened again, this time by a full colonel of Artillery.

'Stand up,' said the Colonel. John stood.

'You are drunk,' said the Colonel and collected a right cross.

John was court-martialled and insisted on conducting his own defence. He had been dropped on his head as a baby, he said, and this had the unfortunate effect of making him lash out at the first person he saw when he was woken from a deep sleep.

The prosecuting officer smiled faintly. 'Perhaps you would tell the court what happens to your batman when he wakes you up in the morning?'

'Nothing,' said John unmoved. 'I have issued him with a fencing mask.'

John left India and the Army and I did not see him again for ten years.

Margie Macdougall left Malta and Trubshawe was saddened. He was comforted by the beautiful Mrs. Tower and rallied strongly. Trubshawe had decided that perhaps the Weasel had a point when he hinted that there were other things that Trubshawe might do better than soldiering.

'When Margie and I marry, old son, we'll live in the depths of the country in some beautiful village. I'll run the cricket club and Margie can hand out pheasants to the tenants . . . of course a lot depends on the local brewer.'

My twenty-first birthday came and went and I was still on that island. Every day it seemed to get smaller. Rumours were constantly flying that the battalion was to be reinforced and sent to Egypt, to China, or to Singapore but nothing ever happened and after each flurry of excitement, the battalion settled further back into its torpor. Trubshawe was now determined to resign his commission within a year so I asked officially to be seconded for service with the West African Frontier Force, a ploy that would have given me an exciting change of scenery and considerably more pay. The Weasel refused to recommend it.

My last year in Malta was enlivened by two things. First, I was made transport officer and as such, spent my days in the stables with several dozen chargers, draft-horses and mules. The mules were a belligerent lot; probably they had an inferiority complex because they did nothing except pull the company cookers. It was a splendid sight to see a company on the march. At the back and always falling further and further behind, were a couple of mules hauling an immense black cauldron on wheels. Inside this, depending on the time of day, was either boiling tea or boiling stew. Both tasted much the same but, at all times, behind the cauldron, was the company cook enveloped in a cloud of steam and stirring the contents as he marched.

Sergeant Fensham was the transport sergeant, a gay bandy-legged little man with the broken-veined complexion that goes with the proximity of horses. He was ready for every four-legged emergency. If the Colonel's horse was too fresh, before an important ceremonial parade, he would calm it down with a jab of tranquilliser. Once he gave it too much and we both watched apprehensively as, with rolling eyes, it tottered about with its precarious cargo in front of several thousand onlookers.

Someone with a distinguished military background died in Sliema and a military funeral was arranged so I was ordered to produce a team and gun-carriage to bear the coffin. Sergeant Fensham paraded the six blackest draft horses we had and towing the black gun carriage, we set off to pick up our cargo.

In the middle of Valletta, one of the horses fell down and grazed its knee. Somehow it knocked off a divot of black hair and exposed a few square inches of hard chalky-white skin. This ruined our carefully arranged black ensemble but Fensham reached into his saddle bag, produced a box of black Cherry Blossom boot polish, and we went on our way without missing a beat.

The other boredom reliever of those last twelve months was the fancy dress ball in the Opera House. It was a predictable show — admirals dressed as pierrots, their wives as columbines. Bo-peeps were plentiful and there was a sprinkling of Old Bills and Felix the Cats among the military. Parties took boxes in the lovely tiered building and everyone tried hard to pretend that it was every bit as gay and abandoned as the Chelsea Arts Ball.

Trubshawe and I went as goats.

First we put noisome rugs on our backs. Then horns on bands were fixed to our heads and finally, between our legs, for the goat fittings, footballs swung with rubber gloves sewn on to them by the regimental cobbler. half a pint of dry martinis apiece and we were ready for the fray.

We arrived just in time for the Grand March for the prize-giving. The judges for the best costumes were on the stage and round and round in front of them, two by two, like the animals going into the Ark, went the clowns with their red hot pokers, the ballet dancers and the Mickey Mice.

106

Rumblings of disapproval rose from the boxes as the two drunken goats joined in at the back of the parade.

'Trubshawe...Niven...goats! Bad show! Damn bad show!' Military moustaches and naval eyebrows bristled from every floor.

I'm getting dizzy, old man,' said the goat behind me after we had completed several circuits.

'Left wheel!'

Obediently, I turned out of the parade towards the empty centre of the floor.

'Now squat!' commanded Trubshawe.

'What?' I asked apprehensively.

'Squat, you bloody fool.'

So there at the very hub of the wheel with a kaleidoscope of colour circling round us and the focus of hundreds of disapproving eyes I squatted. Trubshawe produced a brown paper bag from the folds of his smelly rug and sprinkled black olives on the floor directly behind me.

Except in the box that held David Kilburn and Anthony Pleydell-Bouverie, this flourish was coldly received by the ticket holders, particularly by a party of Maltese students who had a very short fuse when they thought that someone was mocking the local institutions. They jostled and shoved us as we left the floor and made threatening noises.

'Better take off, old man,' said my leader as he headed for the exit and the last I saw of Trubshawe that night he was pounding down the main street of Valletta towards the sanctuary of the Union Club pursued by the hornet students and tripping over his 'udders'.

We were confined to barracks for that little adventure but the boredom of our incarceration was soon relieved by the arrival of a whole new spate of rumours. This time they had a ring of truth to them. The Quarter-Master was seen checking the winter stores and, in the Transport Lines, Sergeant Fensham hinted darkly that he had heard that we might have to find buyers for some of our animals. The Weasel was seen strutting around, obviously having tucked into a sizeable canary.

In fact the battalion had been ordered home to the British Isles – to the Citadel Barracks, Dover. It was like some gloriously prolonged 'end of term' and when the evacuation order was finally given, the whole battalion set about their allotted tasks with a willingness I had not hitherto seen.

'Sixty' Smith, who had become my friend and adviser, was ill in hospital. It started with sandfly fever, then complications and now he was much more sick than anybody realised. Pleurisy had set in and there was no question of him sailing home with the rest of us. I went to see him the day before we embarked on the troopship and was shocked by his appearance.

'Would you ask the Colonel a favour for me, sorr? Would ye ask if the battalion could march a wee bit oot the road on their way tae the Dock so I can hear the pipes for the last time – it's nae far ... aboot five minutes.'

I suddenly felt chilly in the warm little room. 'What the hell are you talking about, Sixty? ... hearing the pipes for the last time?'

'Becos I'm gonna dee,' Sixty replied quietly and I found it impossible to look into his clouded eyes.

The Weasel was oddly sympathetic to the request and when he gave me the answer he told me the Colonel had added that he would like me to be with the old man when the troops passed the hospital the following day.

It was late afternoon when they passed and the sun was golden on the church spires that Sixty could see from his bed. In the distance he could hear the swinging march: 'Wi' a Hundred Pipers ...' and he asked me to prop him up in his bed. Nearer and nearer came the battalion and as he lifted his head to listen, he must have been thinking of a whole lifetime in the regiment he had joined as a boy. Just before the column reached the hospital, the tune changed: changed to the regimental march – 'Scotland the Brave' – and tears of pride slid down his granite cheeks. He sat bolt upright till the last stirring notes faded away into the distance, then he slid down into his bed and turned his face to the wall.

That night Sixty died.

The troopship was a hell-ship of about 11,000 tons and bursting at the seams with men from every regiment on their way home from various parts of the Empire. For four days she was hove-to in the Bay of Biscay in a storm of Wagnerian proportions. Life in the troop decks in the bowels of the ship was unbelievably awful but the Jocks rose above the overcrowding and the smell of vomit by keeping their minds on the fact that at last they were off the island of Malta and headed in the right direction.

We arrived in the Citadel Barracks, Dover, a few days before Christmas. It was a place of undiluted gloom. A grass-covered fortress, high in the mist above the slate-roof Victorian horror of the town below, but as we marched into the barracks, on that drizzly December evening, there was not a man among us who did not rejoice.

The Weasel sent practically everyone in the battalion home on leave. A skeleton party of caretakers stayed behind and as we were still under the cloud caused by the goat episode, the two officer skeletons were Trubshawe and myself. It was really quite enjoyable and a great relief to be de-Weaseled for a while.

Hogmanay at the turn of the year was as boisterous an affair as usual and over at the canteen Cook Sergeant Winters gave the fifty members of the caretaker party a size-able spread of haggis with all the trimmings and, following regimental tradition, the officers waited on the men. Trub-shawe was at his very best belting out an endless stream of songs on the tinny canteen piano while toasts were offered and accepted.

The following day was a day of shock for the Raspberry Pickers. We rose late with appalling hangovers and were gloomily gazing out of the window of the officers' mess whence far below it was sometimes possible to see the English Channel through the murk. After the sauna-bath climate of Malta, the penetrating damp of the Dover heights could only be combated by a concoction of Trubshawe's called 'The Heart Starter' – port and brandy mixed. We were doing our best to get warm when the door behind us opened and the solitary mess waiter stood there making spastic movements of the head and shoulders, rolling his eyes and jerking his thumb over his shoulder. When he stepped aside, the reason for his alarm became clear. Behind him was a real live Major General. A lean and very formidable figure, he walked briskly into the room. The red band on his hat and red tabs on his collar sowed instant alarm in our breasts and this was not diluted by the sight of General Staff armbands on the Major and Captain immediately behind him.

109

'Where is your Commanding Officer?'

'On leave, sir,' said Trubshawe.

'Adjutant?'

'On leave, sir,' said I.

'Who is the senior officer present?'

'I am, sir,' said Trubshawe.

'I don't mean in this room,' snapped the General, 'in the barracks.'

'Still me, sir,' said Trubshawe and tried a misguided smile of welcome. 'Can we offer you a little something to keep out the cold.'

There was an ominous silence while the man treated us to a long, penetrating stare. Then he turned and held some sort of low-keyed high-level military discussion with his staff. The Major and the Captain changed colour noticeably and we got the distinct impression that someone had blundered.

'All right . . . then you show me round,' said the General.

'Well,' began Trubshawe like some obsequious house agent with a prospective client, 'this is the anteroom and the dining room is up these steps to the right, the kitchen is below and the bedrooms, such as they are . . .', he trailed off as the General looked at him speculatively for a long time, tapping his highly polished riding boot with his leather cosh.

'Show me round the barracks,' said the General in a controlled voice, 'that is, if it's not too much trouble.'

'Pray follow me, sir,' said Trubshawe (the greasy head waiter routine now leading way to a bad table). 'Come, Mr. Niven,' he added over his shoulder as an afterthought.

The grisly little procession wound across the almost deserted barrack square; a few bedraggled and hung-over Jocks looked up apprehensively from whitewashing some stones around the guard room.

'Fatigue party "shun",' yelled a corporal rising from behind a sporting paper. Unfortunately, his snappy salute was ruined by the fact that he omitted to take a cigarette out of his mouth.

'Mr. Niven! take that corporal's name,' roared Trubshawe, military efficiency now and pulling the big switch.

'Sir!' I yelled back and rushed over to the offending man.

110

'For Christ's sake,' I hissed at him, 'it's a General doing a surprise inspection – get the word round quick – get everybody looking busy.'

I rejoined the group just in time to see the General pointing towards a squat building.

'What's that?' he demanded.

Trubshawe and I had a somewhat sketchy idea of the layout of the Citadel but it still came as a rude shock when I realised that the Chief Raspberry Picker was shamelessly passing the buck to his trusted lieutenant.

'Mr. Niven,' he said sweetly, 'what's that?'

'Er ... the library, sir,' I faltered hazarding a guess. Trubshawe must have misheard me, 'The lavatory, sir,' he said. We went inside what was quite evidently the band practice room. In the far corner was the pipe major, who hated going on leave, frantically beating life into the bag of his pipes while his trembling fingers groped for the first plaintive notes of 'The Flowers of the Forest'. The General looked grim.

The inspection of the barracks proceeded on its nightmare course. Trubshawe heard my whispered cue of 'latrines', headed in the indicated direction, took one look at several pairs of protruding white spats belonging to Jocks who had decided to seek sanctuary there, lost his head and made the sort of noises reserved for orderly officers in the dining hall at mealtimes.

'Any complaints?' he asked.

Bewildered and aggrieved Scotsmen rose from their individual thrones.

'No complaints, sorr,' they mumbled.

We correctly identified the cookhouse only because Cook Sergeant Winters, in a white apron, was standing outside it beckoning with a heavy-handed helpfulness with a ladle, but we received some timely reinforcements in the shape of Ginger Innes wearing the red sash of orderly sergeant and a smart-looking corporal from Trubshawe's platoon. Our morale rose as, with their whispered help, we successfully fielded searching questions in the quartermaster's stores, the miniature range and the domain of the Pioneer Sergeant.

By now the full complement of fifty caretakers had been mobilised by bush telegraph and wherever we went there were groups of men frantically cleaning, polishing, leaf sweeping and wheelbarrowing.

Trubshawe, as we headed for the General's car, felt that victory was within his grasp. He relaxed and was in an expansive mood when the General fired his last enquiry.

'What's in there?' he asked, indicated a large building with red double doors and FIRE HOUSE written above them. Almost smugly Trubshawe said,

'Why, the fire engine, sir.'

'Get it out,' ordered the General.

'Yes, sir,' Trubshawe looked as though he had been hit with a halibut. Then he turned, almost apologetically to me.

'Mr. Niven, get the engine out, please.'

'Very good, sir,' I said, giving him a real killer look.

'Sergeant Innes – get the engine out.'

'Sir! – Corporal MacQuire, th' engin' – git it oot.'

The buck was now passing with great rapidity.

'Lance-Corporal Bruce, git th' engine oot ...'

'Private Dool, git th' engin' oot.'

The cry echoed round the Citadel.

The General had started once more on that ominous metronome bit with the leather cosh and the riding boots.

'What sort of engine is it?' he asked with ominous calm.

'Oh – a beauty,' said Trubshawe.

'Merryweather,' I piped up from the back.

'Yes,' said Trubshawe, 'made by Merryweather & Company and it has a lot of brasswork and coils and coils of hose.'

'Get it *OUT!*' said the General much louder now.

Trubshawe seemed almost on the point of surrender – then, like a lookout at Mafeking seeing relief approaching, he let out a long sigh. A soldier bearing a huge key was approaching at the double from the direction of the Guard Room but I could hardly believe my ears, when I heard Trubshawe pressing his luck.

'Many's the night, sir, when this trusty engine has been called out to help the honest burghers of Dover.'

'Get it out!!'

At last the key was inserted in the lock and with the flourish of a guide at Hampton Court opening the door of Henry VIII's bed-chamber, Trubshawe pushed open the double doors.

112

Inside, against the far wall stood two women's bicycles: a dead Christmas tree from another era lay in the centre of the floor and in the foreground was a bucket of hard and cracked whitewash from a bygone cricket season.

The General turned and stalked to his car without a word. The staff officers gave us pitying glances before they followed him. In silence they all drove away and in silence Trubshawe and I returned to the officers' mess.

In the next few months a tremendous upheaval took place in the battalion. We received a new Commanding Officer; and there was a change of Adjutant. The new Colonel – Alec Telfer-Smollett, D.S.O., M.C. – was nothing short of a miracle. In no time at all he shook the battalion out of its warm climate garrison complex. The whole atmosphere became charged with a sense of purpose. It became possible to perform the dullest chores and at the same time to feel one was doing so for a good reason.

Telfer-Smollett was patience itself with me, in fact he took special pains with all the junior officers to make them feel at home, and I use that word advisedly because he was a firm believer in an ancient concept of a regiment – that it should be a family.

I found myself often dining alone with the Colonel and his wife and, unbelievably, at least twice a week I was invited to play golf with him. He laughed at my tales of Malta, nurtured my flagging military ambitions, sympathised with my permanent financial straits and cheated blatantly in the scoring.

He was a wonderfully warm and understanding human being and came within an ace of persuading me to become once more a serious soldier but this was quite unwittingly sabotaged by a petite snub-nosed blonde, very pretty American girl with the smallest feet I had ever seen – Barbara Hutton.

In the spring of that fateful year, my grandmother died. For years she had lived in rooms in Bournemouth and as children, my sister Grizel and I had paid her annual visits, travelling from the Isle of Wight on a paddle steamer as day trippers. I remember her as a very beautiful old lady with a cloud of carefully coiffed white hair and a little lace choker at her throat kept high under the chin with bones. She had very pale and strangely lifeless skin on her cheeks which I always tried to avoid kissing. She left me £200 in her will.

I immediately invested about half of this windfall in a second-hand Morris Cowley and gleefully entered the London social scene.

Soon I found myself on the Mayfair hostesses' lists – as they were desperately short of available young men – and every post brought its quota of invitations to debutantes' parties or weekends in smart country houses. Dover being near to London and weekend leave plentiful, I indulged myself to the hilt with the minimum of outlay and became a crashing title snob in the process. For a short while I really believed that dukes and baronets were automatically important.

One evening at a dance I met Barbara. She was spending a few weeks in London with her uncle Frank and at the time she was engaged to Alex Mdivani, a Georgian prince who was to be her first husband. A gay and sparkling creature, full of life and laughter, she became a great ally at some of the more pompous functions. When she left London she made me promise to come to New York for Christmas, an invitation as lightly made as it was lightly taken.

In November I was sent on a physical training course for several weeks at Aldershot. One night I was called to the telephone and found myself talking to 'Tommy' whom I had not seen for over three years.

'Your mother is very ill,' he said, 'she is in a nursing home in London and you should come and see her immediately.' He gave me very little further information except the address.

I quickly obtained leave and rushed to Queen's Gate. Although I had seen her only a few weeks before, she was so ravaged by cancer that I was utterly and completely horrified by what I saw. She did not recognise me before she died.

I went back to Aldershot and completed my course in a sort of daze. I simply could not comprehend what had happened. I had never had to cope with a loss of this magnitude and I endlessly chastised myself for always taking her presence for granted, for not doing much, much more to make her happy and for not spending more time with her when I could so easily have done so.

Alec Telfer-Smollett was a father figure and when I got back to Dover he helped me with great wisdom and infinite patience to get over the worst part. With Christmas approaching and with four weeks' leave coming to me, he suggested that I should go far away somewhere and be with people who could not remind me of what he knew well was a gnawing feeling of guilt.

It was then that I remembered Barbara Hutton's invitation. In reply to my cable asking if she had really meant it, I received one which said – 'Come at once love Barbara.'

I flogged the Morris Cowley, borrowed a little money from the bank and a little more from Grizel who had become a very clever sculptress and was now installed in a tiny house in Chelsea, and ten days before Christmas, I embarked on the one-class liner *S.S. Georgic* and throbbed my way to New York. Throbbed was the word; I had the cheapest berth in the ship – directly above the propellers.

CHAPTER EIGHT

THE trip from Southampton to New York should have taken eight days but we met a gale head on, so it took ten.

My little throbbing box of a cabin I shared with an enchanting middle-aged American who had been making his first ever visit to Europe on the strength of having sold his clothing store in Milwaukee. He was much exercised by the thought of going home to face, once more, the rigours of Prohibition and during the trip he proceeded to make up for the lean times ahead. He was none too fussy either about mixing his intake.

'Dave,' he said, one evening, 'I've gotta a great idea ... tonight you and me are gonna drink by colours.'

We settled ourselves at the bar and he decided to drink the colours of the national flags of all the countries he had visited on his trip — Stars and Stripes first of course. Red was easy — port. White was simple — gin, but blue was a real hazard till the barman unveiled a vicious Swiss liqueur called gentiane. The French and British flags fell easily into place but a horrible snag was placed in our path by the Belgians. Black, yellow and red. Black beer was used to lay a foundation for yellow chartreuse and burgundy, but it was the creme de menthe of the Italian flag that caused me to retire leaving my new-found friend the undisputed champion.

The crossing was my first confrontation with Americans en masse and I found it a delightful experience. Their open-handed generosity and genuine curiosity about others came as something of a shock at first. What a change, though, to be asked the most searching personal questions in the first few minutes of contact, or to be treated to a point-by-point replay of the private life of a total stranger. What a difference as an unknown foreigner to be invited to sit at a table of friends or to join a family. I suppose it is the fact that we have fifty-odd million people crammed on to an island the size of Idaho, and unable ever to get more than eighty miles from the sea, that makes us so defensive. Who else but the British would spread hats, handbags, umbrellas and paper bags on the seats of railway carriages and then glower furiously through the windows at anyone who shows signs of entering and ruining our privacy?

I had my first brush with the American language in that ship. For a partner in the ping-pong doubles championship, I had snagged a delicious lady from Sioux City. 'Now we have a practice tomorrow,' I warned her, 'if you're not on deck by eleven o'clock, I'll come down to your cabin and knock you up.' She put me straight.

I do not, with my poor pen, have the impertinence to try and describe a first impression of the New York skyline because no one I have ever read has done it justice so far, but that forest of gleaming white set against an ice blue sky is something I will never forget.

Barbara had cabled that she would meet me at the dock so, as the Moran tug company's fussy little work-horses pushed and tooted us into our berth, I went below and gathered together my hand baggage.

My Milwaukee friend was there having fitted himself into a strange forerunner of today's space suits. Inside and beneath the armpits were cavernous pockets which concealed large aluminium tanks, each capable of holding about two and a half gallons of Scotch whisky. He was in the process of being topped up by the steward.

He pressed speakeasy cards on me, telephone numbers of friends in New York and issued a permanent invitation to visit with him at his home and meet some lovely people.

'Goddam Prohibition,' he muttered as I left, 'takes a man's balls off.'

I walked down the gangplank and looked back at the good ship, *Georgic*. A few years later she was sunk by the Germans. Barbara was waiting for me at the dock and had brought two or three carloads of friends to welcome this strange young man, with the funny voice. I was a bit of a freak in the United States in those days as the vast majority of people had still never met a Briton nor heard an 'English accent'. Nobody went to see English movies because they couldn't understand them.

They gave me a rousing reception and I am happy to think that several of those I met on that Christmas Eve are still my friends today.

117

Barbara's family lived on Long Island but for a town house they utilised several suites in the Pierre Hotel. I was to be installed there and on the way – it was now growing dark – I beheld a breathtaking sight. The limousine swept round the corner of the Grand Central building and stopped. In the frosty evening, there stretched before me as far as the eye could see, a straight line of enormous illuminated Christmas trees. Also, as far as the eye could see, was a necklace of red lights. Suddenly, these lights changed to green and we shot forward. At that time, traffic lights were only being experimented with in London so I could be forgiven if I was unduly impressed by New York's Christmas decorations.

I was given a very nice room at the Hotel Pierre and Barbara, the perfect hostess, made it clear that she hoped I would spend as long as I liked there but feel perfectly free to come and go as I wished and not to feel bound to her or her family.

That night, she gave a party at the Central Park Casino. The incomparable Eddie Duchin was at the piano leading his orchestra and a very attractive couple of young ballroom dancers were the stars of the Cabaret – George and Julie Murphy. (George later became Senator from California.)

It may have been Prohibition but so far I had not noticed it. A vague pretence was certainly made to keep bottles out of sight and many people made extra trips to the lavatory or to their cars to uncork a flask there, but otherwise it was business as usual.

Christmas Day with Barbara's family and presents for the unknown young man of Homeric generosity. Next a visit to Princeton to watch the annual football battle with Yale. The trip to Princeton was organised by a cousin of Barbara's – Woolworth Donahue – and for the occasion, for our comfort and refreshment, he thoughtfully provided a special coach on the train.

The long ride passed in a flash. The men were all about my own age and the girls were the result of their very competitive selection for this high point of the College year. The result was spectacular. I had never seen such beautiful girls in my life and there were more to come. Jack and Marshall Hemingway were our hosts at Princeton and there the train group joined about forty more for a colossal spread before the game. Finally, we set off for the Stadium and our wonderful, wonderful girls. Coonskin and camel-hair coats were very much in evidence.

I didn't see very much of the game. Once the college bands had left the pitch to the players, excitement was at such boiling point that the moment anything important happened, everyone leaped to his feet thereby obscuring my view. I did not have the same built-in springs in my knees as the others and trained, as I was, in the Twickenham school of indulging in a little polite hand clapping while seated, the most exciting moments were blanketed by vast expanses of coonskin and camel-hair ... but no matter, I had a wonderful day and have since become an aficionado of American football.

The days in New York passed in a blaze of parties, speakeasies and nightclubs with daytime forays to visit people on Long Island, sometimes in specially chartered and bar-equipped motor buses. There were also boxing matches and ice hockey games to see at Madison Square Garden, big Broadway musicals to visit, great bands and singers to listen to.

The headquarters of the group I was adopted by was Jack & Charlie's '21' Club – the best speakeasy in New York run by goodlooking Jack Kriendler and the amiable rotund and folksy Charlie Burns. The doorman was named 'Red' and 'Jim' was the watchdog peering through the bullet-proof door. If an alarm was given of an impending raid by the law, the first thought was to protect the customers – no one would be caught drinking – so waiters were trained to seize all bottles and glasses from the tables and put them on the bar where 'Gus' the barman was in position to throw a switch, the whole bar then tilted up and the offending evidence slid down a chute to the cellar.

No evening was complete without ending up in some dive in Harlem. I don't think I'll try that today.

Prices in New York were bloodcurdling but such was the generosity of my new-found friends, that it was just taken for granted that I was never to be allowed to pay for anything. It was made clear that if I attempted to do so, I would no longer be invited. I didn't feel too bad about this arrangement because there were one or two members of the group who were also financially embarrassed at the time and they too

119

were carried by those in funds. One was a struggling reporter on the *Sun*, a huge teddy bear of a man, named John McClain, destined to become my friend for life. McClain used to point to a slightly older man on the periphery of the group, always with the prettiest girl, a tall, shy, silent, slightly deaf, and compared to the rest of us, very serious minded citizen. 'Let that son of a bitch pay for once,' McClain would rumble. The tall man's name was Howard Hughes.

Phil Ammidown had a Pierce Arrow convertible and was leaving for Florida. 'Come with me, Dave,' he said, 'I have a home in St. Augustine, we can spend a couple of days there, take in a party at the girls' college in Tallahassee, then go down to Palm Beach.'

The night before we set off, A. C. Blumenthal, the diminutive financial genius – once described by Dorothy Parker as 'a pony's ass' – gave a party, just six of us. Blumenthal's wife, Peggy Fears, and two other glamorous members of the Hollywood scene – Mary Duncan and Bubbles Haynes, Ammidown and myself. Blumenthal arrived bearing a suitcase almost as big as himself, a glorified model of Trubshawe's dipsomaniac's delight of beloved memory and the farewell party went on at various places all over town till Phil and I were waved away in the Pierce Arrow en route for Florida.

First stop, Richmond Virginia, and my eyes now gummed together with tiredness, snapped open with amazement when, just as I was signing the hotel register, I noticed a full sized alligator in a small pool about six feet from the reception desk.

Phil was a demon driver and the Pierce Arrow was a very fast car – a combination that provoked a movie-style chase by a speed cop from the State Highway Patrol who was gaining on us with siren blaring when we shot across the State line into Florida and safety.

St. Augustine is the oldest town in the United States, indeed the oldest house in the country is still standing there. Phil's house nestled peacefully in lush woods just outside and for two or three days, I was able to charge up my batteries after the hectic days of New York. I revelled in the peace and charm of the place and after the frenetic pace of the big city,

I sniffed the warm magnolia-scented air, stared at the hibiscus, listened to the cicadas and the lazy drawling voices of the inhabitants and found it hard to believe I was in the same country. The Citadel Barracks, Dover, were every minute receding further and further into their grey clammy and depressing mists.

The party at Tallahassee took place just before the end of the year. The girls of the college had a tradition that during Leap Year they had the right to ask the men to dance and also to cut in on them. I had witnessed this rather barbaric tribal ritual of cutting in at parties in New York and had many times been highly frustrated having cut in on a beauty only to feel, as she melted in my arms, an ominous pat on the back from the next customer from the stag line, watching and choosing his moment from the middle of the floor. I had also suffered, once or twice, by getting stuck with a comparatively unattractive girl and not receiving that now welcome and relieving tap on the shoulder but I had never sunk so low as to dance round with some poor unprepossessing creature in my arms holding a ten-dollar bill behind her back as bribery to a rescuer. However, having sweated out my first invitation to dance, I kept my ears pricked for the rustling of currency behind my head.

Through forest and swamp, the arrow-straight U.S. Highway No. 1 connects Jacksonville with St. Augustine and half way between the two, Phil and I nearly died. Five o'clock in the morning, and travelling fast, we could see the lights of a car coming towards us at least ten miles away. As we shot past the other headlights and into the dark beyond, there was an almighty crash. We were both knocked unconscious. When we came to we were in the swamp on the left hand side of the road, incredibly, the car was the right side up and we were sitting in it pinned against the high back of the seat by the bronze frame of the now glassless windshield bent hard against our chests. The front of the car had been completely demolished. Water and mud were up to the floor boards and we knew we were covered in warm blood. From the swamp beside us came a terrible grunting and splashing –

'Alligators,' whispered Phil, 'don't make a sound.'

As we sat, cowering and waiting for the foul slavering jaws

to come snapping at us through the non-existent front of the car, we felt ourselves all over: the blood could not have come from us, we were unscratched.

'We didn't hit the other car,' I whispered, 'We were past it when it happened.'

The awesome noises continued for a long time then just as the first grey light of dawn was beginning to silhouette the moss-festooned trees, they stopped. The light grew stronger and we saw what had happened.

In that split second when we were blinded by the too-quickly turned up headlights of the other car, two large black mules had emerged from the swamp and we had hit them broadside. Poor brutes, one must have been flung up in the air and over our heads. Its body had bashed us against the high soft seat-back knocking us out, but, by a miracle, not breaking our necks. The noises had come from the wretched animals dying in the swamp. The Sun Life Insurance Company used a photograph of what was left of the car as a warning and a reminder.

Phil Ammidown, if not a man of great means was certainly a man of style – he bought a new car that same day, and in the afternoon, we continued south to Palm Beach.

Phil found us rooms in a small hotel and got busy on the telephone. Soon, the days were flying by, girls everywhere, glorious golden ones, and golf, tennis, fishing in the blue Gulf Stream for marlin, dancing in roofless restaurants – 'How deep is the ocean? How high is the sky?' Parties, love-making, kindness and overwhelming generosity on all sides. Lili Damita, a gorgeous French actress, paraded about with a leopard on a leash and Winston Guest put a shark in his mother's swimming pool. I hoped it would never end but, suddenly, it was Pumpkin Time.

One of the glorious golden girls sidetracked me and I missed the last plane that would carry me north to catch my ship for home. I despatched a cable to Colonel Telfer-Smollett: DEAR COLONEL MAGNIFICENT OPPOR-TUNITY BIG GAME HUNTING WHALE FISHING FLORIDA REQUEST ONE WEEK EXTENDED LEAVE. This would give me ample time to catch the German ship *Europa* but if permission was not granted I would be in deep trouble overstaying my leave.

The answer came back – NO WHALES OR BIG GAME WITHIN A THOUSAND MILES STOP TAKE TWO SMOLLET.

The parties and the hospitality reached a crescendo till finally, deafened and petrified by flying for fourteen hours in a non-sound proofed Tri-Motor Ford through the most hideous weather, I crawled on board the *Europa* and made for another rabbit hutch of a cabin in the bowels of the ship. As I unpacked I realised with a tinge of guilt that I had hardly thought about my mother ... oh! the callousness of youth!

The Great American Kindness went on all the way across the Atlantic. The little cabin was full of goodbye telegrams and Barbara had arranged for a most welcome delivery of champagne. McClain had alerted a friend of his that I was on board and one night I was invited to a dinner in the First Class given by 'Jock' Whitney, a wonderfully intelligent and witty man who can light up a room and who quite lately was one of the most popular and successful U.S. Ambassadors to the Court of St. James.

On another occasion, I was asked to dine in the First Class and my host insisted, after dinner, in cutting me in on his syndicate that was bidding for a number in the ship's sweep. My contribution was minimal, a fiver, I think, all I could afford anyway. I don't know how my host arrived at the result but when his number won, he told me my share was £160.

Thanks to this wonderful and, I am ashamed to say, now nameless man, I arrived back at the Citadel Barracks with more money than when I had left. I had tasted the fleshpots, in fact I had stuck all my trotters in the trough and had gorged myself: it had all been too rich for my blood, and in a welter of false values, I knew that one day, somehow, I would go back to America.

Trubshawe was on his last legs militarily. 'Can't go on much longer, old man. It's getting too much like the Army ... it's hunting four days a week and checking on the young pheasants for me.'

I soon noticed the change myself. Telfer-Smollett was determined to shake the battalion out of its Maltese malaise and bring it to a peak of efficiency and this meant first of all a great sharpening up of the officers.

The Colonel was wonderful to me and the off-duty golf games were as frequent as ever. There was nothing I could not discuss with him. His good advice was boundless. He understood perfectly the itchy feet I had contracted during my flying visit to the United States. He also saw the limited possibilities in the Army for an impatient young man of very slender means. We discussed the possibility of my following Trubshawe's example and resigning my commission, and he counselled caution. 'Give it a few more months', he said, 'don't rush it.' I could become a good soldier but I had seen that grass on the other side of the fence and oh! Brother! was it green!

Trubshawe helped me find an old car. 'A man must have wheels.' We settled for a 1927 3-litre sports Bentley. It had done over a hundred and twenty thousand miles, had a strap over the bonnet, a handbrake outside, a compass, an altimeter, and a pressure pump on the dashboard, a cut-out that made the exhaust roar like an aeroplane and a three-tone horn. With a car like that one could only wear a chequered cap. It was the complete cad's car. It was cheap, because it was about to fall apart and the terms of payment were long. When I had handed over the down payment, I didn't have enough to pay for the licence – £25. Luckily the colour of the licence for 1932 was a light fawn so it was a simple matter to put a Guinness label in the licence holder. Guinness labels at that time were numbered, so from five yards my home-made licence was indistinguishable from the real McCoy.

Although I kept my promise to Telfer-Smollett and worked hard, I also used my wheels to good effect and London saw almost as much of me as Dover.

Ann Todd's career was booming and because of my friendship with her, I began to get a little stage-struck. She introduced me to a strikingly good-looking young actor who was even then electric on the stage. Since then, he has two major claims to fame – he is godfather to one of my children and has become the first in his profession to be made a Baron ... Laurence Olivier.

One day in the spring, I received a letter from Tommy. I had not seen him since my mother died. He suggested a Sunday luncheon at the Carlton Club and thinking that perhaps we were about to find some kind of rapprochement after three years of hostility, I went.

I gave my name to the porter and was led through several gloomy rooms. My stepfather rose from a chair, ignored my outstretched hand and said, 'The solicitors tell me that, so far, you have paid nothing towards the grave.' I did not stay for luncheon and I never saw him again.

Trubshawe decided to leave the Army and get married. Although I had been given plenty of warning of this impending, as it turned out, disaster, I was shattered by the news.

'I'll wait for the Levée and the Caledonian Ball, old man, but I've come to the end of the Tartan Trail.'

The prospect of soldiering on without my friend was horrendous and my thoughts turned even more towards taking the plunge into the unknown civilian life.

The Levée took place at St. James's Palace in June. Officers of all arms holding the King's Commission were supposed to present themselves to their Sovereign once or twice during their careers. Many people in the battalion were due for this ceremony and Telfer-Smollett entered wholeheartedly into the arrangements. The biggest problem was where to find regimental full dress. Some of the older officers had their own, but the rest of us, with few exceptions, had no wish to go £250 into the hole for one morning of peacock glory, so we hired from costumiers.

About ten of us attended the Levée and everyone seemed to have everything on and everything right. The smell of mothballs made our eyes water but we were, I thought, quite an imposing sight as we strode down St. James's Street in the June sunshine, shakos on our heads, McKenzie tartan plaids over our silver-buttoned scarlet doublets, claymores flashing and dirks at our sides. Sir Arthur Balfour was the Colonel of the Regiment and as we followed in his wake, for he was technically there to present us to the King, Trubshawe remarked that we looked like 'a gaggle of Highland Postmen'.

Inside St. James's Palace was most impressive; two large ante-rooms were filled with several hundred officers from all branches of the three services. It was a blaze of colour – Highlanders, Hussars, Greenjackets, Gentlemen at Arms, Indian cavalry officers in turbans, Gurkhas and Maharajas.

There was a suppressed bonhomie in the first ante-room and many old friends were recognised, some from Sandhurst days. The second ante-room into which we were later directed was quiet and one sensed a certain nervousness. In all it took about two hours to percolate through the two ante-rooms and into the Throne Room where we were to pay our respects to King George V.

Finally, my turn came. I was ushered through the door and remembering my minute instructions from Colonel Balfour, I handed my calling card to the Gentleman-at-Arms. Ahead of me was a slowly moving single line of officers, inching forward towards the dais at the end of the long beautiful room. About twelve men were in front of me and as I, in turn, began to move forward, I had plenty of time to take in the scene.

On the dais and standing at the back were about forty very impressive gentlemen – the most senior in the Royal Household and Services. At the centre, on a gold throne, sat the King in Field Marshal's uniform, and standing immediately behind him to right and left, his four sons – the Prince of Wales in the uniform of the Welsh Guards, the Duke of York in naval uniform, the Duke of Gloucester in his Hussar uniform and the Duke of Kent in the sky blue of the Royal Air Force.

I found myself filled with great emotion. When I reached the end of the line, my calling card had miraculously arrived at the same instant and was being handed to a senior official who glanced at it and announced . . . 'Mr. David Niven – The Highland Light Infantry'. I turned to the right, my shako under my arm, praying I would not trip over my claymore and marched the regulation number of steps that would bring me opposite the King, then a smart left turn and I was face to face with my monarch. I bowed. He acknowledged me with a slight inclination of the head. A smart right turn and I marched out into another ante-room. It had been an unexpectedly moving experience for me and for the others too. We gathered in silence till Sir Arthur Balfour joined us and told us that the Colonel-in-Chief of our Regiment, the elderly uncle of the King, the Duke of Connaught, wished to receive us in his apartments behind the Palace.

During the short walk I was brought down to earth by Trubshawe who said, 'I hope the poor old sod doesn't get gassed by all this camphor.' Standing in a line in his dining room, we were presented to the Duke. He seemed a very old man and his German accent was most pronounced.

'It's good to see the old uniform again,' he intoned, peering at us over a white moustache and a huge beak of a nose.

'Jesus!' whispered Trubshawe, standing next to me. 'Somebody's got one of his old ones on.'

The next night was the Caledonian Ball held at Grosvenor House, a most colourful spectacle awaited us. Scots from all over the world were present in full regalia and the pièce de resistance was always the set reels. The huge ballroom was cleared and in the middle the Duke of Atholl's private sixteensome took up position, then around it were placed the eightsomes of the six Highland Regiments, the Black Watch, ourselves, the Gordons, the Camerons, the Seaforths and Argylls.

Trubshawe and I with, luckily, two very special friends, Keith Swettenham and Michael Bell, were the four subalterns selected by Telfer-Smollett to represent the Light Infantry. The four girls we were to partner wore the sashes of their clans and had been carefully selected by the Ball Committee for their territorial connections with the Regiment and not, we noticed, with some alarm, for their good looks. However, we had just arrived from a riotous dinner in a private room at the Mayfair Hotel which Brian Franks had arranged, so we were not too unnerved when introduced to our horse-faced partners from far-away glens. Also, the dinner party was there to cheer us on, headed by Margie Macdougall, Celia Tower, David Kelburn, Anthony Pleydell-Bouverie and Brian Franks.

The Pipe Major had been polishing up our dancing for days before the big night and we were quietly confident of holding up the good name of the regiment in front of hundreds of pairs of critical eyes.

Now, in an eightsome reel, it doesn't matter how well the individuals dance the steps if the whole eightsome fails to stay in its allotted position. The unknown girls were expert dancers and it was the dawning look of horror on their faces that alerted me to a very nasty situation ... somehow our entire eightsome performing perhaps with too much verve and abandon, had started to creep slowly down the ballroom floor towards the Gordons. A crash was imminent. The 'Gay' Gordons turned rather nasty, and hissed oaths came our way. We recoiled and began travelling inexorably in the direction of the Camerons who tried to avoid us and got into a really horrible mix-up with the Seaforths. Having started the rot and cleared a large portion of the floor for our own use, our eightsome settled down beautifully and never moved again. The other eightsomes were left cannoning into each other and generally behaving like goods trains at Clapham Junction often ricocheting off the Duke of Atholls's sixteensome in the centre. Trubshawe observed the Argylls trying to ignore a couple from the Black Watch who were now dancing dazedly in their midst and summed up things – 'Bit of a fuck-up at the other end of the room, old man.'

Trubshawe adhered to his timetable and by midsummer, he had left the regiment and married Margie Macdougall.

The junior officers, non-commissioned officers and men of the battalion were sad to see him go. The senior officers had mixed feelings. For me it was disaster, compounded when, almost immediately, over half of my platoon were drafted to India and I was sent on a course to the Machine Gun School at Netheravon. Gloom descended on me like a blanket.

I was befriended around this time by the Weigall family who lived in a large white Georgian house in Ascot. Sir Archibald was tall, charming, good-looking, pink-faced and vague. Lady Weigall, permanently in a wheel chair, wearing a blonde wig with a blue bow in it, was plump, vivacious, a tremendous gourmet who loved laughing and being shocked. She was attended by two resident doctors, a youngish male social secretary and a mysterious old gentleman called 'C.J.' who read *Horse & Hound* all day long, and who was rumoured to have been Lady Weigall's boy friend before Sir Archibald showed up. Priscilla, the only child, was a flashing brunette with a delicious sense of humour who was quite correctly considered 'Deb of the Year'.

I spent many happy weekends at Ascot and the Weigalls took a great interest in my future. Sir Archie and Lady

Weigall thought it fitting that I should go to Australia as A.D.C. to the Governor General. Priscilla had other ideas.

'You should be a movie actor,' she declared flatly and promptly went to work to promote the idea. First, she introduced me to my boyhood hero, the great Douglas Fairbanks. A chronic anglophile, Fairbanks was enjoying a period of playing the country squire and had rented Mimms, a lovely Queen Anne house in Hertfordshire.

Fairbanks invited me to play golf with him at Sunningdale which I did and basked happily for eighteen holes in his reflected glory. I was so impressed by the gaiety and simplicity of the great man, I never dared mention Priscilla's project.

Undeterred by my cowardice, she next presented me to Bunty Watts, a producer at Sound City, a minute studio nearby, and one Sunday, I appeared in front of the cameras as an extra in a racing film – *All the Winners* with Alan Jeayes as its star. Greatly to Priscilla's disappointment, I was not immediately signed to a million-pound contract and returned to Netheravon in time for parade on Monday morning.

My loathing of the Machine Gun School was only equalled by my pathological hatred of the Vickers Mark IV machine gun, a foul piece of machinery of such abysmal design that it was subject to countless stoppages, all of which we were supposed to be able to diagnose and rectify at a moment's notice. There were about a hundred officers on the course drawn from every conceivable regiment. Henry Clowes of the Scots Guards was my constant companion and although I nearly killed him one day, when the vintage Bentley skidded and somersaulted on Salisbury Plain, pinning us underneath it, he forgave me and did all he could to help me through the hot mornings when I arrived, sleepless, from London.

One such morning was the harbinger of military doom. I had escorted Priscilla to a dance and a night club and I screeched up in the Bentley only just in time to take off my tail coat, jump into my brown canvas overalls, cram my Glengarry on my head and relieve Henry of a hideously heavy tripod before my name was called on the early parade.

'Present, sir,' I puffed.

All morning we laboured, putting that damn gun together then taking it to pieces again.

'All right, gentlemen,' said the chief instructor, a full colonel, 'it's a very warm day, you may remove your overall jackets and work stripped to the waist.'

Sighs of relief all round as the officers peeled.

'Mr. Niven, you may remove your overalls,' said the chief instructor.

'No thank you, sir, I have a sniffle.'

'Remove your overalls, Mr. Niven,' ordered the colonel.

'Yes, sir.'

I stood in the middle of Salisbury Plain unveiled in white tie, stiff collar, shirt and white waistcoat ... Glengarry still on my head.

After that I was a marked man.

The end, militarily speaking, came for me on another stiflingly hot day during the last week of the course. I was much looking forward to a particularly exciting rendezvous in London and my time table was in grave danger of being ruined by a long-winded address being delivered by a visiting major-general. In the hot tin-roofed lecture hut he was droning on about fields of fire, close support and trajectories. Bluebottles were buzzing about and my head was nodding. Finally he closed his notes.

'Any questions, gentlemen?'

My hand went up. I will never know what prompted me to do it, four years of frustration, I suppose, but I opened my mouth and heard myself say,

'Could you tell me the time, please, I have to catch a train.'

'Stand up that officer.'

I stood – 'Your name?' I told him.

'Go to your quarters and remain there.' I departed.

Soon an officer of the Seaforths of the same rank as myself joined me in my room, ominously he was wearing a sword. He was very embarrassed. 'I'm afraid I have been told to ... er ... stay with you,' he said.

'Close arrest?' I asked.

'Looks like it?' he said.

The embarrassment deepened as we sat staring at each other in the hot little room, he in the leather chair, me on the bed. After about an hour, with an exasperated flourish, he took off his sword.

'This is bloody ridiculous,' he said, 'let's have a drink.'

I agreed eagerly and summoned the room orderly who was lurking suspiciously close determined not to miss a moment of this juicy situation. A bottle of whisky arrived from the mess and almost in silence the Seaforth Highlander and I drank it, and when I say 'it' – we drank the whole bottle.

'I've a suggestion,' said the Seaforth as the last dram was drained, and he said it slowly and with great deliberation.

'I'll go to the lavatory, which I badly need to do, and you escape.'

The beauty and simplicity of this plan would have shamed Field Marshal Montgomery's famous 'Left Hook' at El Alamein.

The Seaforth, with brimming eyes, then clasped both my hands in his, shook his head mournfully, and tottered off in the general direction of the latrines. I climbed hurriedly out of the window, closed my eyes and leapt into space. Luckily my room was on the ground floor so I found myself in no time up to my chin in rhododendron bushes.

I ran to the Bentley and drove rapidly, and luckily without incident, to London.

The girl with whom I had a date I never saw again. I arrived comparatively sober and utterly appalled by what I had done. I rounded up two friends, old friends whom I admired ... Victor Gordon-Lennox, an ex-Major of the Grenadier Guards, then the diplomatic correspondent of the *Daily Telegraph*, and Philip Astley who, as Adjutant of the Life Guards, had been asked to resign his commission for committing a heinous crime – he had married an actress – the gorgeous Madeleine Carroll.

The three of us dined at White's, outside, Guinness label gleaming, stood the Bentley. The two ex-Guards officers listened attentively while I told them what had happened. With the port came the inquest.

'How much do you like the Army?' asked Victor.

'I hate it,' I answered.

'You're bound to be court-martialled, why don't you pack up before you're thrown out?'

'Because I'm broke,' I said.

'Do you have any money at all?' asked Victor.

'A few pounds and about half that old Bentley outside.'

They left me nursing a large glass of Cockburn's while they murmured together in a bay window overlooking St. James's Street. I tried to avoid the eyes of an ex-member of White's who stared down on me disapprovingly from a large gilt frame – the Duke of Wellington.

Finally the jury returned to their seats.

'There is no question that you are through in the Army,' said Philip, 'but Victor has a possible solution.'

Victor, lately married to a Canadian girl, then spoke, 'I am sailing on the *Empress of Britain* tomorrow to pick up Diana from her parents' island in the Rideau Lakes, then I'm off to Washington. Give me the Bentley or the part you have paid for and I'll give you a return trip to Quebec – come and stay on the island for a week or two and you can decide what to do next.'

I was stunned by my good fortune.

'Now, we'll go downstairs,' said Philip, 'and you can write your colonel your resignation – I'll help you – I've done it.'

Below, by the porter's desk – the only place in White's where guests can use the Club stationery – I wrote out a cable to Alec Telfer-Smollett at the Citadel Barracks, Dover:

'DEAR COLONEL REQUEST PERMISSION RESIGN COMMISSION. LOVE NIVEN.'

I sailed for Canada in the morning.

CHAPTER NINE

THE *Empress of Britain*, like my earlier transatlantic carrier the *Georgic*, was sunk a few years later by the Germans. She was a beautiful ship and the September crossing was perfect. We ran into fog only once about one day out of the Gulf of St. Lawrence; suddenly, it got much colder and we reduced speed. I remarked on this to a steward.

'Icebergs about,' he said.

'How do you know?' I asked.

'We smell 'em,' he replied.

As yet there was no radar in passenger ships and the steward gave it as his considered opinion that the Captain wetted his pants every time they entered these particular waters.

The fog lifted and everyone was pointing. A mile or so away was a gigantic fortress sailing majestically along. Pale pink in the setting sun on one side and blue-green on the other. It towered out of the water and with nine-tenths out of sight below the surface, imagination boggled at the size of the whole.

Diana Kingsmill Gordon-Lennox was a rarity – a genuine Canadian eccentric. Dark, with beautiful teeth and a lovely smile, she was highly intelligent, smoked small cigars and wore a monocle. She met us in Quebec and we drove and drove to Portland, Ontario. Diana seemed not at all put out that Victor had arrived with an unknown friend, she intimated that her father and mother were looking forward to having me on the island and was delighted when I told her I loved fishing. 'Then Daddy will have a playmate,' she said.

When we approached the island a loon was calling plaintively across the lake. The maples were turning and I had never seen such blazing beauty, great splashes of red, brown, yellow and gold were reflected in the still water and behind rose the foothills of the Gatineau Mountains all clothed in the same breath-taking colours.

The island was of about five acres. The main house was surrounded by perhaps four guest cabins, all of wood.

133

Admiral Kingsmill and his wife were walking down to the boathouse as we arrived. The Admiral was a famous old Canadian sea-dog and with his forthright manner, pointed white beard and ramrod carriage, he certainly looked the part. Diana had heard my story on the long drive from Quebec and had said it would be better to forget my true exit from the British Army. 'Just settle for a straight resigning of the commission when talking to the old man,' she said firmly.

Lady Kingsmill was a gentle motherly creature and I was immediately made welcome.

The days slid by. People came from other islands to visit. The Admiral and I endlessly went fishing for the big green bass, the fighting, jumping, black bass; the giant pike and the ferocious muskellon.

Victor and Diana took me on excursions into the back country and we discussed my future endlessly. Return to England? Hardly. Because of my lack of training in any useful profession the chances of employment seemed brighter in the U.S. than in Canada, so when the time came to move on I made up my mind to cash in my return trip ticket to England and cast my lot in New York.

On the day of my departure I had an agonisingly sore throat. I didn't say anything about it because the Kingsmills might have felt they were getting stuck with a permanent guest so when Victor and Diana headed for Washington, I accompanied them as far as Ottawa, where I said goodbye to my saviour and his wife and visited a doctor who said I had chronically infected tonsils which should come out immediately. I imagine he must have done something about the infection first, but anyway he stuffed me into Ottawa General Hospital. Sodium pentathol not having yet come on the market, the operation was carried out after I had first been rendered unconscious by a mixture of gas and ether being pumped into a rubber mask over my face. After the operation, I lay for days with a throat of greatly increased soreness and to take my mind off my misery, I am afraid I indulged in a little gentle plagiarism.

I hope that the statute of limitations applies in this case and that the Mounties will not be sent to pull me in, and if it will help at all, I offer my belated apologies to the author, Thyrett Drake, who long before had written a book called

Fox Hunting in Canada. I found it in the hospital library, copied some of it assiduously and sold four articles to the local newspaper under the title 'Hunting of the Canadian Fox'. It paid the doctor's bill.

I had met some friends of the Kingsmills, Pete and Ginny Bate, and one day they appeared at my bedside.

'We've talked to the doctor,' they said, 'and he has agreed that we can take you home with us. There's a room at the top of the house you can have while you are convalescing and it'll be much more comfy for you. Besides, we would love to have you.'

I was overwhelmed by such a wonderfully warm-hearted gesture by the slightest of acquaintances, though it is typical of Canadians as a whole.

I had at least a week more to spend in bed – apparently it had been an operation with 'complications' so I jumped at the idea and, swathed in blankets, was installed, as promised, in a bright chintzy room at the top of their house.

On a Sunday night Ginny and Pete came up to see me.

'We're going over to Pete's mother's for supper but we'll be back before eleven. Do you mind being left alone?'

Of course I didn't. I was feeling better and due to get up in a day or so. They left me with a radio and departed.

I went to sleep about ten and woke up some time later literally drowning in my own blood. I had had a terrible haemorrhage in the throat and when I turned on my side, it poured out like a tap on to the floor. The bright chintzy room looked like an abattoir. I had not the faintest idea where the telephone was or what was the doctor's number but I had a vague idea that the operator could somehow help me.

I collapsed at the top of the stairs where the poor Bates found me, mercifully a short while later.

Back to hospital and blood transfusions but finally I made it by train to New York. It was now mid-October and becoming exceedingly cold. I found a room in a cheap hotel on Lexington Avenue – the Montclair – and for a week I lay in bed without the energy to pick up the telephone to try to find some of last year's companions.

Finally, I began to make contact with the old group and although they went through the motions of being pleased to see me, I soon realised that there was a big difference between an irresponsible young man over for a short holiday, and an anxious young man badly in need of a job. The background was none too welcoming for a foreigner either, the United States was still in the grip of the depression and there were millions of United States citizens unemployed. I could not have chosen a worse time for my arrival.

However, good health can overcome the gloomiest thoughts and as my strength returned, my morale improved. I registered with an employment agency and picked up a few dollars here and there working at night for catering companies who handled cocktail parties. It was not a very technical job. The host produced the booze via his bootlegger and the caterers provided the hors d'oeuvres, the barman, the glasses and the waiters. I invested in a white jacket and took great care to check the addresses I was sent to, only accepting jobs where it was very unlikely I would be seen by any of my erstwhile acquaintances.

John McClain, the reporter, was doing better. He had just been given a daily column to write for the *Sun* – 'Up the Gangplank', interviews with interesting arrivals on the ocean liners. One day McClain had a brainwave . . .

'Look,' he said, 'prohibition was repealed in April and is due to be ratified in a few days and all booze becomes legal. Jack and Charlie are going to become wine merchants – maybe they'll give you a job. I'll have a word with them.'

The next day I had a meeting with Jack Kriendler and found myself employed on a forty dollars a week retainer against ten per cent of what I brought in in the way of orders. Jack explained that Frank Hunter of the world champion doubles team of Tilden and Hunter would be president of the company and my immediate boss.

Frank Hunter, a man of great charm and humour, introduced me to my co-worker, a tough professional salesman named Harry Rantzman.

During the months I held my job, I hardly ever topped four hundred dollars a week in sales which would have 'augmented' my 'retainer'. Harry Rantzman ended up owning several apartment buildings, in the Bronx, a real professional.

The first day at work Kriendler sent me to F.B.I. Headquarters to have my fingerprints taken and to be photo-graphed with a number round my neck and to this day at '21' is that picture of me: underneath is written – *Our First and Worst Salesman.*

The products we had to sell were Justerini and Brooks' whole line, Ballantyne's Scotch, George Goulet champagne and a peculiar brandy called Jules Robin.

'Go out now and get the orders,' said Charlie Burns airily. They gave me a price list and told me my beat.

'East of Lexington over to the river and between 42nd St. and 90th St., that's for the restaurants and bars – the private customers you pick up anywhere you can.'

I made my first sale the day before drinking became legal – a case of champagne to 'Woolly' Donahue – he needed it at once, Gus the barman gave me the case out of stock and 'Red' the doorman and I delivered it in a Yellow Cab just before midnight on 4th December – '21 Brands Inc' was in business.

In the days that followed, three things became apparent. The first was that with all the ex-bootleggers and gangsters leaping into the legitimate wine and spirits trade, I was in for a rough time in the very rough sector of the city that had been allotted to me.

Secondly, most private customers, in a sudden wave of self-righteousness, preferred to deal with old-time wine merchants and looked down their noses at the upstarts who had erupted from the gangster-ridden world of speakeasies, though this was an excuse I preferred not to make to Jack and Charlie when my shortcomings as a salesman came up for periodic review.

And thirdly, I found it impossible to try and sell to friends and acquaintances. I just could not bring myself to say 'Thank you so much for having me to dinner – now, how about buying a case of Scotch?'

The Montclair Hotel was pretty awful and the steam heat in my tiny room was suffocating but it was cheap and right on the edge of my 'territory'. The front door of the Montclair was on Lexington Avenue, exactly opposite the back door of the Waldorf-Astoria so during that miserable cold winter, I made it a point to come out each morning from the Montclair, carrying my bag of samples, cross Lexington, climb the long stairs at the rear entrance of the Waldorf, wend my way through the vast gilded lobbies of the most luxurious hotel in New York, descend the steps to the front entrance, pass through the revolving doors and issue on to Fifth Avenue to start my day ...

'Good morning, Mr. Niven,' said the doorman, saluting deferentially.

'Morning, Charles.'

Very good for morale. Then I turned right at the first corner heading for the sleazy restaurants and bars of my domain and making the most of the warmth from the exhausts of the heating plants coming up through grills in the sidewalks, I started my dreary rounds.

'Stand over there and wait your turn – okay, Jerk, let's see your list – what's this crap? Never heard of it. Git yer ass outa here.'

Fourteen degrees below zero outside and stamping into stifling sandwich counters for lunch then off again to try and corner restaurant owners sitting hunched over their meals while 'waiters' in filthy aprons wiped off tables and removed the debris of departed customers.

'Wait till I finish eating for Chrissake. Okay, let's look at the list ... Who expects to get these goddam prices anyway? "21 Brands", never heard of 'em ... Take off twenty per cent and maybe I'll talk to you: now beat it.'

Back at the end of the day with little success.

'Good evening, Mr. Niven.'

''Evening, Charles.'

Up the front stairs – through the warm, rich-people-fragrant lobbies of the Waldorf, down the back stairs, across Lexington, avoiding skidding taxis and clanging street cars and then going to ground like a bedraggled fox in my lair in the Montclair.

Big cities can be the loneliest places in the world, especially when cash is in short supply, but on New Year's Eve I decided to splurge so I took in the show at the Radio City Music Hall and stood myself a decent supper in a bar-grill off Broadway. There I met, or rather picked up, a show-girl who said she had been stood up by her date. We had a few drinks and she asked me to take her up to see the marathon dancers. The Depression had produced some desperate

138

people but none could have sunk to greater depths of degradation than those poor creatures, shuffling round twenty-four hours a day for days on end sleeping occasionally in each other's arms. Zombies with exhausted pinched faces competing for a few hundred dollars in purse money and for the sadistic pleasure of jaded onlookers like my pick-up. She lived in a gaudy apartment on the West Side. A large number of vacuous satin-clad dolls were propped upon her bed. She was attractive in a brassy but curiously vulnerable way. She too seemed lonely.

The next day, I got a call from Jack Kriendler, he must have got the news with his breakfast, he was very highly strung, 'Jesus, kid, you gotta watch your step ... you outta your mind or something? You wanna get rubbed out? ... Lay off that dame you had last night for Chrissake ... she's dynamite!'

He told me the name of the man who had stood her up. It didn't mean anything to me, but McClain whistled when he heard it.

'Jack's right,' he said, 'forget it unless you want to wind up at the bottom of the East River in a barrel of cement.'

An awful lot happened in 1934 and I had a funny feeling that things might be going to get better when one evening in early January, passing homeward through the Waldorf, I ran into Tommy Phipps, an old friend from England. There were three famous Langhorne sisters from Virginia – all very beautiful. One married Dana Gibson, the artist, and became the prototype of the Gibson Girls, another, Nancy, married Lord Astor and became Britain's famous female Member of Parliament representing Plymouth from 1919 to 1945 and was presiding at the very time I met Tommy over the much publicised Cliveden Set. The third, Norah, the youngest, and gayest, married an English Army officer, Paul Phipps. Tommy, the result of this union, had been sent to Eton and now, a few years later, had come to America to live with his mother and a newly acquired stepfather.

Tommy insisted that I leave with him that moment to spend the weekend with his family in Greenwich, Connecticut. While I was flinging a few things into a bag, Tommy filled me in on various details.

139

'Lefty' Flynn had been one of the most famous of all Yale athletes. Full-back and all-American, he had also created impossible records in track, winning everything except the high jump and he only failed to win that, according to Tommy, because he was busy winning the mile which took place at the same time.

He became a leading light in the Yale Glee club and toured with it all over the country. When they were performing in Los Angeles, his monumental physique and good looks caught the eye of William Wellman, the director, and almost overnight Lefty was starring in cowboy pictures.

His instantaneous success had made him, for a while, unreliable and during his third and last film, he had asked one day to be excused in the middle of shooting to go to the lavatory. Eight days later he had been located by distraught studio executives, in an hotel in Oklahoma City, sitting up in bed playing a guitar and painted bright blue from head to foot. In the room with him was a six-piece Hawaiian orchestra which he had picked up en route to San Francisco.

Somewhere during his travels he had met Tommy's mother and the resulting *coup de foudre* had only lately resolved itself and resulted in a new home for Tommy.

I fell in love with the whole family immediately and I am forever grateful to them for the home they gave me from that weekend on. Not a frame house home ... though that was available to me at any time ... something much more important ... a home inside myself from which I felt safe to venture forth and do battle.

Norah and Lefty did not go to parties in New York, preferring the simple life, in Greenwich, but they had a very soft spot for that inveterate international party giver, Elsa Maxwell. One evening they waited for me at the end of my day's work and took me to tea with this legendary figure in her apartment in the Waldorf Towers.

Rumours abounded as to how Elsa managed to pay for all the extravaganzas she presided over. Some said she was backed by the nouveaux riches who picked up the tab in exchange for being launched surrounded by Elsa's formidable list of the socially desired: others, less generous, hinted that she made a good living out of the by-products of these parties and having talked someone into paying for one, she

140

then collected a handsome percentage from the caterers, orchestras and decorators involved. The truth was that she was personally enormously generous and died leaving very little money. I liked her the moment I saw her.

A small, dumpy figure of sixty-odd in a sacklike garment relieved by not a single bauble, she dispensed tea and dropped names with great expertise. She reminded me somewhat of Lady Weigall so it didn't surprise me when she said, 'Selling liquor ... that's no good, no good at all ... get you nowhere ... you should go to Hollywood ... nobody out there knows how to speak English except Ronald Colman.'

Norah and Lefty made encouraging noises so she went on 'Next week I'm giving a party for Ernst Lubitsch, just a small dinner up here for forty ... plenty of people are dropping in after the theatre so you be here about twelve and I'll introduce you to Ernst and tell him to do something about it.'

The following week, I showed up at the appointed hour to find about a hundred and fifty people milling around all with the indelible stamp of self-assurance and wealth. 'If I could only sell each one of them a bottle of Scotch ...' I thought. Instead of trying, I grabbed a glass for myself and looked around for Elsa Maxwell. She was sitting on a sofa at the far end of the room, surrounded by admirers, and didn't seem to show too much enthusiasm when she caught my eye, just lifted a hand in greeting, so I decided to get on with the job myself.

Beside me stood a little dark man with a pale face, slicked down black hair and a huge cigar. He was regarding the social scene with evident distaste.

'Which is Lubitsch?' I asked.

'I am,' he said and moved away.

A few days later, Elsa called me at the Montclair and said, 'I talked to Ernst about you but he says this is not a good moment to start in pictures so I've thought of something else for you – you should marry a rich wife.'

'How do I do that?'

'Become the most popular man in New York, of course.'

'On forty dollars a week?' I said but Elsa started issuing instructions like a demented Field Marshal.

'I'm giving the party of the year for the Milk Fund. It will be at the Casino de Paris. I shall have all the most eligible bachelors in New York as professional dancing partners at a hundred dollars a dance for the Fund, and afterwards there will be a big auction and people will vote with dollars for the most popular man in New York. I want you to be one of the contestants. You will all wear green carnations ... goodbye,' and she hung up.

The Casino de Paris was filled with the brightest, the most beautiful and richest in New York. I had dusted off my ageing dinner jacket and reported for duty as ordered. Elsa gave me my badge of office – the green carnation and stood me in line with about twenty other fellows. I was probably the youngest. I was certainly the worst dancer.

A number of people bought dances from me and I was able to hand over a considerable sum to the Lady Treasurer but I was ill prepared for the shame of the auction.

After a midnight show featuring that classic mime, Jimmy Savo, a huge imitation section of the Big Board on the New York Stock Exchange was wheeled on to the stage.

There were twenty names on it. I remember only five of them, Jock Whitney, Sonny Whitney, Lytel Hull, William Rhinelander Stewart and Clifton Webb, the current rage of Broadway. My name, spelt David Nevins, was at the bottom of the list. As I watched the auction progressing a cold sweat of embarrassment broke out all over me. Blocks of shares worth thousands of dollars were bought and the amount registered in lights beside the name after each sale. For a while I had hopes that people would think I was the maker of the machine or something and in fact NEVINS might have gone unnoticed if Fifi and Dorothy Fell had not felt sorry for me and bought a hundred dollars' worth of stock between them. My value and my shame remained at that level for all to see. The winner, Jock Whitney, notched up a colossal sum for the Fund. Everyone, with one exception, was highly delighted with the evening.

I couldn't take the Montclair any longer – as a matter of fact it was mutual because on the coldest night of the year I managed to loosen enough layers of cracked and grimy paint round the window to open it about four inches at the bottom.

When I woke up my radiator was frozen solid and the heating system for an entire floor had ceased to function.

I found a basement room on Second Avenue. My view was of feet hurrying by and up beyond them, silhouetted against the yellow sky, the rattling, banging Elevated Railway.

The freezing winter seemed endless. Lefty took me skating, something I had never tried before. On a pond near Greenwich I got out of control and charged a girl who was figure skating round an orange. I cut the orange in half and knocked the girl over. Not the best way to start a romance but this was no ordinary girl as I noticed while she was helping me to my feet. She was small, almost tiny, with a wonderfully alive and pretty face, huge brown eyes, and a cloud of auburn hair pushed out from beneath a woolly skating bonnet. We had hot chocolate together and I asked where she lived.

'May I call you when I come back to New York?'

'Sure, if you want to, my name is Hudson and you can find it in the book. My father's a doctor and we live at 750 Park ... Donald Hudson.'

A few days later I called her, 'May I speak to Miss Hudson, please?'

'This is she.'

'Oh, well, this is David Niven – you said I might call you.'

'Who is this?'

'David Niven.'

'I'm sorry ... I don't know your name.'

'Don't you remember me ... cutting your orange in half?'

'I *beg* your pardon.'

'Last weekend ... skating at Greenwich ... don't you remember? I knocked you over?'

'You must be mistaken . . . I've never been to Greenwich in my life and I never go skating.'

'You are Miss Hudson?'

'*MRS*. Hudson.'

'Oh, I'm terribly sorry. You see the Miss Hudson I thought I was calling said that her father was a doctor – Donald Hudson – living at 750 Park ... I looked him up and ...'

She interrupted, 'Well, you found my husband's number and he's a lawyer. Dennis Hudson, and his address is 250

143

Park.' She had a most attractive voice; and safe at the end of the telephone I decided to press on.

'How is he anyway?'

'Who?'

'Your husband, Dennis.'

'Very well, thank you.'

'Is he a *good* lawyer?'

There was a tiny intake of breath but I sensed that she had missed the logical point to put down the receiver.

'Very good, thank you.'

'Where does he work?'

'Downtown.'

'Well, then, how about meeting me for lunch somewhere uptown?'

She still didn't cut me off.

'Certainly not, I don't have lunch with total strangers.'

'That's the trouble with all you middle-aged American women – no sense of adventure ...'

'I'm not middle-aged. I'm twenty-two.'

I settled smugly on my dungeon bed.

'Then that's really awful. I suppose you go off to one of those terrible hen parties, nibbling on a salad and gossiping?'

'Would you please not bother me any more. I'm not going to have lunch with you.'

I said nothing ... just waited.

'I mean ... how do I know that you're not a murderer or a kidnapper or something?'

'I tell you what I'll do,' I said. 'I'll wear a blue and white spotted scarf and a red carnation and I'll stand on any street corner you name at one o'clock. Then you can walk or drive by and you'll know me but I won't know you. You can take a good look and if what you see seems all right and not like a murderer or a kidnapper then we'll have lunch uptown ... how about that?'

A long, long pause. Finally she said,

'Madison and 61st Street, one o'clock,' and hung up.

I was well pleased with myself so I bought a dozen roses for Mrs. Hudson and a few minutes before 1 o'clock took up my position, round my neck my blue and white scarf, in my buttonhole, my red carnation.

Keep moving in sub-zero weather whatever happens.

144

Don't stand on windy street corners. By one-thirty, I was shivering and blue. By a quarter to two, I couldn't feel the end of my nose and the roses were turning black. I was beginning to feel pretty stupid.

Just before two o'clock, a girl walked by and smiled sweetly, 'Good afternoon, Mr. Niven.' Off came the hat ... she kept going. Next three came by, arm in arm. 'Good afternoon, Mr. Niven', they chorused.

Two went by on bicycles and four more in a taxi – she must have been awfully busy rounding up her friends but her masterstroke was the singing group from Western Union.

'Mr. Niven?'

'Yes.'

'We have a message for you sir. One! two! three! Happy lunchtime to you ... happy lunchtime to you ... happy lunchtime, dear David ... happy lunchtime to you.' I wish I could report a romantic aftermath to that episode but there was none.

In March I dropped in at a bar on 58th Street hoping to pull off a big sale. I didn't and was soon sipping a consoling drink and staring at the back-view of the first cowboy I had even seen. He sported a black ten-gallon hat, black shirt with white buttons, a white kerchief at his throat and black levis tucked inside heavily worked high-heeled boots. He also wore a large pair of spurs. From the back he didn't look much like the traditional, tall, lean, leathery man of the saddle. There was a white pudginess about his neck and a very definite bulge at his waistline. He stood no more than five feet four inches.

He finally got his drink and turned away from the bar, a bad move because his spurs became locked together, his drink went flying and he fell into my arms.

Doug Hertz, for as such he introduced himself, had a round, white face, small black eyes and a little black pencil moustache. It seemed doubtful that he could ever have been west of Brooklyn. The stories he told later of his childhood were conflicting, but I am sure I detected in his accent a mixture of the Mersey and Whitechapel somewhere under the other layers.

'Sorry, pardner,' he said, 'some dude gave me the elbow.'

Doug Hertz was a promoter of extravaganzas and sporting

145

events. As the evening wore on it appeared that he had gone down with the *Lusitania*, bobbed up again and had the top of his head blown off in the Argonne.

'Under this,' he said, rapping two knuckles on a thick black thatch of curly hair, 'you'll find a steel plate ... hair grows like moss ... pull it out tonight and it's back in the morning.'

He had also it seemed worked as ranch hand, circus roustabout, oil rigger, bouncer and strike beater. Looking at his small soft hands, I was doubtful.

'You got any dough, son?'

'None, I earn forty bucks a week.'

'That's tough, find me forty grand and I'll make you a million.'

The scheme he uncorked was wondrous.

'You've seen a rodeo, son, and you've seen a horse race. I'm gonna combine the two. Races that will last fifteen minutes.' He leaned forward, conspiratorially – 'INDOORS,' he hissed.

'Tell me more,' I said.

'You kidding? I'm on to a goddam goldmine and I'm not giving it away to some jerk in a bar ... You come up with some heavy dough and I'll make you a partner. I'm gonna make me a fortune so if you want "in" ... scratch around and come up with some rich pals. Here's my card – I'm at the Astor Hotel.'

I called Hertz early the next morning and invited him to meet me at '21' for lunch.

'You outta your skull?' he said, 'eating in joints like that? Boy, have you gotta lot to learn.'

He suggested I meet him in the lobby of the Astor and he would then show me the way to eat less expensively. I found him and we started walking. I told him about Lefty Flynn and Hertz immediately sparkled to the idea that Lefty with his connections was the ideal man to enlist in the project. Then he initiated me into his cheap eating plan. It was beautiful in its simplicity. He chose a big busy restaurant around 48th Street. I entered alone and sat at a table for two. Then I ordered a cup of coffee and a doughnut and opened my daily paper. After a suitable interval, Hertz came in and joined me. Not a flicker of recognition passed between us.

Hertz then commanded a huge meal of soup, steak, potatoes, pie and coffee. I continued reading my paper, drank a second cup of coffee, and nibbled at my doughnut.

When Hertz had finished eating, he summoned the waitress and called for his check. This was my cue.

'Would you give me mine too, please?'

The waitress slapped the two checks on the table. When she had moved away and was busy elsewhere, Hertz picked up my check for the doughnut and two cups of coffee, marched briskly over to the cashier, paid and went out into the street.

I took my time, finished my reading, then picked up Hertz's very sizeable account.

'Oh! waitress . . . look, there's a mistake here! I haven't had all this steak and pie and stuff . . . I've just had a doughnut and a couple of cups of coffee.'

Consternation and consultations followed but there was nothing for them to do but write out a second bill for two cups of coffee and a doughnut. I paid and joined Hertz at a prearranged street corner far away. A second busy restaurant was selected and there, following the same routine, Hertz got the doughnuts and coffee and I tucked in to a sizeable repast.

Lefty Flynn was always becoming involved in schemes to make his fortune overnight, so it was only natural that when I told him about Doug Hertz, he insisted on meeting him the very next day.

They made an extraordinary couple walking side by side down Fifth Avenue. Lefty towered over Doug by a good twelve inches in spite of Doug's high-heeled boots and high crowned hat.

Doug was obviously impressed by Lefty and could see that he agreed with me that this great ex-athlete with his mass of friends could be more than useful in finding backing for his dream. Horse races lasting fifteen minutes! Over coffee he explained it to us in detail.

'Simple,' said Doug, 'you have four jockeys in each race and each jockey rides fifteen horses for one minute.'

Lefty's arithmetic was no stronger than mine and his fingers were working like a Turkish bazaar dealer's on an abacus.

'Why, that's sixty horses for each race,' he said finally.

'You said it ... so we'll need about 150 horses all told for a card of six races – each horse running several times. Mind you this is the time to buy ... polo ponies! That's what we want for this set up. Who needs polo ponies in the winter? Nobody wants to feed the sons of bitches ... Polo ponies: that's what we have to get.'

'That's right,' echoed Lefty, slapping the lunch counter. 'We need polo ponies!'

I looked at him out of the corner of my eye ... there was no question ... he was hooked.

'It's just like a relay!' said Lefty, eyes gleaming.

'Just like a relay,' repeated Hertz, 'except the jockeys will have to ride a different way, for each minute, one bareback, another facing the pony's ass, another changing saddle, another changing mounts without touching the ground and so on.'

'Gee whiz,' said Lefty.

'And get this,' said Hertz, 'we'll be having betting concessions, peanut concessions, liquor, hot-dogs – kids, we're gonna clean up', said Hertz.

Later that day we formed our company – *The American Pony Express Racing Association* – and pencilled in its officers. President Maurice B. Flynn, Secretary and Treasurer, D. Niven. The experienced D. Hertz prudently kept his name off the books.

'We'll open in Atlantic City,' said Hertz.

'Where do we get the ponies?' I asked.

'Sales. Pick 'em up for peanuts. So long, as they're sound, doesn't matter how mean they are.'

'Who's going to ride them?'

'Cowboys – I'll find them, a few ads in Montana and Oklahoma and we'll have all we want ... thirty'll be enough.'

Lefty and I sat goggle-eyed as Hertz expanded.

'Atlantic City, Municipal Auditorium, then the Boston Garden, then the big one – Madison Square ... we need working capital right now for offices and my living expenses so you fellas can get going and raise that dough. Forty people putting up a thousand bucks each'll do it.'

Lefty and I were mesmerised by Hertz. We became like two schoolboys who had wandered into a power station and pulled a switch. Everything suddenly started to happen.

The first person Lefty decided to approach was Damon Runyon.

Runyon loved the idea, promptly bought a thousand dollars' worth of stock and gave us a word of warning.

'Skip Atlantic City.'

'Why?'

'Unless you can make a deal with the guy who runs it.'

'Who's that?'

' "Pinkie", he runs the numbers, the protection and the whores. He even gets a piece of every slot machine on the Steel Pier ... nobody gets into Atlantic City without Pinkie ... don't try it.'

When we reported this conversation to Hertz, he pooh-poohed it. 'Oh, Pinkie won't bother us.'

Armed with our first thousand dollars, and with Damon Runyon's name as an investor, we soon found that it was not all that difficult to raise some more. Jack and Charlie bought a few shares and stifled sighs of relief when I told them I was leaving. Elsa Maxwell campaigned for us and the sudden arrival of two old friends from England, Dennis Smith-Bingham and Ian Galloway who both became shareholders and officers of the Board, helped to lay a fairly solid financial foundation.

Many people however were sceptical of our chances and at 1, William Street, the headquarters of Lehman Brothers, we had to throw in our reserves. I went downstairs and retrieved Hertz. We had left him sitting in full regalia in a waiting room.

Hertz was subjected to a barrage of technical questions about cash flow, contracts and projected earnings. He fielded them admirably but the day was not won till I remembered the steel plate on the top of his head.

'Oh, Doug ... tell Mr. Lehman about the Argonne.'

Hertz went into his routine about the hair growing like moss but still Lehmann wavered.

'Pull a little out for Mr. Lehman,' suggested Lefty.

Hertz was as brave as a lion. Without a murmur he seized a great hank of his forelock and pulled it out by the roots. Victory was ours. The hair never grew in again, of course. We didn't use this impressive 'ploy' too often but even so, by the time we had raised twenty-five thousand dollars, Doug Hertz's head looked like a diseased moorhen.

Hertz made a deal with a decaying Polo Club at Poughkeepsie, eighty miles away up the Hudson River. There was a ramshackle hotel on the property and Hertz persuaded the proprietors that they should give us free stabling for our ponies. In return we would provide a rodeo every Sunday for which they could sell tickets. The advance guard of ponies went to Poughkeepsie followed by a bus load of cowhands from Carland, Oklahoma, and six Indians whom 'Colonel' Zack Miller had persuaded to leave their reservation. I went up to take care of this group while Lefty and Hertz went to Atlantic City. A week later they returned, flushed with success, having landed a contract with the Municipal Auditorium for a Grand Opening in May.

Smith-Bingham and Galloway, both expert horsemen, moved up and training started with a vengeance ... it was needed. The cowboys, mostly old rodeo and circus hands, operated in a haze of bourbon and rye whisky, and the ponies bought at an average price of around a hundred and twenty dollars, though sound in wind and limb were mostly quite mad.

'Excellent,' said Hertz, 'we'll have 'em running through the orchestra and jumping into the ringside seats.'

Our spartan life at Poughkeepsie was enlivened by the appearance of Hertz's blonde, statuesque wife who took an instant shine to Ian Galloway. One night there was an ugly scene when Hertz accused Ian of trying to seduce her in the stables. It ended with everyone getting drunk in the hotel and swearing eternal friendship but in the middle of the celebrations, Dennis Smith-Bingham rushed in. 'Come on, quick! somebody's left the door open and about forty ponies have got out ... they're all over the bloody country.' We dashed out.

It was a pitch black night so it took hours to round them up. The only casualty was Hertz who ran very fast straight into a large carthorse which was standing perfectly still in the middle of a field. The impact knocked him cold.

Training progressed and in a few weeks, we could see that we had a very exciting spectacle on our hands: the only problem was money. We were approaching our Grand Opening in Atlantic City and the cost of moving the whole cavalcade from Poughkeepsie was going to be astronomical. Hertz called an emergency meeting.

'We're in trouble, boys, we've gotta have another ten grand to get us to the opening. From there on in the show'll pay for itself but I've gotta have ten big ones this week or we fold.'

We were silent.

'Get down to New York fellas and beat the bushes – I mean it – or we fold.'

Somehow we raised the money, and set off for Atlantic City on the appointed day.

The advance man had done his job with enthusiasm. Hoardings and walls were plastered with announcements of our coming and promises of what we were going to deliver. 'CHILLS, SPILLS AND THRILLS' – screamed the posters. Doug Hertz organised a parade from the railway station and tied up traffic all over town as a result. He rode at its head himself, an oval pouter-pigeon figure rolling slightly in the saddle as his round thighs tried to grip: he didn't really ride, he 'conned' horses into letting him sit on them.

The American Pony Express Racing Association was in Atlantic City for a week before the Grand Opening and Lefty and I often broached the subject of Damon Runyon's warning about the mysterious Pinkie which still nagged us.

'Nothing to worry about at all,' said Hertz confidently, 'I've seen the police, nobody's going to interfere with us.'

'How do we get any betting? It's illegal in the State of New Jersey.'

Hertz winked broadly. 'Everything is just Jim Dandy.'

On the night of the Grand Opening, it was pouring with rain but the lines were at the box office and by the time the parade started, the auditorium was packed – fifteen thousand people. Dorothy Fell and McClain came down with a big party from New York to cheer us on but we were so short of cash that we couldn't afford an orchestra for our opening night. The best we could provide was an organist. The organ blared out stirring music as the parade trotted round the arena.

A Master of Ceremonies, wearing full fox hunting regalia, explained over the loud speaker the finer points of the races. The teams of ponies were guaranteed to be evenly matched, he said, so it was a question of picking the jockey with the most prowess.

I had a feeling of cement in my stomach when the teams came out for the first race, but Hertz waddled about exuding confidence.

'Good luck, kids,' he said, to the riders, 'you're gonna be great.'

The ponies sensed the tension and acted up like thoroughbreds. One or two which had been tubed whistled loudly through holes in their necks. Suddenly the auditorium went dark except for the bright floodlit track. Crack went the opening gun and away went the first race. The entire audience rose to its feet. Terrible chances were taken at the sharp turns. The cowboys excelled themselves, the courageous Indians staged some hair-raising falls and at the end of the evening we listened almost unbelievably to loud and prolonged applause.

'We're in business, kids,' said Hertz, clapping Lefty and me on our backs. 'Next stop, Boston, then the Garden!'

The morning after, I was sitting in our little office in the Auditorium smugly reading the reviews of our show in the local press when four extremely hostile characters barged in. They wore fedoras and tight double-breasted suits.

'Where's Hertz?' they demanded.

Almost before I could answer the avocado shape of our leader appeared in the doorway behind them. When Hertz saw his visitors, he went the colour of cat-sick.

'Okay,' said one of the hostile men to me, 'we don't need you – beat it.' I left with what dignity I could summon.

For about twenty minutes, I watched the approach to our office from a discreet distance and when I saw the men depart, I hurried back in. Hertz was sitting slumped behind the desk. He looked stricken.

'What did they want?' I asked.

Hertz smiled wanly.

'It was a shakedown,' he said, 'but nothing's gonna happen. Like I said, I'm right in there with the cops.' He didn't sound too confident and in the event, a number of things did happen. That second night, we had a 'house' only slightly less well filled than the previous one. Everything was going according to plan and the audience was enjoying itself hugely. Suddenly, in the middle of the second race all the lights in the Auditorium went out. For a while chaos reigned, ponies were crashing into each other, cowboys were swearing and women screaming. The lights stayed out for fifteen minutes and the slow handclaps started. Finally, the lights came on again and we restarted the show. During the fourth race, the same thing occurred – only this time, when the lights went on again the people were streaming towards the exits and many went to the box office and demanded their money back.

On the third night, it was discovered that at least half the cowboys had packed up and left during the day.

The next day, the forage for the animals never arrived and during the night a large number of saddles mysteriously disappeared.

On the fifth night, the lights went out again. More cowboys defected the next day and on the Saturday night, our show was pitiful. It didn't matter any more, the audiences had eroded to a point where only a handful turned up.

Hertz, who had certainly never lacked courage, was stoic in defeat, but all chances of selling the show to other Auditoriums in the country had evaporated. We were living on a shoestring. Everything had depended on making a big profit during that first week.

It was decided to liquidate our assets immediately and salvage what we could from the wreck.

Lefty could take all the disappointments except the desertion of the cowboys. He had loved them dearly and he couldn't believe that they had allowed themselves to be induced to sink us. Sadly, he left for Greenwich and I stayed on to help Hertz arrange a sale of the livestock and remaining saddlery – all the assets we had. They didn't fetch much and by the time we had tied everything up in Atlantic City, I am afraid our gallant band of backers did not see very much of their original investment.

When I came to think of it, I, too, was in far worse financial shape than when I had first become involved with the American Pony Express Racing Association and in addition, I had given up my job with Jack and Charlie but please don't feel at the end of this chapter, you are leaving me, like Pearl White, strapped to the financial railroad tracks, because, thank God, succour was already puffing towards me aboard the American Express.

CHAPTER TEN

BACK in New York, I found a letter from Grizel. My mother, it appeared, had left everything to 'Tommy' in trust for the four of us, but she had stipulated something very important. Max had once borrowed £300 from her to bail himself out of debt, so if either Joyce or Grizel or I were in desperate need, the small estate must try to provide the same amount for us.

Within a week, I had collected my share. It came to a little over eight hundred dollars – I was rich.

Lefty and Norah had gone to Bermuda where they had rented a small cottage at Devonshire Bay. Lefty met me in Hamilton and I spent several blissful weeks on that spectacular island at a time that must have been its golden era. No cars, no motor cycles – just bicycles or horse-drawn carriages, no muttering groups at street corners, no sullen looks from under pork-pie hats, no cut-off conversations, just smiling happy faces and music everywhere.

Joe Benevides was our carriage driver, a mixture of negro and Portuguese blood. He had bright blue eyes and the broadest smile I had ever seen.

As we clip-clopped along the dazzling white coral road, we passed through orchid farms and dense plantations of palm trees. Bright hued little birds darted in and out of the oleander and giant hibiscus bushes and when we arrived at the cottage, the bay in front of it was aquamarine and the seagulls flying lazily in the blue above had long graceful forked tails.

'Norah's got a big surprise for you, Davey,' said Lefty, 'somebody very special is coming to supper tonight.'

In a day spent swimming on a pink sand beach, reminiscing about our ill-fated venture and laughing – oh! how much we laughed – I forgot about my big surprise until Anthony Pleydell-Bouverie walked into the cottage, accompanied by a diminutive Finnish wife called Peanut.

Anthony was now flag lieutenant to Admiral Sir Ernle Erle Drax, commander-in-chief of a large fleet based on Bermuda. It was a classic reunion.

A week later, Tommy Phipps arrived. He had lately come back from California and was full of stories of Hollywood. He had also sold his first piece of writing, a short story, to *Harper's Bazaar*. The days flew by. We bicycled off in the mornings to various beaches or explored the Islands. We were never out of the water and became burned the colour of mahogany. I fell slightly in love with a dark haired beauty of eighteen from Richmond, Virginia. She wore a camellia in her hair on the night I took her for a romantic drive in the full moon. Joe Benevides, though himself the soul of tact on these occasions, sitting bolt upright in his box and staring straight ahead oblivious to what was going on behind him, had unknowingly sabotaged my very delicate preliminary moves by feeding his horse some wet grass. It is quite impossible to impress a beautiful girl with your sincerity if your carefully worded murmurings into a shell pink ear have to compete with a barrage of farts.

A lot of the time we spent planning our lives. Lefty and Norah had made up their minds to leave the suburbia of Greenwich for the real country. They had masses of places to choose from and plans and prospectuses went with us everywhere. Their hearts were more or less set on the little village of Tryon, North Carolina, nestling at the foot of the Smokey Mountains. There they had their eyes on a delicious low white frame farmhouse called Little Orchard.

Tommy had more or less decided to follow a literary career and looked like installing himself in New York.

I was the problem and much of the planning time was allotted to my future moves. A letter from Dennis Smith-Bingham decided them.

Lefty's stories of his time in Hollywood had fired my imagination. Then Tommy had stoked the fires. Now Dennis's letter clinched it.

Immediately after Atlantic City, he had left for California: 'This is a great spot. Come out and see for yourself,' he wrote. 'I'll find you a place to live.'

Deep down I had a sneaking feeling that I might be able to make a go of it in the movies. Norah and Lefty urged me on when I broached the idea but Tommy was more forthright – 'Your legs are too big,' he said.

Big legs or not, at the end of July, I packed my worldly

155

belongings in my suitcases and the Flynns, Tommy, Anthony and the Peanut came to see me off. I sailed on a dirty old freighter for Cuba.

I had a week to wait in Cuba before the *President Pierce* sailed for the Panama Gulf and California.

Havana enthralled me and I loved the gay jostling mobs but there was a strange undercurrent of uneasiness and much that I did not understand. A lot of heavily armed soldiers were about and almost as soon as I arrived I witnessed a very brutal arrest.

One night in Sloppy Joe's Bar, I met an Irishman. He explained what was going on. The power behind President Mendieta was his Chief of Staff, Batista – 'a ruthless bastard' according to my informant. 'He won't even let them have an election.' The Irishman was fascinating and, I think, a little mad. I met him every evening. He tried to sell me the idea of becoming a soldier of fortune with him and joining some strange group who were forming 'to fight for the rights of the people'.

One night, on my way to Sloppy Joe's, an English voice spoke to me from a doorway near the entrance to my cheap hotel.

'May I have a word with you?' The man was about 35 and wore a white linen suit.

'Of course.'

'You hold a British passport do you not?'

'Yes.'

'I'm from the British Embassy – how long are you planning to stay here?'

'I'm sailing on the *President Pierce*, the day after tomorrow.'

'Good. I hope you'll do just that. You've been seen with a man whom the local authorities don't view too highly. We got the word from them this morning. I suspect you have been followed, because they told me where to find you. Take my tip, don't miss that ship.'

He refused to join me for a drink and hurried away. I avoided Sloppy Joe's that night and was the first in line when the gangway of the *President Pierce* was lowered.

When travelling I have always lived in the hope that I will find myself seated on planes next to the most beautiful girl. It never happens. Usually it is a mid-European business man who spreads himself over my seat and smokes a foul cigar.

I knew I would be sharing my cabin on the *President Pierce* with someone and I prayed that the agents might have slipped up and that I would find myself with one of the several attractive ladies I noticed going through the Immigration. My room mate turned out to be an Indian male – a Red Indian male but this was no lean copper-coloured warrior, mine was about two hundred and fifty pounds of pure blubber and he smelled like a badger. According to the purser, he had just become a millionaire because oil had been found on a small plot of land he owned in Oklahoma.

The *President Pierce* had started her cruise in New York so by the time I joined her everyone was more or less acquainted and I was the new boy in the school. Most of the passengers were elderly but there was a few families headed for Panama and California. It came as a rude shock when I realised the ship was 'dry'. I was fascinated by the passage through the Canal and at Panama, where we spent a day, I went ashore and played golf in a thunderstorm.

The smell of hot Indian was so overpowering in my cabin that I regularly slept in a deck chair behind a funnel.

I spent a great deal of time and energy avoiding the cruise director, a man who looked and behaved like a games-mistress.

'Come, come,' he would say, clapping his hands. 'Who's for shuffle board ... we don't want to get "pepless" do we? You look like a perfect ping-pong type', he said to me, just as I was settling down to a good book. 'This is Miss Weyhauser from Toledo, Ohio. 'She'll give you a good game ... come ... come ...'

Miss Weyhauser had a small brother of nine and he became the bane of my existence – a really horrid little boy who wore white plus-fours, a white shirt with a red bow tie and a white peaked cap with a pom-pom on the top of it. His name was Cyrus – Cy for short – he never left my side. He was intrigued by my 'English accent' and followed me round all day saying, 'Pip-pip, old chappie. Jolly good show – what! any teabags anyone ...?'

His father, not surprisingly, was a Hollywood scriptwriter. Finally, after several warnings, I hit him. I was playing ping-pong with his sister and when Cyrus was not picking up the ball and throwing it overboard, he was pinching my bottom and crying out 'The Redcoats are coming,' so I let him have one really hard with the flat of my hand. It made a noise like a pistol shot. Everyone looked up from their chairs to find Cyrus lying on the deck holding the side of his face, and pointing and howling, 'The Limey hit me! The Limey hit me!'

Miss Weyhauser took a backhander at me with her ping-pong racquet and said, 'Oh! how dare you strike a child!' The cruise director materialised as if by magic.

'Well, we all thought you were a gentleman,' he swished off and picked up the blubbering little brute and cradled him in his arms.

That night the cruise director said he thought it might be a nice gesture if I apologised publicly to Cyrus and his mother after dinner. I had nothing to lose; no one was speaking to me anyway, so in the lounge, I stood up and asked for attention. I said that I was really sorry that it had happened and begged them all not to think it was typical of my race. 'I am an orphan,' I said. 'I was abandoned in a cemetery by my mother when I was a few weeks old. I never knew who my father was. I was brought up by the parson but he drank the Communion wine and beat me every Sunday night.' I went on along those lines. I was good – there was no question, and as I warmed to my work, I saw several good ladies sniffling and taking out their handkerchiefs. I began to wonder if my trip to Hollywood might perhaps not be in vain.

I sat down to rapturous applause. My apology was accepted with smug bad grace by Cyrus and his mother and for the remaining days of the voyage, he redoubled his efforts to annoy me. I got even with the little sonofabitch on the day we docked at San Pedro.

'I'm really sorry, Cy, about what happened,' I said.

'Oh, that's okay, Limey, forget it.'

'No really Cy, to show there's no hard feelings, come and have an ice cream soda with me.'

'Okay.'

We sat on two stools at the only bar in the ship.

'Banana split with cream?'

'Okay.'

Then a little later,

'How about a chocolate sundae with pistaccio nuts?'

'Okay.'

'A nice prune whip and caramel sauce?'

'Okay.'

I must say it was an expensive revenge. He was a veritable human disposal, but finally, after about seven mountainous concoctions his colour began to change.

His mother's last-minute packing must have been very interesting.

Dennis had cabled that he would meet the ship and there he was with a beautiful golden-haired girl. I recognised her at once as Sally Blane, a fast-rising young star of the movies.

The usual shipboard reporters were sniffing around for stories. They spotted Sally and I found myself improvising about the pony racing and my plans. The next day, there was a picture of me in the Los Angeles *Examiner* with the caption – 'BRITISH SPORTSMAN ARRIVES, PLANS TO BUY OVER A HUNDRED HEAD OF POLO PONIES.'

Sally was marvellous, endowed with a lovely open face. 'It's all arranged,' she said. 'Mom's got a room for you. You are going to come and visit with us till you find somewhere to live.'

Mrs. Belzer was Sally's mother and with her three other daughters she lived in a charming colonial style house on Sunset Boulevard between Holmby Hills and Westwood.

On the drive up from San Pedro, we passed first through oil fields and citrus groves, then we stayed on the Coastal Highway with the endless sandy beaches and pounding Pacific surf on the left. In the distance, were the high hills behind Los Angeles and far away to our right, the snowy top of Mount Baldy.

Mrs. Belzer was a beautiful woman, wonderfully sweet and seemingly vague with an impeccable taste in antique furniture. The girls all worshipped her.

When I met the others I gaped. They were all spectacular beauties. Blonde Georgiana was the youngest, only about eleven. Polly Ann Young, an excellent and successful actress, was the oldest, probably twenty-two, a glowing brunette. Then there was Gretchen. Gretchen was already a big movie star and her working name of Loretta Young was known all over the world.

There has never been in my experience such a beautiful family to look at, and the beauty came from within because each and every one of them was filled with concern for others, and kindness, and generosity.

They have never changed.

It was impossible to lie to people like these so when Dennis, a few days later, left suddenly for England, I confessed one night to Mrs. Belzer and the girls that I was hoping to break into movies. I felt an idiot doing it in front of three already established professionals but they took it in their stride and took great care not to put me off by telling me too many facts that I was soon to discover for myself.

The next day I got my first taste of a major studio. Loretta was making a picture at Fox, something about hospital nurses and it was arranged that when the family car came to fetch her in the evening, I would be smuggled past the eagle-eyed police at the gate lying on the floor under a rug.

Once inside the gate it was a dream world. The car slipped through Indian villages, jungles, sections of Venice, complete Western streets, New York streets and past a French château and a lake with a large schooner and native canoes on it.

The studio buildings, the executive offices, cutting rooms, fire department, casting office and the huge towering sound stages seemed like a miniature city and everywhere the streets teemed with cowboys, Indians, Southern gentlemen, soldiers, policemen, troupes of dancers and tall willowy show girls. I just gaped and gaped and wondered if I could ever be part of it.

Loretta's driver took me inside stage 19 and I watched fascinated from a dark corner while she was powdered and primped and prepared for a close-up. What a strange, wonderful secret world! It pulled me like a magnet.

I really cannot remember what I was using for money at that time. I know I didn't borrow any and I don't remember stealing but I do know that within a very few days of arrival I realised the vastness of the distances and the urgent necessity for some wheels and for an augmentation of my funds.

The girls took me to a used car lot in Culver City and I

160

bought a very old Auburn for ninety dollars. It went quite well on the flat but hated hills and the small incline of the Bel Air driveway could only be negotiated in reverse.

They also helped me in my search for a place to live. They never gave any sign of it but they must have prayed that I would soon be successful. It is with great embarrassment that I have to record that nothing suitable was found for a considerable time.

The Central Casting Office was down on Western Avenue. It handled only the 'extras'. Anybody who spoke lines was a 'bit player' or a 'small part actor' – these the studios employed through agents. In the Auburn I drove to Central Casting thinking that all I had to do was enrol myself and go to work. It was a forbidding moment. Outside the building was a large sign.

'DON'T TRY TO BECOME AN ACTOR. FOR EVERYONE WE EMPLOY, WE TURN AWAY A THOUSAND.'

I stood in a long line and finally was interviewed by a brisk elderly woman with protruding teeth and glasses so dark that I could not see her eyes.

'Yes?'

'I'd like to be a movie actor.'

'So would millions of others. What professional experience have you?'

'None, I'm afraid.'

'Nationality?'

'British.'

'Do you realise how many Americans there are looking for work these days?' Before I could answer, she went on, 'Well, the studios are making a lot of British stories right now so we might find something for you ... fill in this form and mail it to us ... you got a work permit okay?'

'Work permit?'

'You can't work without one – it's against the law. You got one?'

'No.'

'Give me back that form ... the way out's over there.'

There is an antidote to everything, even, we are told, hopefully, to the Intercontinental Ballistic Missile, and usually when those old Chinese weeds we wrote about earlier start clogging up the garden and things look pretty hopeless, out of the blue comes a weed-killer.

The weed-killer at this point was Alvin Weingand, later a highly respected Congressman from California, but then a junior reception clerk at the Roosevelt Hotel on Hollywood Boulevard. My search for cheap accommodation had not been going well and Al gave me a room between a service elevator and a huge machine that shrieked and thumped all night as it inhaled warm air, cooled it and belched it downstairs for the benefit of the guests. When I say 'gave' me the room, he charged me so little that it amounted almost to a gift. I had a bed, a shower and a telephone, I needed no more.

Unpacking, I came across a telephone number – a girl I had met in New York, Lydia Macy who lived in Montecito eighty miles away. I called her and was invited for the weekend.

Not feeling I could trust the Auburn to undertake such a long trip, I packed my bag, including my frayed and frightful dinner jacket, and thumbed a ride up the U.S. Highway 101 arriving in Montecito in a fruit truck, in plenty of time for dinner. Montecito has more resident millionaires per acre than any other community in the United States. The houses are beautiful; the mountains behind them are purple in the evening light and between them and the white sandy beaches lies a palm-covered plateau inhabited by charming lotus-eaters.

On the Saturday morning, I looked out of my bedroom window and, riding at anchor in the bay, off Santa Barbara, I beheld an old friend, H.M.S. *Norfolk* a county class cruiser. She had been in Malta when I was there and more lately, I had found her again in Bermuda. Now, she was on a goodwill tour of the West Coast of Mexico, the United States and Canada.

I told Lydia that I would love to go and visit her as I knew several people on board – 'Well, you're going tonight,' said Lydia. 'The officers are giving a party and all of Montecito is going.'

That night, in a dinner jacket that had been rejuvenated by Lydia's maid, I escorted her on board *Norfolk*.

162

A huge awning covered the after-deck and she was dressed with garlands of lights and bunting. The Royal Marine Band was grinding out a foxtrot ... I looked around for a familiar face and nearly fell over the side – there stood Anthony Pleydell-Bouverie. Apparently, Admiral Sir Ernle Erle Drax had decided to join the cruise and his flag lieutenant had come too.

Poor Lydia! I didn't behave very well. The reunions were continuous and strenuous and I spent far too long in the wardroom. She left without me. All guests were asked to be off the ship by three a.m. At about that time, I mumbled to Anthony that it was time I left.

'Nonsense,' he said, 'don't go ashore ... we'll look after you ... there's a bunk you can have ... go to bed and have a nice rest.'

It sounded fine and I was past being analytical anyway, so I removed my clothes and fell immediately into a deep black sleep.

Next morning, about ten-thirty, I woke with a mouth like the inside of a chauffeur's glove – nobody was around. It was Sunday and the ship's company was at Divine Service. I looked out of the port-hole and couldn't see much except sea and the sea was passing the window at a great rate.

I lay there wondering what to do next. Whatever Anthony had said, it made no sense to be at sea, in the middle of the Pacific, in one of His Majesty's county class cruisers ... in broad daylight ... in a dinner jacket.

I continued to lie there. About noon a sailor poked his head round the door.

'Compliments of the Ward Room, sir, the officers would like to see you.'

I doused my head with cold water, donned my crumpled suit and followed him through the humming interior maze of the ship. Sailors gave me surprised glances as I passed.

Several of last night's drinking companions were already at the bar.

'Morning, Niven – pink gin?'

'Yes, thanks.'

'Enjoy yourself, last night? Pretty girl you had with you,' – small talk, chatter, more pink gin, no sign of Anthony and nobody bringing up the question of why I was still with them.

I thought to myself 'Well, I'd better just play this by ear ... if they're not going to mention it – I'm not' – so I relaxed, joined in the small talk, accepted the pink gins and closed my mind to the future.

At last, Anthony appeared. 'Sorry,' he said. 'I've been with the Admiral. He wants to see you!'

'Like this?' I said, looking down.

'You look fine,' said Anthony, 'let's go – he's waiting for you.'

By now I was sure I was going to be made to walk the plank.

In the Captain's dining-room, the Admiral was waiting, a spare, ruddy, typical sailor.

'Morning, Niven.'

'Morning sir.'

'Enjoy yourself last night?'

'Very much thank you, sir.'

'Care for a pink gin?'

'Thank you, sir.'

There I stood in my dinner jacket, wondering, and there half an hour later, I sat having luncheon, still wondering. Small talk, shop talk, Malta talk, Bermuda talk but the subject of my presence never broached.

Towards the end of the meal, a signalman knocked and entered. He handed the Admiral a message using the flat white top of his headgear as a tray.

'H'm,' said the Admiral, 'H.M.S. *Bounty* off the starboard bow ... Niven, look out there and see if you can see her, will you?'

I moved to the indicated port-hole wondering if delirium tremens was always so fascinating. I had just finished reading Nordhoff and Hall's brilliant historical novel which Lefty had taken to Bermuda.

Sure enough, I beheld the *Bounty* with all sails set, moving gently on the Pacific swells. Suddenly, little white puffs of smoke like cotton wool erupted from her side, followed by the champagne cork pops of her cannon. H.M.S. *Norfolk* slowed to a dead stop. The *Bounty* came close and I could see her crew wearing pig-tails and striped stockings, then victory cheers floated across the water. I turned towards the Admiral and Anthony and they both burst out laughing.

'This is where you get off, young man,' said the Admiral.

As he led me on deck, Anthony explained that the great Metro Goldwyn Mayer producer, Irving Thalberg, was about to make a film of *Mutiny on the Bounty*. A complete replica of the original eighteenth-century warship had been built and now, as a publicity stunt for the promotion of the picture, a meeting with its modern counterpart had been arranged in the Catalina Channel.

A rope ladder was dropped over the side and, an incongruous figure in my dinner jacket and cheered on by Anthony and a large number of the ship's company, I clambered nervously down on to the deck of the press tender which had materialised alongside.

Several of today's Hollywood Press Corps, including Jimmy Starr of the Los Angeles *Herald Express* and Bill Mooring of *Tidings*, witnessed my arrival and I got the reputation of being the first man to crash Hollywood in a battleship.

Also on the tender were Frank Lloyd, the director of the picture, and Robert Montgomery, one of the reigning Hollywood stars. Clark Gable and Charles Laughton who were to make the film as Fletcher Christian and Captain Bligh were not present. Bob Montgomery had come along for the ride. The camera crews, the press, Frank Lloyd and Montgomery were most hospitable to their unexpected charge and as *Norfolk* gathered speed and resumed her course south, I was carried unprotesting for the second time in about three weeks to the port of San Pedro.

Montgomery had a new sports Bentley – very impressive for me to see this beautiful machine so far from home and very helpful to me when he offered me a lift to M.G.M. studios, which lay some hundred miles north.

We arrived at about seven o'clock just as the day's work was coming to an end. The departing crowds of extras stood, respectfully, aside as Montgomery was saluted through the main gate by the studios' police.

Frank Lloyd offered me a drink in his office and there I met another great director of the day, Edmund Goulding.

Goulding had lately completed the epic *Grand Hotel* with

165

Garbo, John Barrymore, Joan Crawford, Wallace Beery and a host of other great names as his stars. He was about to start a film with Ruth Chatterton.

Goulding was about five feet ten of square stocky build, sandy hair and a broken nose spread halfway across his face. About forty, a man of enduring charm, I owe more to him than to anyone else in the business.

Goulding was wearing the Goulding uniform – sweat shirt, silk handkerchief round his neck, a blue blazer and white slacks turned up at the bottoms displaying highly polished loafers. He laughed with a deep rumble when he heard from Frank Lloyd about my arrival on *Norfolk*.

'Ever done any acting?' he asked.

'None to speak of.'

'Good. I'm looking for a new face to play the drunken, dissolute, younger brother of Chatterton. Will you make a test for me tomorrow?'

I thought it better with this wonderful opportunity being dangled before me to leave nothing unsaid that ought to be said so I told him about my abortive trip to Central Casting a few days before.

'No problem,' said Goulding, 'you don't need any permit to make a test ... if it works out, the studio will arrange things.'

'What do I have to do?'

'Just be yourself ... Harry Bouquet, the test director, will make it – he'll give you something easy to do.' Goulding then invited me to his home for dinner. He was married to the famous dancer, Marjorie Moss. Even then she was dying. Goulding knew, she didn't.

After dinner when I made a move to go home, Goulding and Marjorie would have none of it.

'Why?' they asked.

'To sleep, shave and change.'

'You can sleep and shave here,' said Goulding, 'but I want that test made exactly as you are now – in that dinner jacket.'

The next morning at 8.30 a.m. I presented myself to Harry Bouquet on stage 29. I had been painted a strange yellow ochre by Bill Tuttle in the make-up department and my eyes and lips were made up like a Piccadilly tart – I felt ridiculous.

Harry Bouquet, a frustrated man, was in a hurry. 'Christ,' he said, 'I've got six of these goddamned things to get through by lunch time; waddaya gonna do?'

'Mr. Goulding said you'd give me something easy,' I said.

'Jesus! nothing's easy in this business! Okay, stand over by that table while they light you.'

The set was decorated as a New York apartment. Under the bright lights I could vaguely make out the outlines of the camera and about forty people. A man with evil-smelling fingers stuck a light meter immediately beneath my nose.

'Light 'em all,' came a voice from the camera – 'Okay, Harry, let's go.'

Bouquet loomed out of the shadows.

'Okay now, start off facing the camera, then turn slowly when I tell you – wait a beat at each profile. Then wind up facing the camera again, got it?'

'Yes sir.'

'Turn'em over.'

I stood blinded by the lights and stared in the direction of the camera like a dog watching a snake.

'Turn slowly,' said Bouquet, 'hold the profile, goddammit ... Okay, now hold the full face ... try to come alive for Chrissake ... tell us a funny story.'

Out of my panic and my subconscious came a very old school boy limerick. I recited it.

There once was an old man of Leeds
Who swallowed a packet of seeds,
Great tufts of grass
Shot out of his arse
And his cock was covered in weeds.

'Cut!!!'

Bouquet loomed up again. 'Whattayou trying to do for Chrissake! Get me fired? Everyone sees these things ... L. M. Mayer ... Mannix, the whole bunch.'

He softened and smiled, 'Okay, kid, now relax, we'll pick it up from there ... think of some little story. When you're ready tell me and we'll shoot it ... clean it up though willya.'

Finally I recounted a story that had happened to Tommy

167

Phipps when he first went into an automat. Not knowing how it worked, he put five cents in the slot machine for a cup of coffee and collected a jet of hot fluid in the fly buttons. Later somebody ate his sandwich and somebody else dunked their doughnut in the coffee he had finally managed to collect in a cup.

I had laughed when Tommy told it and there was, I thought, quite a gratifying reaction when I had finished this homely little tale.

The next day, Goulding called me and told me to meet him at his office.

'That test was really pretty bad – apart from the natural bit when you told the limerick. Except for that you were all frozen up. You won't get the part this time ... L.B. wants Louis Hayward anyway ... but I think you can make it and I'm going to help you. I'll be through with my picture in about twelve weeks, till that's over I can do nothing – call me in three months and we'll see what can be done.'

Al Hall was Mae West's director and she was about to start a picture at Paramount – *Going to Town*. Goulding told Hall about me. Hall got hold of my test and a week later I got a call from the Paramount Casting Office. Mae West would like to interview me as her possible leading man.

I was welcomed at Paramount almost with eagerness. Anybody Mae West might want, they might want too, so before I was even seen by Miss West, I found myself being asked if I would be interested in a seven-year contract with options. Did I have a work permit? – 'No.' – 'Never mind, we can fix that.'

I was ushered into a huge office and seated behind a Mussolini-type desk was a small round platinum blonde woman flanked on one side by a large American-Irish manager, and on the other by the diminutive Al Hall.

She never spoke. The men asked various questions. Then, after a whispered conversation Al Hall said, 'Would you mind taking off your coat? And your shirt?'

'Now turn around, please.'

More whispers, then the manager spoke.

'Who is your agent?'

'I don't have one.'

Incredulous looks were passed.

'We'd like to see you again. Please be sure that Casting knows where you are.'

The men rose and shook hands cordially, Mae West said nothing.

The next day, I had an urgent call from the Paramount Casting Office. I also had a visitor. A pale-faced man in a dark suit was waiting for me in the hotel lobby.

'I'm from United States Immigration Service, Mr. Niven. Now let me see ...' He had some documents, 'you arrived in San Pedro four weeks ago. You asked for and were granted a ten days' visitors' visa. You are, therefore, now in this country illegally. We also understand you are contemplating signing an employment contract with a U.S. firm, so you are about to break the law on a second count.'

'What do I do?' I asked.

He was a kind man but a tired one. He must have been through this a thousand times. His voice was weary.

'You have twenty-four hours to be off United States territory – you understand that don't you?'

'Yes.'

'Then sign this.'

I glanced at a mimeographed slip, it was a statement admitting that I had been told to leave and that I understood the dire penalties involved if I did not comply.

'Where the hell do I go?'

'That's your problem, son. If you want to work in this country you must get a Resident Alien Visa. So long now.'

Al Weingand advised me and that afternoon I boarded a train that clanked and bumped for hours through a sandstorm to the border post of Calexico. There I left the United States and walked on foot into Mexico.

Mexicali may be a thriving metropolis by now. I hope it is, for its own sake. In late 1934, it was the most awful dump I had ever seen. A single dirt road ran through the centre of the small township and petered out at each end into dry brown hills. In the centre of the town there was one dilapidated hotel, a few broken-down lodging houses, a grocery store that must have been the official breeding ground for all the flies in Northern Mexico and one small clean-looking house, the American Consulate.

The American Consul was a busy man, mostly because he

had to cope with the problems and grievances of the sad daily flow of underpaid Mexicans who crossed the border to be driven in stinking buses to work crippling hours picking fruit, cotton and vegetables in the Imperial Valley.

He advised me kindly that he would be able to arrange a visa for me as a Resident Alien in the U.S. but first I must produce my birth certificate and a copy of my police record from Scotland Yard.

I took a room for a dollar a night in a loathsome lodging house and sent my sister Grizel a cable – 'SEND BIRTH CERTIFICATE IMMEDIATELY.' She got the cable two weeks later when she returned from a trip to Spain. She did not distinguish herself by her reply – WHOSE BIRTH CERTIFICATE? I really had to sweat it out – there was little transatlantic air mail in those days. The mail service in Mexicali via Mexico City must have gone by donkey. My little pile of money was dwindling alarmingly but many Americans came to Mexicali to hunt quail and other game in the surrounding brown hills. I became the 'gun man' in the only moderately clean bar in the town and in exchange for chili or tortillas, I cleaned and polished the guns while their owners drank and boasted. Sometimes I was given a tip. I never refused.

It was just after New Year's Day 1935 when I triumphantly presented myself at the U.S. Border at Calexico, in my hand was my Resident Alien Visa – my permit to work.

I jumped trucks back to Los Angeles. Al Weingand let me have my old room back and manfully swallowed the difficulties of payment.

I telephoned Goulding, but he had finished his picture and gone to New York. Mae West, I learned, was halfway through her picture with an unknown English actor called Paul Cavanagh playing opposite her.

I visited Central Casting and after an agonising wait of several days, was finally accepted and enrolled as 'Anglo-Saxon Type No. 2008'.

Such was the efficiency of Central Casting that the first call I got to work as a professional actor, was as a Mexican.

Los Angeles is one of the largest cities in area in the world. The film studios are mostly strategically placed in far away suburbs miles from its centre. Universal Studios is in the

San Fernando Valley. I was told to be there at 5 a.m. The Auburn broke down the night before so I started a zig-zag journey across the city by street car at 3 o'clock.

Once at the studios, I was handed a chit through a small window and instructed to report to wardrobe. There, I waited in line, showed my chit which was stamped, and was issued with a baggy white suit, a large sombrero, some sandals and a blanket.

I changed in a huge barn-like dressing room. Other 'Mexicans' were putting on their outfits. 'Indians' were also preparing themselves and honest townsfolk were getting into tailcoats, top hats and bowlers. The women 'extras' were dressing in an adjacent barn.

I followed my fellow 'Mexicans' to the make-up department and once more stood in line. While those, including myself, who had fair skins were sprayed with a brown mixture from a spray gun, on some of us they glued moustaches. The 'Indians' lined up opposite were being similarly treated all over their bodies with a reddish colour. Somewhere the Chinese were getting it in yellow.

There was not much happy chatter, I noticed.

At six-thirty, we were all marshalled by an assistant director and loaded into buses for a one hour drive to a remote movie ranch where the permanent Western town had been erected, there we were positioned by other assistants and told when to move slowly, when to scatter in alarm, etc., etc. The cowboy star, whoever he was, appeared and at eight o'clock sharp shooting started. The director's name was Aubrey Scotto. He did not bother with us, we were pushed around all day by a harassed assistant.

At one o'clock we were given a cardboard box and told we had half an hour to eat. The contents consisted of a piece of chicken fried in batter, some cookies, an orange and a small carton of milk. After lunch we resumed shooting till the sun became too low and its light too feeble to continue.

There had been a lot of pushing and pulling by the extras during the filming of the last scene, it being essential to be 'established' so that you would automatically be called back the following day.

Back at the studios, I waited my turn to wash the make-up off in a basin. When I handed in my moustache and clothing, my chit was stamped again – then a last long wait at the cashier's office to present my chit and be paid.

I was lucky enough to get a lift back to Hollywood from a group who had lived there but even so it was ten o'clock before I sat down on a stool in the drugstore for the '50 cents Blue Special'. My salary for my first day as a professional actor amounted to two dollars and fifty cents.

My fellow extras, I discovered during the next few weeks, fell into two distinct categories. There were the professional 'crowd artistes' and the actors who were 'would-be stars'.

The professionals were content to remain extras. They had no acting ambitions. They worked all the angles and were not above slipping a percentage of their daily salaries to unscrupulous assistant directors to guarantee being 'called' next day. Among these 'professionals', could be counted the specialists such as the mounted extras, who worked almost exclusively in Westerns, and the Dress Extras. This last named group were much more highly paid, getting as much as twenty dollars a day because they provided their own modern wardrobe for every occasion, including evening dress for the women, white tie and tails for the men, beach outfits, city outfits, and the correct clothes for race meetings, football games, fox hunting and graduation days.

The acknowledged leaders of the professional Dress Extras were two elderly English people, Mrs Wicks and a white-moustached ex-Indian Army man known as 'the Major'.

This couple were in great demand, lending dignity and refinement to the drabbest pictures. They had their own little coterie of friends and, sitting in full evening dress, they all played bridge together from morning to night.

There were a few younger professional Dress Extras also totally devoid of acting ambition and perfectly content to put on their smart clothes and work two or three days a week. Stuart Hall was one of these. Born in Cyprus, he had been brought to California as a child and had drifted into the movies. Stuart was a striking looking man of my age. He was constantly being offered small speaking parts: he always refused them.

I did not have the finances to set myself up as a Dress Extra but Stuart became a good friend and if we were called to the same studio, he always gave me a lift.

The 'would-be stars' did everything decently or indecently possible to get themselves placed in foregrounds with a chance of being noticed, and people in this group were occasionally singled out to say a line or play a small 'bit'. At night they went to acting schools or formed small theatre groups. The studios sent talent scouts to cover these showcases. Unless you were a big star brought out specially from Broadway, the only door into Hollywood was within Hollywood itself.

These were the golden days. The movie business was booming. Hundreds of films were being made each year and there was little competition in the entertainment world. Television had not been heard of. Night football and night baseball were in the future. Nobody played bingo or went bowling.

This was the era of the Great Stars. The studios had not yet been emasculated by the Supreme Court in anti-trust suits and the newspapers still had several pages each day devoted to nothing but Hollywood news and gossip.

The studios looked ahead and carefully built up their stables of favourites. When I worked in crowds at Metro Goldwyn Mayer I used to stare in awe at the names on the dressing room doors ... Garbo, Gable, Norma Shearer, Jean Harlow, Joan Crawford, W. C. Fields, Wallace Beery, Spencer Tracy, Hedy Lamarr, William Powell, Myrna Loy, Louise Rainer, Robert Montgomery, Lionel Barrymore, John Barrymore, Charles Laughton and the Marx Brothers.

The supporting actors were a powerful lot too. Frank Morgan, Louis Calhern, Robert Young, Franchot Tone, Reginald Owen, Lewis Stone, H. B. Warner. And the 'babies', some of them doing their school work in little canvas cubicles on the sound stages – so many hours each day by Californian law ... Elizabeth Taylor, Mickey Rooney, Lana Turner, Judy Garland and Ava Gardner. All those under contract to one studio at the same time.

Other studios had their stables too. James Cagney, Pat O'Brien, Edward G. Robinson and Bette Davies were at Warners, Gary Cooper, Charles Boyer, Claudette Colbert and Marlene Dietrich at Paramount, while Fred Astaire, Ginger Rogers and Cary Grant reigned at R.K.O.

Small wonder that young people with stars in their eyes flocked to Hollywood from all parts of the world. There was hardly a beauty contest winner anywhere who didn't hopefully book a one way ticket.

Small wonder ... outside Central Casting ... 'DON'T TRY AND BECOME AN ACTOR FOR EVERYONE WE EMPLOY WE TURN AWAY A THOUSAND'. And small wonder that behind cosmetic counters, serving as car hops and waitresses, selling theatre tickets, swim suits, ice creams, or their bodies were the most beautiful girls in the world.

I soon got the feel of it and was able to take short cuts. Friends among the extras tipped me off about jobs that might be coming up, and riding very much with the Sandhurst 'forward seat', I worked in a number of Westerns.

I got to know a few assistant directors and they put me on their personal lists. I also made the rounds of all the studio casting offices when the Auburn was in the mood.

Once or twice a week, I worked as deck-hand on a swordfish boat operating out of Balboa.

Chet Leibert had a forty-five foot charter boat rigged up for marlin fishing with rod and line from the stern and a ten-foot spear platform forward for tackling the giant broadbill. He was a dour, rather unpleasant man, but a wonderful fisherman, and generous. He gave me six dollars a day, more if we had fish to sell, and allowed me to keep my tips. I enjoyed the fishing more than the filming.

I don't believe this is one of the thoughts of Chairman Mao but breaks, good or bad, do come when you least expect them.

I had been doing a fruitless round of the studio casting offices and my last port of call was the United Artists studio on Santa Monica Boulevard. ... 'Nothing just now, call next week' ... So that the sanctity of the studio could be preserved, the entrance to the Casting Office was separated from the main gate by a twelve foot high wall of wire netting. I was walking out again when I was hailed from a large limousine on the other side of the cage. 'Hi! how's the golf?' It was the great Douglas Fairbanks himself. He never forgot a face but he had the greatest difficulty in coming up with a name to match it.

Soon I was on his side of the barricade and setting him right that I was not Bobby Sweeny. He asked what I was doing in Hollywood and I told him. He thought for a moment and said kindly,

'Gee, I hope you make it . . . I'm here with Sylvia at the Beach House and we'd love to see you any time you like. I'd like to take you to play at Bel Air – it's a great course. Come around, I mean it, any time but please don't ask me to help you with your career.'

This was the completely honest expression of a completely honest man and a breath of fresh air in a place where the empty promise was the easy way out.

'Now,' he said, 'I'm going to take a steam – come on in and join me.'

Actually, I would have preferred the offer of a good hot meal but I gratefully tagged along. He greeted everyone he passed with a wide smile and 'Hi! how are you'. It was obvious that he was greatly loved but he was never quite sure who was loving him.

Inside the steam room, I was introduced to various mist-shrouded figures and I found myself sitting stark naked on a marble slab between Darryl Zanuck, the head of Twentieth Century, a new thrusting company which he was just forming, and Joe Schenck, his partner. Opposite sat Charlie Chaplin and Sid Grauman, a famous theatre owner. Present too were Bill Goetz, another associate of Zanuck's, Lew Schreiber, his casting director, Bill Dover, Sam the Barber and Aiden Roark.

The sight and proximity of these great men, combined with the intense heat was almost too much for me but I decided to sit there if it took all night. It might lead to something. They were used to these steam baths. I wasn't. After ten minutes, my lungs felt scalded and my head was spinning.

Fairbanks, above all, loved jokes of any sort, funny jokes, practical jokes, any jokes. He had, of course, caught on that I was practically broke so he couldn't resist saying,

'Oh, Niven, what are you planning this winter? Playing polo or bringing the yacht round?'

'Polo . . . polo,' I croaked and made for the exit. Sam the Barber grabbed me before I fell to the marble floor and put me forcibly into the ice-cold plunge. I was reviving when the others came out of the steam room.

'Doug says you played for the British Army,' said Zanuck.

'Well, I played a bit in Malta,' I mumbled.

'Come and play a few chukkas on Sunday. We'll have a good game.'

'Er ... my clothes haven't arrived yet, I'm afraid.'

'Aiden here will fix you up.'

Aiden Roark was a ten goal international. He and his brother Pat both played for Great Britain. Now he was employed by Zanuck in some capacity and organised Zanuck's polo team. A quiet, dark haired, olive-skinned Irishman, he looked more like a South American. I decided to tell him the truth and in a corner, I explained my limitations.

'Don't worry about it – I'll lend you all the stuff you need. Just play a couple of chukkas – you'll have fun.'

So it was arranged. I was to play polo at the Uplifters Club the following Sunday afternoon with Darryl Zanuck. How many two dollars and fifty cents 'extras' were getting that break?

On the fateful day, Aiden Roark lent me some jodhpurs that were much too tight and drove me to the ground. The first thing that worried me was when I noticed that the stands were full of people. Douglas Fairbanks and the gorgeous Sylvia Ashley were in a box. The second thing which unnerved me was the sight of the other players. Among them were 'Big Boy' Williams, a formidable performer, Elmer Boseke and Cecil Smith, both ten-goal internationals. The final thing, and this nearly completed my disintegration, was the sight of 'Saint George'.

'Saint George' was a white Arab stallion. He bit savagely at everything in sight and at that moment, a groom was struggling to put him into a muzzle.

'You can play Saint George,' said Aiden. 'Play him in the first and fourth chukkas. It's only a pick up game. You play at number one and I'll hit the ball up to you ... Mark Darryl, he's playing back on the other team ... wear the red vest.'

The bell went. It was a nightmare. I didn't know who was playing in which position on what team. Those great experts were hitting the ball like a rocket from every direction but during that first chukka, I was far too busy stopping Saint George from leaving the ground altogether to care. When

Aiden passed the ball up to me, I made vague flourishes at it with my stick but quickly needed both hands again to control the brute. It was during one of these mad dashes that Saint George kicked a goal.

Zanuck I tried to cover but generally passed him at high speed without making contact.

At the end of the first chukka, Aiden was laughing so much he could hardly change ponies.

'Come back in for the fourth one ... you'll find him easier now he's worked some of it off.'

I toyed with the idea of slinking from the ground but I still hoped that I might impress Zanuck and further my movie career so I waited apprehensively for my next appearance. My riding muscles, suddenly forced into violent action, were not reacting and causing me to shake like a leaf. This did not go unnoticed by Saint George when I mounted him once more for the fourth chukka.

I was determined to make my mark on Zanuck and I stayed as close to him as Saint George would let me. I even hit the ball a couple of times which encouraged me enormously. The experts continued to charge about playing a spectacular game shouting oaths and instructions at each other but Aiden, I suspected, had deliberately stopped sending the ball up to me. It all seemed more peaceful.

Suddenly, 'Big Boy' Williams, renowned as one of the longest hitters in the game, connected from the far end of the ground and the ball sailed over Zanuck's head towards the goal. Zanuck turned fast and galloped off to backhand it away. I chased after him to try and ride him off the line, and if miracles could happen, to score. The two of us were now the focal point of all eyes. People were shouting and clods of earth were flying up into my face from Zanuck's pony's hooves.

Saint George was the faster and we gained inexorably.

As we drew almost level and I was getting into position to bump Zanuck off the line of the ball, Saint George leaned forward and through his muzzle sank his teeth into the seat of Zanuck's breeches. Zanuck roared with alarm and pain and in the ensuing shambles, his pony trod on the ball. It became embedded in the turf. I caught a momentary glimpse of the white mushroom top passing below us and, trying to

ignore the embarrassing action at the front end of my steed, I
made a vague swipe at it as it fell astern. I missed and my
stick passed beneath Zanuck's pony's tail. His mount being
extremely sensitive in that area, with a maidenly reaction,
clamped its tail to its behind. The head of my stick was thus
imprisoned. I was attached by a leather thong around my
wrist to the other end of the stick. Saint George had a firm
grip on Zanuck's buttocks and our horrible triangle galloped
past the stands.

Zanuck was good about it. I was not invited to play polo
with him again but he mentions it to this day when I see him.

Goulding came back from New York and kept his word ...
he really tried to help me.

'You must stop being an "extra" and have a good agent,'
he said.

He talked to Bill Hawks, an important man in that line
and I found myself with a representative. It was vitally
important to 'have something on film' so I was delighted
when I was given 'tests' for various roles. I did tests with
Mady Christians, with Elizabeth Allen and with Claudette
Colbert but I never landed the parts I was being tested for.

Three men did the same test on the same day with
Claudette Colbert for *The Gilded Lily* – a scene on a park
bench complete with popcorn and pigeons. The other two
both got contracts at Paramount but nothing happened to
me ... their names were Fred MacMurray and Ray Milland.
I was a new face and the life blood of movies is 'New Faces'. I
also had a good agent and a powerful director pushing me;
furthermore, I was meeting 'the people who mattered'. I was
interviewed and tested for dozens of roles at all the major
studios. I had the contacts and the chances, none could have
had more, but I was a hopeless amateur and in front of the
camera, I congealed with nerves.

As the weeks went by, I changed from being 'a new face' to
being 'a face that's been around and hasn't made it'.
Invitations to the houses of the great became fewer. Tests no
longer came my way and it began horribly to dawn on me
that after all, it might be beyond my reach.

Irving Thalberg had been the boy genius of Hollywood.
Now just in his mid-thirties, he was the undisputed master

producer of Metro Goldwyn Mayer. Married to the beautiful Norma Shearer, they were the golden couple of Hollywood.

Production of his epic *Mutiny on the Bounty* was getting under weigh and having been told by Goulding of my bizarre connection with his ship, Thalberg decided that, as an additional drop in the publicity bucket, it might be worth while to sign me up as one of the non-speaking mutineers.

He happened to phrase it more glamorously at some Friday night gathering:

'I'm thinking of signing David Niven to a contract on Monday.'

That did it. The word went round. If the great Irving Thalberg was going to put me under contract, then I must be worth having. Three studios sent people looking for me but I was out chasing marlin. When I got back on Sunday night, Al Weingand gave me a sheaf of messages. I called Goulding and told him of the sudden activity. He and Bill Hawks came over to the hotel and held a council of war. Then Goulding fetched my original and only relaxed test from the M.G.M. studios vault, put it in his car and went directly to the house of Samuel Goldwyn, Hollywood's legendary and most successful independent producer.

Goldwyn ran the test there and then while Frances, his wife, listened sympathetically to Goulding's sales talk.

On Monday morning, Goldwyn sent for me. He sat behind a huge desk in a tastefully furnished office. He was almost entirely bald, very well dressed, with small intense eyes set in a brown face. He was about fifty and looked extremely fit. He spoke without smiling in a strangely high-pitched voice.

'I'm giving you a seven year contract,' he said. 'I'll pay you very little, and I won't put you in a Goldwyn picture till you've learnt your job: now you have a base. Go out and tell the studios you're under contract to Goldwyn, do anything they offer you, get experience, work hard, and in a year or so, if any good – I'll give you a role.'

I was ushered out in a daze and taken to see the head of publicity – Jock Lawrence, a dynamo.

'Jesus,' said Jock, 'you realise what a break you've got? Mr. Goldwyn never signs unknowns. He only has three people under contract – Eddie Cantor, Anna Sten and Ronald

Colman. Colman's leaving next month and he's taking on Gary Cooper and Joel McCrea.'

He looked at me quizzically, 'What do you think of Mr. Goldwyn?'

'He didn't give me time,' I said. 'I was in and out of there in about two minutes.'

'He's the greatest,' said Lawrence. 'All his pictures are hits and he is the only producer in Hollywood who uses his own money – Mr. Goldwyn never goes to the banks – he's the greatest all right but boy! can he be rough sometimes. Now, he's told me to build you up so let's hear all about you.'

I gave Jock Lawrence a brief résumé of my life so far while he made notes.

'Mother?'

'French.'

'Good, we can use that.'

'Father?'

'Killed in the war.'

'*Great*! What rank?'

'Lieutenant.'

'Jesus, that's terrible, we'd better make him a General.'

I was taken to see Reeves Espy, Goldwyn's assistant, a gentle, intelligent man who explained that my contract started at a hundred dollars a week for the first two years, with twelve weeks' lay-off each year. During the first two years, Goldwyn had an option every three months to terminate the contract. In the third year, a little more money and fewer options and so on for seven years. I hardly listened ... it was all too unbelievable. I was taken to see Bob McIntyre the Production Manager and Lola Unger his assistant. Lola said, 'We have a nice dressing room for you' and gave me a key. 'We'll put your name on the door tomorrow.'

I found my little cubby hole and sat there in a wicker chair for a long time. Then I wandered about the studio, the same United Artists Studio where Fairbanks had invited me to take a steam.

Near the Main Gate was a familiar high wire fence. On the other side was a shuffling line of extras enquiring for work at the Casting Office.

The Auburn had finally collapsed altogether so I walked to

180

the hotel and told Al Weingand the good news. He was genuinely overjoyed but he also said, 'Thank Christ, now you can pay your goddam bill!'

Together we crossed Hollywood Boulevard to the showroom of the Ford Motor Company. The new models were in the window and priced at just under five hundred dollars. I told the snooty salesman I had just signed a seven year contract with Samuel Goldwyn and at the magic name, he became, immediately, deferential.

'I'll take that one,' I said, pointing. He gave me some forms to sign to do with monthly payments. Then he pulled a chain – the whole window moved aside and I drove out into my Brave New World – and took Goulding and Al Weingand to lunch.

CHAPTER ELEVEN

GOLDWYN SIGNS UNKNOWN! – that was the headline of super-powerful columnist, Louella Parsons, the next morning. The *Hollywood Reporter* and *Daily Variety*, the twin bibles of the industry, similarly alerted their readers to this earth-shaking occurrence.

In my new Ford, I drove out to bask in the congratulations of the Belzer-Young family.

Within a week I had evacuated from Al Weingand's haven and found myself a tiny, brown cuckoo-clock of a chalet at the top of North Vista Street, with a view looking over the whole of the Los Angeles Basin. I shared the chalet with several scorpions and black-widow spiders and a garage with the Madam of a well-known whore house situated immediately below me.

I joined the Hollywood Cricket Club.

There were twenty-two cricket clubs in California at that time. The Hollywood Cricket Club was deservedly the most famous and crashes were frequent on Sunset Boulevard on Sunday afternoons when amazed local drivers became distracted by the sight of white flannel trousers and blazers on the football ground of U.C.L.A.

Hollywood was going through a 'British period' and the studios were indulging themselves with such epics as *Mutiny on the Bounty*, *David Copperfield*, *National Velvet*, *Bengal Lancers*, *Edwin Drood*, *Disraeli*, *Lloyds of London* and *Sherlock Holmes* ... it was a bonanza for the British character actors. The captain of the Hollywood Cricket Club was the redoubtable, craggy C. Aubrey Smith. A famous county cricketer, he had a penchant for suddenly nipping out from behind the umpire and firing down his fast ball. ... He had been nicknamed 'Round the Corner Smith'. His house on Mulholland Drive was called 'The Round Corner'; on his roof were three cricket stumps and a bat and ball serving as a weather vane.

Ernest Torrance and his wife Elsie were other leaders of the British colony. Henry Stephenson, E. E. Clive, Eric Blore and H. B. Warner were members. Later arrivals, Basil Rathbone and Nigel Bruce, were fiercely independent of the label 'British colony' and Herbert Marshall spent all his time with Gloria Swanson and Reggie Gardiner with Hedy Lamarr while, aloof from it all, living the life of a hermit in his house at the end of Mound Street, was Ronnie Colman. There he entertained only his intimate circle – William Powell, Richard Bartlemess and Noll Gurney. He had just overcome an unhappy marriage and was trying not to fall in love with Benita Hume.

The hard core British colony took tea on Sundays at the Torrances or the Aubrey Smiths ... the atmosphere was very like the Marsa Polo Club in Malta.

Nigel and Bunnie Bruce became, for me, the Norah and Lefty of the West Coast.

'Willie' Bruce, immortal as Doctor Watson in *Sherlock Holmes*, was fat and jovial and generous. Bunnie was thin and gay and generous. They both adored their two little girls, Pauline and Jennifer. They kept open house in an old Spanish-style mansion on Alpine Drive and happily spent every penny that Willie earned.

It was Willie who made me join the Hollywood Cricket Club. He was keen and had played first class cricket before he collected eleven machine-gun bullets in his left leg at Cambrai. After the war he went on the stage and appeared often with Gerald du Maurier and Gladys Cooper. Once he was invited for the weekend to play country house cricket at some ducal monstrosity.

He arrived the night before the match and was shown his room by the butler with that subtle mixture of alarm and condescension reserved exclusively for actors. Out of his window, Willie saw the house party gathered round the Duke, sitting under a giant yew tree, tea cups and cucumber sandwiches were in evidence and Willie shuddered.

Finally, he plucked up courage to go down and meet his host and fellow guests but to put off the evil moment as long as possible he made a detour through the orchards and greenhouses. There he came across a small peach tree bearing one solitary peach. He ate it and continued on his way to the giant yew. Nobody, including the Duke, took the slightest notice of him so he huddled miserably at the back of the group and toyed with a piece of fruit cake. The butler appeared and announced, 'The Gentlemen of the Press are here, your Grace'. This caused considerable excitement and an anticipatory buzz arose. Willie tapped his nearest neighbour.

'What's all the excitement?'

'Oh, haven't you heard? The Duke is the first man in the world to succeed in growing a full-sized peach on a miniature tree.'

Willie tiptoed away, packed and left before dinner.

Having a highly publicised contract with Goldwyn made it obvious that I was not about to parlay an invitation to dinner or tennis into an embarrassing hint for work. New doors were ajar. I played tennis with Constance Bennett and Gilbert Roland, with Dolores del Rio and Cedric Gibbons, golf with Jean Harlow and William Powell. When Garbo was not nursing him, I spent sad afternoons with John Gilbert who was fighting a losing battle with the bottle in his hilltop hideaway. The Thalbergs, Douglas Fairbanks and Sylvia became close friends; so did Merle Oberon of unbeatable beauty. Ronald Colman slowly made me persona grata at Mound Street and a lasting bond was formed with Phyllis and Fred Astaire.

John McClain suddenly arrived from the East with a contract to write scripts for R.K.O. and my cup overflowed.

My social life was picking up nicely but my professional career was not in top gear. My first speaking part was at Paramount in *Without Regret*. Elissa Landi was the star and I said 'Goodbye, my dear,' to her on a station platform.

Howard Hawks produced *The Barbary Coast* with Miriam Hopkins – I got the part of a cockney sailor, with drooping moustache.

'Orl rite – I'll go,' I said, and was thrown out of the window of a brothel in San Francisco and into the mud. Miriam Hopkins, Joel McCrea, Walter Brennan, thirty vigilantes and some donkeys walked over the top of me.

I was employed by Woody Van Dyke to play a whole scene with Jeanette MacDonald in *Rose Marie* at M.G.M. She and Nelson Eddy were the stars and a lanky young actor from New York was making his debut in the same picture. James Stewart was his name.

This looked better — a whole scene in a big important musical!

It was a short piece so I was not given a complete script, just a couple of sides with my stuff on it. It took place in a theatre in Toronto. Jeanette MacDonald had just come off the stage from singing some aria to a packed house and was rushing to the arms of Nelson Eddy, her lover in the Mounties, who was supposed to be waiting in the dressing room.

She flung open the door expectantly and all she found was a top hat protruding above a screen. Underneath the hat was a drunken stage-door Johnnie (me) who, after a short altercation, was forcibly removed.

Van Dyke seemed happy enough with my efforts and by eleven o'clock I was out of the studio.

He was a very fast worker. M.G.M. sent me two tickets to the preview and I took a girl friend along.

'What's the story,' she asked.

'I've no idea, but when they get to Toronto — that's me after the song — a top hat behind a screen. I'll tell you when it's coming.' We settled back expectantly.

The picture trailed on and finally it was clear that the song in Toronto was over and Jeanette MacDonald was heading for her dressing room.

'Here I come,' I whispered. The girl held my hand.

'There! . . . there's the hat — this is me!!'

The hat moved and a perfectly strange man stepped out from behind the screen and played my scene.

Apparently, I had been so bad that they had got rid of me early and sent for another actor to come and do it correctly.

Van Dyke was a very fast worker.

Al Santell was a director at Columbia and I have blessed him forever. He was directing *A Feather in Her Hat* with Ruth Chatterton. I was employed to play a long and difficult scene in a big party sequence. Leo, the poet, was my character.

The party had been in full swing for some time with much build up towards the arrival of Leo, the poet.

'I *wish* Leo would come, he'll liven it up', etc., etc.

Finally, all gaiety and light, I had to burst in through a door and for at least three minutes, I was supposed, single-handed, to raise the whole tempo of the party, with a wise-crack here and a kiss there. The scene was in a continuous shot with the camera on a rail moving with me from group to group.

The 'extras' on the set, some hundred or so, were Dress Extras. Stuart Hall was there full of encouragement but most of the others were of the highly critical 'would-be star' category. It was an appallingly difficult scene and I hadn't slept all night from anxiety.

I didn't own the tail coat I needed for the occasion so Herbert Marshall lent me his. 'Bart' Marshall had lost a leg on the Somme so for some technical reason, his fly buttons did up the wrong way, like a woman's coat. I was shaking so badly in the wardrobe department that a seamstress had to do my flies up for me with a button hook.

I waited around in an agony of apprehension till finally, I was sent for to do the scene. Santell was kindness and patience itself and walked me gently through many rehearsals but I still couldn't relax.

This was my big chance but I was rigid with terror.

'Okay, Dave, let's take a crack at it – do it just like that last rehearsal – that was just fine.'

Miserable and sweating, I stood outside the door and listened to the happy sounds of the party inside. After an eternity, a red light glowed – my signal to burst in.

I did. My toe caught in the track and I nearly fell over. I bumped a dowager in a chair; I spilled somebody else's drink and said all the wrong lines to the wrong people but somehow, I staggered through to the end.

Everyone on the set applauded.

I couldn't believe my ears. Santell rushed up.

'Hey, that's great, Dave! Just what I wanted ... perfect! Now we have that one in the can we'll just take another for safety ... Oh! this time don't hit the track, and watch out for the old dame's chair ... one or two little changes ... just clean it up a little ... but it's great and we have it already – this one's a luxury.'

I stood outside the door looking at that red light ... I couldn't wait for it to go on. 'This is easy,' I thought, 'this is fun!'

I sailed through the second take, loving every minute of it, completely relaxed.

At the end of the day, Stuart Hall and I were celebrating in a bar: he told me the secret. Santell had addressed the whole 'set' while I had been shivering and shaking in my dressing room.

'The boy who's playing Leo – this is his first big scene in a picture and we've all got to help him loosen up. After the first take, however bad he is, I want you all to applaud then I'll put some film in the camera.'

Santell is in my private Hall of Fame.

'Go get yourself experience,' Goldwyn had said ... so I went to the Pasadena Playhouse. This was by far the most highly regarded of all the 'showcases' and almost impossible to break into. The magic name of Goldwyn opened the door.

I was welcomed by Gilmour Brown, the Playhouse director, and given a minute part in *Wedding*.

It was all very 'arty'. The curtain was up when the audience arrived. It never came down between acts and it remained up when they left.

I was one of the guests. There were sixty others and most of them were queer. One with whom I shared a cubicle dressing room was different. He was an ex-footballer from Notre Dame with a forgettable Polish name. When last heard of he was a dentist in Lancing, Michigan. He was a devotee of Scotch whisky and had a large stock of a brandy called 'Mist o' the Moors'.

It tasted like rubbing alcohol. I think it was made in Japan.

My part was as follows: Early in Act I. I sauntered on carrying a large bowl of punch. This was a very important prop as there was an urgent message for someone underneath it. I arrange the bowl carefully on a table and sauntered off again.

Act II. I had to enter left looking distracted, suddenly see off stage someone I was looking for, smile with relief and exit hurriedly, right.

Act III. Was my big moment. I had a snatch of conversation with my Footballer Friend.

Niven: 'I tell you the King of Siam *does*.'

F.F.: 'Well, I *know* the King of Siam ... and I tell you he doesn't.'

Niven: 'I see.' EXIT

During the two weeks' rehearsal, I went to many parties in Hollywood and without actually lying I propagated the idea that I was starring in a play at the Pasadena Playhouse – good propaganda ... 'Yes, I am opening with a very interesting girl at the Playhouse next week ....I think she'll go a long way ...' That sort of thing, not lies really.

On opening night, thanks to the ever present Mist o' the Moors, I was completely relaxed. When my moment came, I picked up my bowl of punch and wandered on stage.

I received a thunderous ovation.

In alarm I shielded my eyes from the footlights, an unforgiveable thing to do, and saw that 'Bart' Marshall had brought a surprise party of about thirty people to witness my great star debut. I caught a glimpse of Gloria Swanson and Charles Laughton among other famous people filling the first three rows and tottered off the stage with the bowl of punch, thereby ripping irreparable holes in the plot.

Downstairs in our cubicle, the F.F. tried to calm me.

'Have a little Mist, Dave, don't worry about 'em ... screw 'em ...'

He gave me a great umbrella stand full of the stuff.

Act II. I thought 'they mustn't see me' – so I shot across the stage from left to right like a meteor.

Act III. And after several more calming draughts of Mist, I had changed considerably – 'Many of these people', I said to the F.F. 'have come from as far as Malibu to see me ... let's go.' He blinked and shook his head in a dazed way, then followed me meekly on stage for our snatch of conversation.

We swayed on and I led him by the arm right down to the footlights.

'Now look,' I said giving him an intimidating stare, 'I don't want to impose my rather strong personality on your very dull brain ... but I have it ... on the very finest authority ... straight from the horse's mouth ... that the KING OF SIAM *DOES*.'

The F.F. looked utterly stunned, then in an awed voice he said, 'Jesus Christ!'

Gilmour Brown was waiting for us in the wings – 'Get out of my theatre – both of you.'

Reactions to my performance were mixed. 'Bart' Marshall said he wouldn't have missed it for the world; Charles

Laughton gave me an angry lecture about 'bastardising my profession'. Goldwyn treated me to a mild dressing down. He had been pacified in advance by the news that the great Ernst Lubitsch had just seen my 'relaxed' performance as Leo, the poet, and wanted me to start immediately at Paramount in a very good part in *Bluebeard's Eighth Wife* with Gary Cooper and Claudette Colbert.

Working with Lubitsch in the company of such professional experts and such privately wonderful human beings as Gary Cooper and Claudette Colbert was a joy that lasted for about three months.

The screen play was by another expert – Billy Wilder.

Lubitsch sat, like a little gnome, beside the camera, perched on a small step ladder, giggling and hugging himself at all his own wonderful inventiveness. A vast cigar was always in his mouth. He was patient, understanding and encouraging: what more could any actor ask?

I learned major lessons about playing comedy during that time and will forever remember a statement of his: 'nobody should try to play comedy unless they have a circus going on inside.'

Thank You, Jeeves was the next. I was borrowed from Goldwyn by R.K.O. to play Bertie Wooster and the indelible Arthur Treacher played Jeeves. But it was a 'B' picture, a curtain raiser on the programme for the main feature. It was my first leading role, however. Virginia Field was the leading lady.

Then I was sent for by Warner Brothers, where Michael Curtiz was testing actors for *The Charge of the Light Brigade*. Errol Flynn was the star – his second picture. His first had been a smash hit – *Captain Blood*. Now he was the big white hope of the studio.

Curtiz had a reputation for eating actors for breakfast. An ex-cavalry officer and very Prussian in his approach to subordinates, he was a daunting sight when I reported for work, outfitted in riding boots and breeches and carrying a fly whisk.

I was testing for the part of Flynn's friend: destined for a sticky end in the Charge. The whole scenario was a loose adaptation of the true story and the Charge itself took place on the North West Frontier of India, but no matter, those

189

were the days when Hollywood was reshaping British history to conform to budgets and available locations. I was to play the test scene with Olivia de Havilland so, I realised with dismay, were a dozen other hopeful young actors all dressed in exactly the same uniform as myself ... all standing around and, a refinement of sadism, allowed to watch each other perform.

By the time the scene had been played half a dozen times, and six actors curtly dismissed by Curtiz, everything I had hoped to do had already been done. My mind was a blank when Curtiz, with heavy accent, called out, 'Next man.'

I was led out of the shadows by an assistant and introduced to Miss de Havilland and Curtiz. She smiled a tired resigned smile and shook hands. Curtiz said,

'Where's your script?'

I said 'You mean the four pages I was given for the scene,'

'Yes ... where is it?'

'Well,' I said, hoping it was true, 'I've learnt it, Mr. Curtiz. I don't have it with me.'

'I asked you *where* it is!'

'Well, it's in my dressing room at the other end of the studio.'

'Run and get it,' he shouted.

My uniform was thick and tight. It was 100° in the shade and the sound stage was not air-conditioned ... also, after witnessing the efforts of the others, I reckoned I had no chance of getting the part anyway.

'You fucking well run and get it,' I said.

His reaction was instantaneous.

'Dismiss the others – this man gets the part.'

We got along famously all through the picture ... 'that goddammed Sandhurst man' Mike called me and built up my part.

My friendship with Flynn dated from that picture. I had met him once or twice at Lili Damita's bungalow in the Garden of Allah and we had reacted to each other with wary distaste. Now he was married to Lili and we made a new appraisal of each other.

Flynn was a magnificent specimen of the rampant male. Outrageously good looking, he was also a great natural athlete who played tennis with Donald Budge and boxed

190

with 'Mushy' Calahan. The extras, among whom I had many old friends, disliked him intensely.

They were a rough lot too, the toughest of the riders from Westerns, plus the stunt men who specialised in galloping falls. Flynn, they decided, had a swollen head, having made too big a success too soon. They were the 27th Lancers. Flynn was their commander; I was the second in command.

One day they were lined up on the parade ground of our fort, somewhere in the San Fernando valley. Flynn and I were slightly in front of our men when one of them leaned forward with his lance, rubber-tipped to cut down accidents, and wriggled it in Flynn's charger's dock.

The animal reared up and Flynn completed the perfect parabola and landed on his back.

Six hundred very muscular gentlemen roared with laughter.

Flynn picked himself up, 'Which of you sons of bitches did that?'

'I did, sonny,' said a huge gorilla of a man, 'want to make anything of it?'

'Yes, I do,' said Flynn. 'Get off your horse.'

Nobody could stop it and the fight lasted a long time. At the end of it the 'gorilla' lay flat on his back. After that everyone liked Errol much more.

Goldwyn decided that I was ripe to appear in one of his own super-pictures and cast me as Captain Lockert in *Dodsworth* with Walter Huston and Ruth Chatterton. Walter had created the role on Broadway and had now moved to California. His son, John, then a script writer, also worked on the picture. He and his father were wonderful to me, so was Ruth Chatterton. William Wyler, the director, was not.

As his record plainly shows, Willie Wyler is one of the world's all-time great directors. Practically without exception, his films have been hugely successful, both critically and financially. He may have mellowed by now but in 1936 he was a Jekyll and Hyde character.

Kind, fun and cosy at all other times, the moment his bottom touched down in his director's chair, he became a fiend.

Some directors, especially those touched by the Max Reinhardt School, believed in breaking actors down completely so that they became putty in their hands. As practised by Willie, he even managed to reduce the experienced Ruth Chatterton to such a state that she slapped his face and locked herself in her dressing room.

I became a gibbering wreck.

Whenever I was working it was perfectly normal for Willie to sit beneath the camera reading the *Hollywood Reporter* and not even look up till I had ploughed through the scene a couple of dozen times – 'just do it again' he'd say, turning a page.

The picture was a big hit in spite of my wooden performance. I have only kept one 'review' during my life. It is of *Dodsworth* and appeared in the *Detroit Free Press*.

In this picture we were privileged to see the great Samuel Goldwyn's latest discovery – all we can say about this actor (?) is that he is tall, dark and not the slightest bit handsome.

It has the place of honour in my lavatory.

Irving and Norma, like all the top movie people, had a private projection room in their home. One night Lubitsch brought down a print of *Bluebeard's Eighth Wife* and they ran it after dinner for their friends.

I sat squirming with embarrassment throughout the showing but after it was over, everyone, with one exception, was overly flattering and enthusiastic. Fairbanks and Sylvia, Merle, the Astaires, Paulette Goddard and Frederick Lonsdale, all puffed me up most pleasantly. One guest sat silent in his chair. Finally, I could stand it no longer.

'What did *you* think, Mr. Chaplin?'

His answer constituted the greatest advice to any beginner in my profession.

'Don't be like the majority of actors ... don't just stand around waiting your turn to speak – *learn to listen.*'

By the autumn of 1936, I was very much involved with a G.B.S. (Great Big Star).

The G.B.S. was doing a week of publicity in New York for her latest vehicle and we had a rendezvous to meet there.

I made a side trip to see Lefty and Norah, by now blissfully happy in 'Little Orchard' at Tryon, North Carolina.

With my father the day he left for Gallipoli, 1915

Nessie's friend—18½ years old, just commissioned in the H.L.I.

Stock Certificate, Pony Express races, Atlantic City, 1934

Hollywood Cricket Club, 1934
(l to r) D.N., Unidentified, Nigel Bruce, C. Aubrey Smith,
Merle Oberon, Cecil King, H. B. Warner and David Torrance
(Photo: Tom Kelley)

My first speaking part—one line as a cockney sailor in *Barbary Coast*, 1935. The script girl was Patsy Ruth Miller, an old-time silent star

Farewell party given by Douglas Fairbanks Jr., September 1939. Among others: Cary Grant, Ronald Colman, Nigel Bruce, Herbert Marshall, Brian Aherne, Laurence Olivier, Robert Coote, Basil Rathbone, George Sanders and Reginald Gardiner

Primmie with David Jr., 1942

Phantom Reconnaissance
Regiment: 'A' Squadron,
commanded by D.N.
(left), being inspected by the
Duke of Kent, 1942
(Photo: The Times)

Normandy, June 1944

Wedding picture of Hjördis

At the Pink House, 1950 (Cupid developed otitis as a result)

Bogie and Betty. Aboard *Santana*, 1953 *(Photo: D.N.)*

Welcomed on arrival
at the Palladium for a
charity show by D.N.
dressed as a doorman
to surprise them

With Susan Hayward, co-winners of the 1958 Oscar

With the boys in Honolulu (David Jr. and Jamie)

Guns of Navarone
(l to r) Gia Scala, Irene Pappas, James Darrin, Anthony Quinn,
D.N., Gregory Peck

At Jamie's wedding, Southampton, Long Island—Hjördis,
Kristina, Fiona and D.N., with *(behind)* 'Betty' Bacall

Hjördis in Malaga resting outside hotel with encouraging name

Our most favourite neighbours, Prince Rainier and Princess Grace

At their Scorpio party with Liz Taylor, Monte Carlo, 1970

Tommy Phipps was there and his highly talented sister, Joyce Grenfell, was over from England. Lefty took me to see the local high school football games and among the glorious colours of the Fall, I rode with him along the foothill trails of the Smoky Mountains. It was a wonderful few days and a most salutary contrast to the life I had been leading in Tinsel City, but I fear the lesson passed almost unnoticed and I hurried off to keep my tryst with the 'G.B.S.' in the St. Regis Hotel.

The 'G.B.S.' was gorgeous and quite adventurous.

'Let's not fly back to California – let's take the sleeper to Detroit – buy a Ford and drive it out.'

She bought the car – I drove and the first night we spent together in Chicago.

She disguised her well-known face with a black wig and dark glasses and called herself Mrs. Thompson. In the lobby nobody recognised her. Though it was highly unlikely that anyone would recognise me, I went along with the game and called myself Mr. Thompson.

The desk clerk handed G.B.S. a telegram,

'For you, Mrs. Thompson.' I was mystified.

'How could that happen?' I said.

'I promised Jock Lawrence I'd tell him exactly where we'll be all the way across in case the studio needs me urgently, then I can hop a plane.'

She opened the envelope – 'TELL NIVEN CALL GOLDWYN IMMEDIATELY JOCK.'

'Forget it,' said the G.B.S. 'call him tomorrow – it's too late now.' We went to bed.

The next night we spent in Cedar Rapids, Iowa.

'Telegram for you, Mrs. Thompson,' said the desk clerk.

TELL NIVEN CALL ME TONIGHT WITHOUT FAIL GOLDWYN.

We didn't want the idyll spoiled even though the new signature gave me an eerie feeling of impending doom.

In North Platte, Nebraska, the wording was crisper –

ASK NIVEN WHAT HE THINKS HE'S DOING HAVE HIM CALL TONIGHT OR ELSE GOLDWYN

Still we pressed happily on across the country, and the telegrams became more alarming at each stop. The one at the Grand Canyon was very unattractive indeed –

193

TELL NIVEN HE'S FIRED GOLDWYN

The G.B.S. was made of stern stuff –

'He can't do that,' she said, 'and anyway he wants me for two more pictures. We'll call him when we get to California – not before.'

I was so besotted by the G.B.S. that I even managed to enjoy the rest of the trip except when we turned off the main road in the middle of New Mexico and got stuck in the desert at sunset.

Finally, the ten-day trip ended and we crossed the State Line into California. From a motel in Needles, with great apprehension, I called Goldwyn.

'Do you know what you're doing, you stupid son of a bitch?' he yelled. 'You're doing about a hundred and thirty-five years in jail. Ever heard of the Mann Act and taking women across State Lines for immoral purposes? Think what Winchell would do to that girl, too, if he got the story – you're through I tell you ... you're ...'

His voice was pitched even higher than usual. The G.B.S. leaned across the bedside table and grabbed the phone out of my hand.

'Sam, darling,' she purred, 'I've had a simply gorgeous time so don't be angry with David ... I'll explain it all to you when we get back tomorrow ...' She motioned me to go out of the room and finished her conversation alone. When she found me later, she said,

'Sam's sweet really, everything's okay again, you've been reinstated.'

The 'actor's nightmare' is the role of Edgar in *Wuthering Heights*. Soon after I came back from my trip with the G.B.S., Goldwyn called me in and told me he had cast me to play it. 'Laurence Olivier will play Heathcliffe and Merle Oberon, Cathy,' he said.

'But it's the most awful part ever written,' I said, 'and one of the most difficult; please don't make me do it.'

'You'll have the best director in the business,' said Goldwyn. 'He'll make it easy for you.'

'Who?'

'Willie Wyler.'

I could not afford it, but I immediately asked to be put on

194

'suspension' – the combination of 'Edgar' and Wyler was too daunting.

On paper, if a contract actor refused to work, he could not, of course, complain if his weekly salary was suspended, but what happened in practice was that the actor was suspended not only for the duration of the picture (four months for a big one), but the producer had the right to suspend him for half that amount of time again as a punishment, then the whole six months was added on to the end of the original contract. In studios with unscrupulous managements who purposely gave actors assignments which they knew would be refused, players were sometimes trapped for twelve or fifteen years working off a seven-year contract. Years later, Olivia de Havilland fought this and took it all the way to the Supreme Court. She won, and thereafter, if someone refused to work, he didn't get paid but it became illegal for the length of his contract to be altered without his consent.

Olivia struck a great blow for freedom and everyone in the industry should bless her but she hardly ever worked in Hollywood again.

Goldwyn did not offer people roles in order to prolong their contracts, and he found it hard to understand my intransigence.

One day after I had been on suspension for two or three weeks, Willie Wyler called me.

'Come and have dinner at Dave Chasen's,' he said.

Over drinks he asked,

'Tell me truly, why you don't want to play Edgar?'

'Because it is such an awful part,' I said.

'It's not, you know,' said Willie, 'and you are one of the few people in the business who can make it better than it is.'

Now that was pretty heady stuff coming from one of the great directors to someone with my minimal experience.

'There's something else, isn't there?' Willie said.

'Honestly, Willie, I love you, I love being here with you but I was so bloody miserable working for you on *Dodsworth* – I just couldn't go through it again. You're a sonofabitch to work with.' Willie laughed.

'I've changed,' he said, 'come and play the part – it's a

wonderful cast ... it'll be a great picture and I'll make you great in it.'

I weakened at once, of course.

'Okay, under one condition – that the night before I start work, you come and have dinner with me here, and I'll remind you that you've changed – that you're no longer a sonofabitch.'

It was arranged.

I reported to the studio next day and did all the costume fittings and renewed my acquaintanceship with Laurence Olivier who had arrived that morning from England.

Larry appeared with a fantastically beautiful kitten-like creature on his arm – Vivien Leigh.

Viv had come out to be with Larry during the shooting of our picture and within a week of that day, she met David O. Selznick, was tested and over the furious heads of all the big established female stars was handed the role of Scarlett O'Hara in *Gone with the Wind*.

The night before I was to start filming, Willie Wyler kept his word. We had a good dinner at Chasen's and played ping-pong on the back patio.

As we bade each other good night, Willie laughed.

'Don't worry – you'll have fun ... I'm not a sonofabitch any more.'

The shooting next day was on location in the San Fernando Valley. Goldwyn had reconstructed Wuthering Heights in rolling hills, and except for the fact that the heather of the moors was about four feet high, it looked wonderfully like Yorkshire. In the first scene, I had to drive up in a two horse buggy with Merle looking very demure as Cathy at my side. Once I had stopped at exactly the right mark, the dialogue commenced. Wyler was up on a rostrum about fifty feet in the air, with the camera.

A few rehearsals to practise that tricky stop and we made the first 'take'.

The horses halted just right.
Cathy. 'Come in, Edgar, and have some tea.'
Edgar. 'As soon as I've put the horses away.'
Wyler. 'CUT! Just play it perfectly straight, David – this is not a comedy, you know.'

After a long drive, breasting through the heather, we arrived back for the second 'take'.

'Come in Edgar, and have some tea.'
'As soon as I've put the horses away.'
'CUT! What's so funny, David? This is not a Marx Brothers picture. Do it again!! Off we drove.

Forty something times I drove those damn horses round the San Fernando Valley. Finally, Wyler said,
'Well, if that's the best you can do, we'd better print the first one I suppose.'
'Willie,' I said, 'remember last night at Chasen's?'
'Yea, I remember – what about it?'
'You really are a sonofabitch, aren't you?'
'Yes – and I'm going to be one for fourteen weeks!'
No one was spared by Willie. The girls were reduced to tears on several occasions and even Olivier was brought up all standing.

The most talented and most reasonable of performers, after being told twenty or thirty times to play some long scene once again, without any specific instructions as to how to alter it, he finally confronted Wyler.
'Willie, look – I've done it thirty times – I've done it differently thirty times – just *tell* me, that's all. *What do you want me to do?*'
Wyler considered this for a long moment –
'Just . . . just be *better.*'
When Cathy was lying dead in her big bed with her family all around her, and a lot of great performers they were too – Flora Robson, Geraldine FitzGerald, Hugh Williams, all weeping silently and Larry circling purposefully round the fireplace, I glanced nervously at the instructions in my script.
(Edgar breaks down at foot of bed and sobs)
'Willie,' I whispered, 'I can't do that.'
'Do what?'
'Sob. I don't know how to.'
'Speak up.'
'I don't know how to sob, Willie.'
'Speak up . . . louder.'
'I DON'T KNOW HOW TO SOB,' I yelled.
Wyler addressed the whole set –

'Well, you've all heard it – here's an actor who says he doesn't know how to act ... now ... SOB.'

I tried and it was pretty grisly. 'Tam' Williams got hiccoughs bottling his laughter and Larry looked up the chimney.

I tried again.

'Jesus,' said Wyler, 'can you make a crying face?'

I made some sort of squashed-up grimace.

'Oh, God,' he groaned, '*Irving!*'

Irving Sindler, the prop man, was instantly at his side.

'Give him the blower,' said Wyler.

Greg Toland, the cameraman, gave his signals and the film started passing through the sprockets.

'The blower, Irving!' said Wyler.

Through a handerchief, Sindler puffed menthol into my open eyes.

'Bend over the corpse,' said Wyler. 'Now make your crying face ... Blink your eyes ... Squeeze a little ... Bend over the corpse. Heave your shoulders.'

A terrible thing happened. Instead of tears coming out of my eyes, green slime came out of my nose

'Ooh! How *horrid!*' shrieked the corpse, shot out of bed and disappeared at high speed into her dressing room.

Thanks to Wyler, the picture was a big hit and has remained one of the all-time classics. And incidentally any time Wyler wants me to work for him – I'll be there.

There was an excitement and generosity of spirit in Hollywood – a minimum of jealousy and pettiness, everyone felt they were still pioneering in a wonderful entertainment medium.

The premières of the big pictures were black tie events and all the big names turned out to cheer on their friends. Outside, 'bleachers' were erected to enable the screaming fans to catch a glimpse of their favourites and searchlights waved weaved patterns across the sky. After the show, a loudspeaker alerted the fans to the departing of the great – Mr. Clark Gable's car!

Miss Marlene Dietrich's car!

Miss Constance Bennett's car!

Miss Shirley Temple's mother's car! and on one glorious occasion –

Mr. Alfred Hitchcar's cock!

Some of the conveyances were a trifle exotic. Connie Bennett sat inside the wicker-box body of a Rolls Phaeton with a spotlight on her ... outside in all weathers sat her chauffeur.

Tom Mix drove himself in a white open Packard wearing a white ten-gallon hat.

Marlene Dietrich had a black Cadillac driven by a chauffeur named Briggs who carried two revolvers and in winter wore a uniform with mink collar.

Marlene, the most glamorous of all, was also one of the kindest. Once, I was ill with flu in my chalet shack on North Vista Street. She hardly knew me but Briggs was a friend and he told her I was sick. Marlene arrived with soup and medicine. She then went to work and herself cleaned the whole place from top to bottom, changed my bedclothes and departed. She came back every day till I was well.

Goldwyn continued my build-up and gave me a good part in *The Real Glory* with Gary Cooper. Then I was loaned to Darryl Zanuck to play two important roles at Twentieth Century Fox, both with Loretta Young, still as sweet and as generous as ever. The whole Young family turned up for the first day's shooting. John Ford directed one of these, an experience actors prayed for. So incredibly sure was his touch that he cut the film with his camera as he went along. All the editor could do was join the pieces together in the correct order and there was the picture.

Ford, like many movie greats, had a soft spot for the practical joke. I had a birthday during the picture and Loretta presented me with a cake which the whole crew devoured.

'David,' said Ford, 'tomorrow you have very little to do – you'll just be background so tonight go on out and enjoy yourself – really tie one on.'

I hate getting drunk but I felt that I had more or less been ordered to do so and I did my best to oblige. I started slowly, after work, in Tyrone Power's dressing room, then home where Flynn joined me enthusiastically, continued at the Trocadero with Mike Romanoff, then I visited two German lesbians in Encino and after making the rounds of Chasen's, the Brown Derby and various bars in Hollywood, I finished up in Doc Law's All Night Café in Santa Monica. From there, I went directly to the studio at eight o'clock in the morning, very drunk indeed and thinking how pleased John Ford would be.

We were rehearsing the first scene. All I had to do was bind up George Sanders' arm who had been shot. Suddenly, I heard Ford say,

'Hold it – what's the matter with you, Niven? Why don't you stand still?'

'Sorry, Mr. Ford.'

'Just a minute – are you drunk or something?'

'Well, I did have a few, Mr. Ford . . . I thought you said . . .'

'Cut the lights,' said Ford.

'Send for Mr. Zanuck. Tell him I have a drunken actor on my set – ask him to come down right away.'

I was sobering up rapidly but still not registering too clearly. All I knew was that people were backing away from me, not wanting to be part of the impending showdown.

Zanuck marched on to the set, looking ferocious, followed by his henchmen.

'What's the problem, Jack?'

'Goddam Limeys,' said Ford, 'they're all alike . . . give 'em an inch . . . this actor reported for work drunk.'

'Let me see a "take",' said Zanuck.

'Put a white coat on him,' said Ford, 'and give him the first aid box . . . 'all right, now try to pull yourself together for Christ's sake . . . on your cue pull the stethoscope out of your pocket, then open the box and take out a dressing – okay, let's go.' White coat? Stethoscope? dressing? – these were new instructions.

The camera turned and George Sanders and Richard Greene played a lengthy scene. Out of the corner of my eye, I could see Zanuck watching intently. I tried to concentrate on my cue and when it came, I put my hand in the pocket for the stethoscope and pulled out a large snake. Trying manfully to continue the scene, I dropped it on the floor and opened the first aid box when I saw it was full of little green turtles. I let out a yell and flung it in the air.

'Print it,' yelled Ford, amidst the ensuing guffaws. The scene which Zanuck had been a party to was run constantly in private projection rooms thereafter.

By now Flynn had separated from Lili Damita and I was looking for new quarters so together we rented Rosalind Russell's house, 601 North Linden Drive and settled in to a fairly ostentatious bachelor existence.

'601' became a hotbed of fun and bad behaviour, the booze flowed freely, the girls formed an ever changing pattern and after Flynn came back from a trip to North Africa, we went through a long period when we smoked or chewed kif.

Kif had strange effects on me, sometimes everything seemed hilariously funny, sometimes I became quiet and introspective, sometimes I experienced pleasant imaginings or hallucinations. I got bored with it one day and just stopped taking it. Nowadays it is known as marijuana.

Flynn had a more lucrative contract at Warners than I had with Goldwyn so he paid the most rent and consequently had the big double bedroom. I was allowed to borrow it for 'special occasions'.

Fairbanks had a small ranch down near San Luis Obispo, where the super newspaper tycoon, William Randolph Hearst, had built himself a hilltop castle dominating some two hundred thousand acres.

His sons, George, Bill, Jack, Randy and David, invited me up there constantly. They were all about the same age as myself and all were either just married, about to become engaged or sliding down the other side into divorce. The girls were beautiful, the boys were great fun and I spent some of the happiest times of my life at San Simeon.

W. R. Hearst lived there openly for years with the blue-eyed beauty, Marion Davies. The sons loved their mother who lived on Long Island. They also loved their father and they liked Marion enormously. It was impossible not to ... a warm-hearted scatterbrain who worshipped 'W.R.'

Mr. Hearst fascinated me. He was an avid collector of antiques on a massive scale. An entire Greek temple had been dismantled, shipped over and reassembled by the swimming pool. Glorious frescoes, paintings and tapestries were everywhere. Often I slept in Richelieu's bed. Hearst had repositories of treasure still not unpacked and a large private zoo. He enjoyed going for rambles with the young and discoursing on every subject under the sun. One heard rumbles that he was utterly ruthless in business but, rather naturally, I saw no sign of that.

In the huge, panelled dining hall, flanked by monks' stalls, and decorated up high by sixty or seventy ducal banners from Venice, Siena and Florence, it always intrigued me that down the centre of the largest refectory table in the world stood clusters of H.P. sauce, Heinz tomato ketchup and paper napkins.

At the end of 1936, Irving Thalberg died. He was thirty-seven years old. He had caught a chill playing cards out of doors, pneumonia followed and very quickly he was gone. Hollywood was stunned. It was a staggering loss.

Fairbanks organised the ushers at the funeral service at the synagogue, B'nai Brith. He told me to help at the entrance and said that he would seat the family personally in the front as he knew them all by sight. Knowing his penchant for putting the wrong name to the wrong face, this made me rather nervous, a condition that increased when I walked down the aisle to ask his advice about something and he showed me into a pew.

By Hollywood standards, the funeral was conducted with great decorum: the fans were kept at bay so nobody had a chance to repeat an earlier disaster when the widow had her veils ripped off – 'Let's see your face, dearie.'

The only sour note was when some moron in the M.G.M. publicity department saw to it that the child actor, Freddie Bartholomew, who had just completed the name part in the film showed up in his black velvet Little Lord Fauntleroy suit.

It was probably the same source of good tase which, when Jean Harlow died, took out full page 'ads' in the trade papers showing the Metro Lion dressed in white tie and tails with tears pouring down its face, placing a wreath on a tombstone: JEAN HARLOW IN MEMORIAM – and below on a scroll, the full list of her screen credits.

Norma was inconsolable and disappeared from view for months.

David O. Selznick was as big an independent producer as Goldwyn so when he borrowed me to play Fritz von Tarlenheim in *The Prisoner of Zenda*, I was very excited. Not

202

only was it to be one of the biggest pictures of the year, it also had a spectacular cast – Ronald Colman, Madeleine Carroll, Raymond Massey, Douglas Fairbanks Jr., Mary Astor and C. Aubrey Smith.

Colman was now very close to me and I did not doubt that on my behalf, he had put in his two cents' worth with Selznick. Doug. Jr. I was meeting for the first time and we immediately struck up a friendship which is just as warm today. An added bonus was that Madeleine's husband, Philip Astley, was coming out to spend three months with her in Malibu.

My part was excellent. Seemingly the only comedy relief, I had never had it so good.

John Cromwell, the director, was rather solemn and steadfastly refused to let me play my part for comedy. I ploughed on, playing it straight as ordered, but was pretty sure the result was dim. Colman found it hard to be encouraging.

After about a week, I decided to make a stand and upon completion of a scene, I said, 'Mr. Cromwell, would you let me do it again – my way?'

This was unheard-of insubordination and the entire crew shuffled about looking embarrassed.

'All right,' said Cromwell. 'Do it once more – your way.'

By now, whatever it was I had dreamed up felt profoundly unfunny but I did it anyway.

'Next scene,' said Cromwell with no change of expression.

That night David Selznick called me.

'I'm sorry, David, but somehow you're not giving the part what I thought you would ... I'm afraid I have to replace you.'

My legs turned to water. I went up to my room and sat on my bed in the dark. So I really couldn't do it after all – Lubitsch and Wyler might have pulled me through but the first big chance had found me out ... What was I going to tell everyone?

My next option with Goldwyn was just coming up ... he would surely drop me. I felt panic rising. I heard Flynn come back about two o'clock and still I sat there.

At nine in the morning, Selznick called me.

'I want to see you at once ... come on down.'

I was taken straight to his office. With him was John Cromwell.

'Look, David,' said Selznick, 'we have just seen yesterday's stuff . . . the last thing you did was exactly what I want from you and John here agrees.'

'I certainly do,' said Cromwell. 'It's my fault entirely and David and I are going to build up the part so that we can get much more fun out of it . . . you'll be great . . . go and get dressed.'

How many big directors are really that big, I wonder? Cromwell is another for my private Hall of Fame.

It was a long picture – over four months – and every day was fascinating. We all felt we were making a success and the enthusiasm ran high.

I was given my own 'stand-in' for the first time. I asked Stuart Hall if he would like the job and for years thereafter he stood patiently being lit by cameramen so that I would be fresh when the moment came to play a scene.

I had problems with my old chums among the extras. At 6.30 at night, they automatically went on a quarter extra salary. If I was playing a scene around that magic hour, they would make it clear they expected me to 'blow' my lines and put them safely into overtime. My loyalty to David Selznick, who would have to pay them, also came into question . . . it was very tricky.

In the coronation procession, Colman and Madeleine were in the royal coach, C. Aubrey Smith and I rode alongside and the two heavies, Doug. Jr. and Ray Massey, rode behind us.

Knowing the fixation that studios have that leading actors should be seen riding highly strung prancing steeds, I had a little chat with the Head Wrangler and exchanged mine for a quiet old mare. Unfortunately, she was in heat and the stallion that Ray Massey was riding decided to mount her, and me, in the middle of a 'take'. I heard snapping teeth behind my head and just caught a glimpse of Ray's appalled expression far above me as I flung myself to the ground.

Towards the end of the picture, King George VI and Queen Elizabeth visited President Roosevelt.

Someone had the bright idea that the British colony should do a special radio show on the Sunday which would coincide with a hot dog picnic which the President was giving for his royal guests at Hyde Park up the Hudson River.

We rehearsed for days and bashed our brains out being loyal and talented.

Olivier gave the 'Into the breach...' speech from *Henry V*, Brian Aherne recited Rupert Brooke's 'The Soldier', Aubrey Smith, Nigel Bruce and Roland Young sang 'Three Little Fishes', Reggie Gardiner imitated a train: Ray Noble's band played and the rest of us – Vivien Leigh, Flynn, Colman, Madeleine, Cary Grant and myself, all did something.

I had an unexpected moment alone with Her Majesty a few years later and asked her how they had all enjoyed our efforts.

'Oh, wasn't it awful,' she said, 'the President's battery ran down just before it came on.'

At the end of *Zenda*, Goulding called in a high state of excitement from his house in Palm Springs.

'Come at once – I have good news, I think.'

I drove down to the desert to find Goulding hopping up and down in the driveway.

He led me down to his pool. There was a naked figure in it.

'Oh, I forgot,' said Goulding. 'Garbo was coming over for a swim ... we'd better go back up to the house.'

Up there he told me the news.

'You've got it!' he said. 'They just called from Warners and confirmed it.'

'Got what?'

'Scotty in *Dawn Patrol* – it's the best part ever written for an actor.'

Warners borrowed me from Goldwyn and Goulding was right. It was a marvellous part ... World War I story of the Royal Flying Corps. Flynn and I were pilots. At one point I was hungover and late and went up in my Sopwith Camel in red and white spotted pyjamas. I was shot down and fell in a lake. The officers' mess was plunged in gloom at the loss when I suddenly walked in, still in pyjamas with an armful of champagne bottles. This was a true incident that had happened near Arras to a certain Flying Officer Pope.

Basil Rathbone played the C.O. and Donald Crisp was the Adjutant.

Goulding was a most sensitive and inventive director. The

picture really hit the jackpot and he achieved what he had always promised – he launched me in a great part in a great picture.

After that, things moved rapidly. I was given star billing and borrowed by Twentieth Century Fox to do a picture in England with the beautiful French actress, Annabella.

Trubshawe came to Southampton to meet the ship. He was now the Squire of Barton Hall in Norfolk and Margie had presented him with two daughters. For old time's sake, he carried the dipsomaniacs' delight. He also displayed a placard:

BARTON HALL VILLAGE FETE

CRICKET MATCH

SIDE SHOWS

RAFFLE

BOWLING FOR THE PIG

CAWSTON SILVER BAND

TO BE OPENED BY FAMOUS HOLLYWOOD STAR

DAVID NIVEN

'Better come, old man,' he said. 'It's tomorrow and I've stuck these bloody things up all over the county.'

It was marvellous to be home again.

The picture was shot at Denham. Angie and Ken Thornton let me be a 'paying guest' in their lovely old house at Ascot, near the Weigalls, and a hundred old threads were picked up. I had time to go to Bembridge. Everyone made a great fuss of me and I wallowed in it.

On the return journey in the *Ile de France*, I met an Austrian named Felix Schaffcotsh. He was on his way to Sun Valley, Idaho, where, at the request of Averell Harriman, he had designed and built a new ski resort.

A handsome and affable 'Graf', he was also a dyed-in-the-wool Nazi. He spent hours extolling the virtues of Hitler, sympathising with his problems and enthusing over his plans. I listened politely but took none of it seriously. I was far more interested in the script of my next film.

Shortly before sailing, I had been advised that Goldwyn had loaned me to Walter Wanger to co-star with Loretta in *Eternally Yours*.

Felix said that he was bringing over a dozen good ski instructors from near his home in Austria – 'all Nazis too'. I promised to go to Sun Valley after I finished the picture.

I arrived back in Hollywood to find that Flynn and Lili Damita had signed a truce and I had to find somewhere else to live.

John McClain was at the Garden of Allah so I rented a bungalow there, and although I missed F. Scott Fitzgerald, who had moved to Malibu with Sheila Graham, I had the great joy of meeting Robert Benchley and Dorothy Parker.

Benchley was one of the wittiest men alive but unlike most people full of funny things to say, he was rather retiring. Long the theatre critic for the *New Yorker*, he was now bravely putting on the other hat and embarking on a highly successful career as an actor. He loved to drink ... 'I must step out of these wet things and into a dry martini ...'

There had lately been a big influx of 'Easterners' and with McClain and Benchley, I spent fascinating evenings at Cole Porter's house where it was quite usual to listen to Cole or Irving Berlin or George Gershwin playing numbers from the half-written scores of their future smash hit musicals.

When McClain moved back to New York, I moved down to Santa Monica and rented a small guest beach house from Marion Davies. I shared this with Robert Coote, an excellent English actor, and a mysterious Australian named Walter Kerry Davis.

Bob was quickly making a big name for himself as a character actor and Walter was hovering hopefully on the fringe of Los Angeles and Pasadena society where, rumour had it, he was trying to snag a rich wife. He so often failed to pay his share of the rent that he must have been finding the going very uphill.

It was a very happy combination, however, and we entertained twenty-four hours a day ... so much so that Carole Lombard, Alice Faye, Ida Lupino and Cary Grant christened the house 'Cirrhosis by the Sea'. We had this painted on a board outside the front door where it remained for over a year till we received instructions from W. R. Hearst to take it down.

Fred Astaire and Ginger Rogers decided to make no more musicals together and the whole world mourned.

207

Fred went on from strength to strength with a series of different dancing partners and Ginger decided to return to straight acting. They were the king and queen of R.K.O. so it was immensely flattering for me when Goldwyn told me that he had loaned me out to co-star with Ginger in her first solo for a long time, *Bachelor Mother* to be directed by the immensely talented writer-director, Garson Kanin.

'Everyone's going to expect you to dance,' said Goldwyn 'show them that you can act instead.'

The script, by Norman Krasna, was a dream and Goldwyn decided that this picture was so important that he would not put me into anything else before it. It was then February 1938.

I kept my promise and went skiing at Sun Valley. The resort was just open, new and small. Only two hotels were built, 'The Lodge', very good and very expensive and 'The Challenger Inn' where I went, very gay and much cheaper.

Averell Harriman had his own charming chalet and others were building. The skiing was perfect and I had a wonderful six weeks. Felix had made a huge success of the place. Given half a chance he was still liable to lay down the law about 'Lebensraum' but he was a most agreeable companion. Towards the end of my stay, I was surprised to get a phone call from Norma Shearer who had been virtually incommunicado since Irving Thalberg's death.

She sounded desperately lonely so I persuaded her to come on up and booked her a suite in the Lodge. When she arrived Averell Harriman went out of his way to make life pleasant for her. She fell in love with the place, with skiing, and a few years later with a great skier and happily remarried.

Bachelor Mother took most of the summer to shoot and was a most happy assignment. Thanks to Garson's sure hand and novel ideas, the result surpassed the highest hopes and it was widely acclaimed as the best comedy of the year. It went straight to my head, of course, and I bought a Leica and went all over Los Angeles taking pictures of my name and likeness on the billboards.

During the filming, Garson said something that gave me pause for thought.

'Do you realise,' he said, 'that I am the director of this

picture and you are the co-star but between us we are being paid less than half what the cameraman is getting?'

There was no doubt that every time Goldwyn loaned me out he demanded huge sums for my services but I was still basically amazed that I was being paid at all and Goldwyn, after all, had given me a chance when nobody else would touch me. Nevertheless, the flea was in my ear so I had a talk with Leland Hayward, the top agent in Hollywood.

'Leave Goldwyn to me,' he said, 'you're making a fortune for him – I'm going in there to ask for a lot of money and a contract for five years straight with no lay-off and no options, a limited number of pictures and six weeks' guaranteed vacation each year.'

On the day of Leland's meeting with Goldwyn, he went in to the office brimming with confidence. I waited in the ante-room.

Two minutes later he was back.

'Did you get it?' I asked.

'Not exactly,' said Leland. 'Goldwyn has barred me from the lot – now I can't even talk to him.'

A really ridiculous war of nerves then started with Goldwyn. He didn't speak to me when I met him and when I turned down what I thought was a really awful script, I was promptly put on suspension.

One day I saw a headline in Louella Parsons' daily gossip column read avidly by the whole industry – 'NIVEN IMPOSSIBLE SAY FELLOW WORKERS.' It went on to charge that because of recent successes I had got such a swollen head I refused to speak to old friends in the studio.

I was appalled and when I discovered through a secretary in the publicity department that the story had emanated from there, I confronted Jock Lawrence.

As usual he was urbane.

'Remember that first day you came in here?' I told you then Mr. Goldwyn is the greatest but he's rough sometimes.'

Being suspended, I started earning a nice amount by working on the radio in the Lux Radio Theatre and other programmes – very serious they were too, with a week's rehearsal and the performance given before a live audience of several hundreds to an unseen one of fifty million.

Reeves Epsy spoke to me: poor man, he hated to deliver bad news.

'Dave, Mr. Goldwyn says that you have been working on radio without his permission. Under the terms of the contract he has the right to everything you earn. However, he'll let you keep half.'

The next radio show I did was with Bing Crosby; the sponsor was Kraft. At the end of the show, as was often the custom, I was presented with a large hamper filled with all the Kraft products, cheeses, spreads, and sardines.

When I got home, Coote helped me, and we meticulously removed half the spread from the jars, cut every cheese in half, every sardine in half, then with an envelope containing a cheque for half my salary from the show, I sent the lot to Goldwyn inside half the basket.

It was ridiculous and childish and I was behaving like a small boy attacking a heavy tank with a water pistol but rather enjoying it.

Fred and Phyllis Astaire arranged a ceasefire and Goldwyn sent for me. All smiles, he received me in his office – he had immense charm. He told me that he wanted to give me a new seven-year contract, mentioned the figures which seemed colossal to me and added that the first picture I would do would be *Raffles*.

I had always wanted to tackle the part of the famous gentleman crook; now it was being dangled before me like a carrot. It all seemed perfect.

'I'll call Leland and have him come over and we'll make a deal,' said Goldwyn. I left in a high state of excitement.

I remember that September evening very vividly because in the car park, outside Leland's office, I listened to the hysterical voice of Hitler, addressing the Nuremberg Rally. The doom-filled tones of the commentator, Gabriel Heatter, left one in no doubt as to the intentions of the man and the rolling Sieg Heils of his massed Storm Troopers underlined them in an ominous and frightening way.

I thought about Felix and his dire prognostications.

Leland blithely turned down Goldwyn's offer.

'You've got to have some guts,' he said, when I remonstrated. 'Sit him out – play it uninterested – your contract is running out. He doesn't want to lose you – he's just playing games – I know Sam – we'll get the deal we want.'

I just hoped that Leland knew what he was doing, and went sailing with Flynn on one of our weekend jaunts to Catalina Island in his ketch *Sirocco*. Normally, the arrangement was that we provided the booze, and the girls, whoever they were, brought the food. There was one lady who had made a habit of showing up with nothing but a loaf of bread and a douche bag.

We were on our way back to the mainland on the Sunday evening. The sea had kicked up quite considerably.

About fifteen miles out of Balboa, we sighted a large cabin cruiser. She was stopped and wallowing about and signalling to us frantically.

When we came near enough, we could see her name *Jobella* and sitting in the stern with a cigar clamped between his teeth, was the owner, Harry Cohn, the head of Columbia Studios.

'Give us a tow for Christ's sake,' yelled Cohn. 'Goddam engine's broke down.'

Jobella was a heavy boat and we didn't bring her in to Balboa till well after midnight.

Cohn in his rough, tough, East Side way was only moderately grateful so the next day I thought I'd have a little fun with him. I persuaded a lawyer friend to send him an official letter quoting maritime law on the question of asking for help at sea and, mentioning the Salvage Act of 1912, I claimed one half of the *Jobella*.

No answer came and I forgot all about it. One day Leland called me. 'What the hell have you done at Columbia – you've been barred from the lot for life!'

'I haven't set foot in the place for three years,' I said.

'Well, you must have done *something*,' said Leland.

Then I remembered and told him about the lawyer's letter. 'But it couldn't be that,' I said.

'Knowing Cohn, that's exactly what it is,' said Leland, 'you'd better call him up and explain.'

I called Cohn and couldn't get him on the phone. I left messages – he never called back.

I became nervous. There were only six major studios. Goldwyn was highly displeased with me at the moment and he had an option coming up in a few days. Suppose Goldwyn dropped me? Out for life at Columbia!! And the 'black list' really did exist. Too many actors who had quarrelled with their studios had sunk without trace. I might never work again anywhere. I panicked.

Leland tried to calm me down but it was obvious that he, too, was concerned.

Finally, Cohn consented to see me and I was granted an interview at 9 a.m.

He kept me waiting in the outer office all morning. At lunch time, he walked out, right past me and never said a word. But I was frightened. I was chicken. I didn't have the guts to leave too.

After lunch, Cohn came back. He never looked at me. All afternoon I sat under the pitying eye of a secretary. Finally at 6.30 – 'Mr. Cohn will see you now.'

In his big office he growled at me,

'Waddaya want?'

I said, 'About that night Errol and I towed you home ...'

'Yeah ... well whattabout it?'

'... did you get a lawyer's letter about the salvage?'

'Yeah, I got it. D'you want apologise?'

'Look, the idea was to make you laugh – if it made you unhappy, of course, I apologise.'

'Okay, I accept the apology – now get your ass outta here.'

I didn't work at Columbia till after Cohn died twenty years later.

The ridiculous war of nerves with Goldwyn continued, though I suspected that the nerves were strictly on my side.

I was called to the studio to make some costume tests for a picture with Gary Cooper. I began to notice a man hovering about in white tie and tails. He was posing for stills with Bob Coburn, the Goldwyn photographer – posing, I saw, half way up a ladder with a revolver in one hand and a pearl necklace in the other ... obviously he was meant to look like 'Raffles', the gentleman crook.

During the afternoon, I approached the man and asked him what he was doing. He was a little mystified himself.

'Well, I've been told to put on these clothes and follow you around having these pictures taken.'

The 'ploy' was pretty juvenile – to get me to rush off and

212

sign the Goldwyn offer for fear of losing *Raffles*. After
I sent Goldwyn a Boy Scout's outfit.

The name of the man was Dana Andrews.

Finally, in the spring, Goldwyn and Leland made a deal.
Goldwyn, who had a great capacity for letting bygones be
bygones, welcomed me to his office with open arms and Jock
Lawrence had pictures taken of the two of us signing the
contract ...

Goldwyn, himself, escorted me to one of the huge star
suites and ordered it to be redecorated to my taste. Olivia de
Havilland was signed to play opposite me and Sam Wood to
direct.

I was pampered and spoiled and my every whim was
catered to. When I asked for some of my old 'extra' chums
to be employed in the English country house sequences, they
were immediately and when I walked on the set, I thought it
was the Crystal Palace. To a man they were sporting
monocles. When Sam Wood fell ill, the picture was
completed by a gentle and helpful Willie Wyler.

We finished shooting on September 1st. The picture
looked good and Goldwyn was delighted. My contract was
munificent. Goldwyn's plans for me were most exciting ...
and all this had happened in less than four years ... but at
that very moment when I was preening myself, something
bigger than a weed was blowing into many people's gardens.

Hitler, without a declaration of war, was invading Poland.

Doug Junior with his attractive new Virginia-born wife,
Mary Lee, had chartered a yacht for a weekend trip to
Catalina. On board were Larry Olivier and Vivien Leigh.
Ronnie Colman and Benita Hume were anchored nearby in
Colman's ketch, *Dragoon*. Coote and I were supposedly
sailing across to join them in a small sloop, the *Huralu*. Coote
and I drank an immense amount of rum at a party in the
Balboa Yacht Club and did not quite 'make the tide'.

We were woken up at 6 a.m. by a man in a dinghy banging
on the side of our boat.

'You guys English?'

We peered blearily over the side. 'Yes.'

'Well, lotsa luck – you've just declared war on Germany.'

We never spoke a word ... just went below and filled two
tea cups with warm gin.

ally arrived at Catalina and joined the others,
nbre group. Nobody knew quite what to do;
over the world, it was beginning to dawn on
pawns in a game that had got out of control.
my couple of days, Coote and I sailed back. I
Felix Schaffcotsh from New York.

'Hello, enemy,' he said gaily, 'what are you going to do?'

'I'll go back to England, I suppose,' I said, very gloomily.

Felix sounded very bright. 'I'm leaving for Germany the day after tomorrow, let's go together.'

The next day, I told Goldwyn that I had been called up and had to leave immediately. Goldwyn, as usual, was far smarter than I gave him credit for. Within half an hour he had checked with the British Embassy in Washington and had been told that nobody outside the British Isles had yet been called up: and furthermore, that all British subjects should continue a normal life until such time as they received a summons. Luckily, nobody told Goldwyn that, having resigned my commission, I was no longer on the Reserve and in all probability would never be called up at all.

I cabled my brother Max with certain instructions and was able to show Goldwyn a cable which read –

REPORT REGIMENTAL DEPOT IMMEDIATELY ADJUTANT.

Doug Jr. gave me a splendid send-off – a bachelor party complete with pipers. The guests included Colman, Nigel Bruce, Olivier, Brian Aherne, George Sanders, Cary Grant, Roland Young, Kerry Davis and Coote, and the next day, I took off from the Burbank airport for New York.

As the plane circled over the San Fernando Valley, gaining sufficient height to cross the mountains, the whole of Los Angeles stretched out below me in the early morning light. Warner Brothers and Universal Studios were easy to pick out. I had a nasty feeling that I might be seeing them for the last time. I also wondered what the hell I was doing up there.

Felix had gone ahead and made a rendezvous with me in Rome.

Dreading the idea of being back again in the British Army, I decided to save time and money by offering myself to the Canadian Army instead so from New York, I went to

Washington to ask the advice of the military Attaché at the Embassy.

The Military Attaché was sympathetic, but explained that the few divisions at present being raised in Canada were already over-subscribed nine times down to cooks. 'Anyway,' he added, 'the Ambassador would like to see you.'

Lord Lothian was flattering, but gave me a very peculiar directive: 'It is, of course, admirable that you want to join up, but if you really would like my advice, the best thing you can possibly do, is to go back to Hollywood and represent your country on the screen.'

The ship was fairly empty except for a group of extremely hostile young Germans who made it obvious that the war had already started. I was delighted when a British destroyer stopped *Rex* outside Gibraltar. Officers boarded her, interrogated all the passengers and over the vehement protestations of the Italian captain, removed several of the young Germans.

Felix met me at Naples and we embarked on a week of liquid farewells in Rome.

He seemed very well connected and twice I found myself at the Golf Club di Roma, playing with Count Ciano, the Foreign Minister and son-in-law of Mussolini.

Ciano was a highly attractive man, and both times we played, beautiful Roman ladies walked round with us twittering like birds. When he heard that I was on my way to England to join up, he wished me luck very solemnly and said that he was sure it would all be settled very soon.

Felix and I decided that we would both leave Rome on the same day. The night before, he arranged a glorious finale. It started with drinks in somebody's Palazzo and continued through a series of visits to the houses and apartments of Felix's smart Roman friends.

In the early hours, we took two carefully selected girls to a night club – a Spanish one for Felix – a Norwegian for me, and all the time we drank, and drank without getting drunkards' drunk or noisy drunk – an evident danger on this occasion. Towards dawn Felix said: 'Let's go to the Vatican and all kiss a Swiss Guard.'

When we arrived, the sky above St. Peter's was changing from black to palest blue and the iridescent beauty of the place was almost unearthly. The Spanish girl surreptitiously crossed herself, the Norwegian whispered irreverently in my ear, 'Every time I've been in the place, I've been groped.'

Soon they were both asking to be taken home.

Ungallantly, we did not accompany them but this was our night and they sensed it.

Alone in a little 'bistro' in Trastevere, we drank Fontana di Candida as though they were never going to make any more – still we didn't get drunk. Felix talked about the new ski lifts he was planning for Sun Valley and I talked of the pictures I was going to make. A long silence enveloped us. We watched the newly awakened swifts wheeling and darting and miraculously missing each other in the darker blue sky. Suddenly, Felix slammed his glass down on the table and jumped to his feet.

'Let's say goodbye now,' he said almost angrily.

I stood up. I think we both wept, anyway, drunk at last, we embraced and parted quickly. A few hours later, Felix headed north-east for the Brenner Pass to join the S.S. and I headed north-west for the French border at Modane to join God knew what.

Felix was killed in Russia.

CHAPTER TWELVE

DUCE! Duce! On every station in letters ten feet high and the train services in Italy were running perfectly. By way of Genoa and Turin, I was quickly transported to the French border and crossed into Savoie at Modane.

Not a bomb had yet fallen on the French railway system but chaos was reigning supreme.

I had the greatest difficulty convincing a pompous little official that I was not a spy.

'Why does an Englishman come from Italy, monsieur?'

At last I persuaded him I was trying to be on his side if only he would let me and with a shrug of resignation, he stamped my passport and wrote a special pass.

'*Se rend en Angleterre pour faire la guerre.*'

The distance between Mondane and Paris is a little over five hundred miles. The train took three full days. It was packed with drunken reservists and if I ever found a seat, I vacated it only 'in extremis'. The corridor was jammed with eagle-eyed opportunists. At night, train and stations were blacked out and we stumbled about bitterly cold platforms looking for bread and cheese and wine being sold by ill-tempered ladies with flashlights and no change.

Most of the time, the train stood in sidings. Nothing seemed to go past and rumours of bombings farther up the line ran up and down the coaches.

I was constantly told by thick garlic-laden voices 'that the whole thing was the fault of England, and now, having forced France to join them against the Germans, the English would never show up to fight – 'just like the last time'.

I thought of the three million British Empire casualties including my own father, and finally, through pure exhaustion, I placated the accusing red faces by explaining that I was half French anyway.

On arrival in Paris, I managed to find a room in an hotel on the Left Bank and slept for twenty-four hours.

Refreshed, I decided to give myself a week in Paris, and then join the R.A.F. I wondered if, perhaps, I could do this in

France so I called at the British Embassy but it was a seething mass of expatriate British looking for permits, visas and transportation so I gave up and contacted Claude.

Claude had appeared in Hollywood for a very short period and had twice made the hazardous crossing to Catalina aboard *Sirocco*.

She had been a model in a famous Paris fashion house and had graduated to become the mistress of a rich industrialist. He had, rather sneakily, sabotaged her movie ambitions by sending her to Hollywood with a return ticket and just enough money for three months. She was now once more under his roof ... actually, if not technically. He had built an apartment building in Neuilly and lived on the top floor with his plump wife and two children. Directly beneath, he had installed the beautiful Claude. She was given a certain amount of freedom but he was adamant that she must never receive gentleman friends alone in her flat.

Although 'Monsieur' paid the concierge on the ground floor, he paid her so poorly that instead of being a built-in spy system for him, she had beome the *gardienne* of Claude's freedom.

Once 'Monsieur' was home for the evening, 'en famille', he never made surprise visits below, explaining to Claude, with Gallic logic, that he would never insult his wife. Claude's only enemy then was the extreme cheapness of the materials which 'Monsieur' had used in the construction of his building: he could hear everything, even the squeaking of bed springs, and once had questioned her closely as to why she had got out of bed and used her bidet at four in the morning.

Bumping about for long periods in motor cars, trains or planes always had a strange exuberant effect on my sexual ambitions: the problem now was how to gratify them without making a sound.

If 'Monsieur' had had the foresight to install a pane of glass in his floor, he could have gazed down on the ridiculous spectacle of two people thrashing around below with handkerchiefs stuffed in their mouths. As it was, it was a miracle he didn't come down to investigate because Claude, towards the end of the evening, decided to freshen me up with an alcohol rub. She intimated this in sign language and

218

fetched a large bottle of eau de Cologne. Unfortunately, as I turned over to have my back done, I knocked the bottle out of her hand with my elbow and most of its contents went straight up my behind. Shrieking agony in whispers is a difficult thing to accomplish.

Noël Coward had come to visit my beach neighbour, Cary Grant, about six months previously and, like hundreds before and since, I had fallen under his spell within a few minutes of meeting him. Quite apart from the searing talent and biting wit, there is a largely unknown gentleness and a kindliness backed by lots and lots of guts. He also has a tremendous sense of loyalty and is a tiger in defence of friends or causes.

When I had last seen him, we had lunched together at 'The Cock 'n Bull' on Sunset Boulevard and he had been quite definite in his prognostications that Neville Chamberlain and his government were leading us all unerringly into war.

Now he was appointed to a job in Naval Intelligence in Paris, though he later had a misunderstanding with Winston Churchill who was never on his wavelength. He was for the moment installed in a beautiful apartment in the Place Vendome.

I went to see him one evening. The apartment was filled with a mixture of French and British diplomats and a sprinkling of officers in uniform. One of them, a very tall R.A.F. Group Captain, cornered me and introduced himself by the name of Pope. 'It might amuse you,' he said, 'but that character you played in *Dawn Patrol* was me! — and I still have the pyjamas.'

Pope told me that I was probably too old to be taken on and trained as a fighter pilot but thought I might get fitted in elsewhere in the Service. I was only twenty-nine so this came as a rude shock. However, he recommended that I go to see John Acheson, the Air Attaché, at the Embassy, and I presented myself promptly, the next morning.

'No way to join up here in France,' said Acheson, 'you'll have to get to England ... keep your mouth shut and I'll get you on the mail plane – it goes every evening.'

He signalled me later in the day and I found myself

clasping my suitcase, sitting on a pile of mail bags and gazing down on, of all things, the white cliffs of Dover topped by those ghastly Citadel Barracks.

It was a gloomy, grey, drizzly evening in late October and as the pilot circled over Hendon aerodrome, I caught my first glimpse of the barrage balloons flying like monstrous grey toys over the city. I had not let anybody know I was coming and by the time I found Grizel's studio flat in Chelsea, it was black-out time.

We sat for hours and she brought me up to date. Max had joined my father's old regiment, the Berkshire Yeomanry and was billeted underneath the grandstand of Newbury Racecourse.

Joyce was making camouflage nets and driving for the Women's Volunteer Service and, pointing down at her own coarse blue trousers, Grizel said, 'I've joined the Chelsea Fire Service.'

Max lent me his little flat in Queen Street and, after contacting a few friends and being given a great deal of conflicting advice, I set about the business of getting into uniform myself. There seemed to be a certain amount of difficulty over this because it was the time of the 'phoney war'. The Navy, indeed, was fully involved but the R.A.F. was confined to dropping leaflets on the Germans suggesting politely that it would be much wiser for them to quit before they got hurt and the Army was stagnant on the Belgian border. All reservists had been called up, plus sufficient classes of conscripts.

An added snag was that my face was all over London. *Dawn Patrol* and *Bachelor Mother* were enormously successful and the publicity department were excelling themselves. Everywhere, I was grinning out of newspapers or leering down from billboards. It was impossible to go unnoticed and the press quickly caught up with me.

To save myself from endless harrying, it seemed wiser to get the whole thing done at once so I telephoned Goldwyn's representative and, still being Hollywood-minded, I allowed him to arrange a press conference with one or two newspapers. He set it up in the Odeon Cinema, in Leicester Square, and over a hundred reporters and photographers showed up.

I explained that I had come to join up and added that I hoped to get into the R.A.F.

The next morning Grizel called in a state of shock. When I read the front pages, I wanted to cut my throat.

'HOLLYWOOD'S FIRST RECRUIT!' 'RELAX! THE DAWN PATROL IS HERE!' 'NIVEN SPURNS ARMY!' ... 'IT'S THE R.A.F. FOR ME!'

I stayed hidden with friends in the country for a week to give things time to settle down and then visited the Air Ministry to make enquiries ... On the way, I noticed with rising panic that the 'ads' for *Bachelor Mother* had been altered ... above my name, red stickers had been added –

THE STAR WHO CAME HOME TO JOIN THE R.A.F.

I was directed to the office of a certain Group Captain. Unfortunately, I was swept into it on the crest of a giggling wave of secretaries, clutching pieces of paper and pencils.

The man restored order and eyed me with distaste. He knew who I was. Unless he had been blind he couldn't have avoided it. Nevertheless, he went through the motions of asking my name and occupation and what I wanted to do.

'Ever heard of Wilfrid Lawson?'

'Yes ... he's a wonderful actor.'

'Maybe ... we took him on and we've had trouble, nothing but trouble ever since ... Drink.'

I said, 'Look – all sorts of people drink, but I've come seven thousand miles at my own expense and I'd like to join the R.A.F.'

'So I've read,' he said nastily, 'but we don't encourage actors to join *this* service.'

For a moment I sat there stunned, then I felt anger rising from the soles of my feet.

'Then fuck *you*!' I said.

'Get out of my office,' he shouted. 'Get out!'

We were standing toe to toe when an inner door opened and an Air Commodore appeared.

'What the devil's going on in here?'

'And *fuck you too*!' I shouted unreasonably and made for the door and the giggling crowd outside it.

A week passed. I heard that Henry Clowes, who had nearly been killed five years before when the Guinness label

221

Bentley overturned on Salisbury Plain, was now Adjutant of the Scots Guards.

Philip Astley was separated from Madeleine Carroll and he offered me a room as a paying guest in his flat at the top of Hay Hill.

'It won't work,' he said, 'they have blinkers on about the theatrical profession in the Brigade – look at me – I was Adjutant of the Life Guards when I got engaged to Madeleine, but I was out of the regiment before I married her – don't try it – it's a waste of time.'

I did try it and I asked Henry Clowes if he could get me into the Scots Guards.

'No problem at all,' said Henry when I warned him about the footlight barrier – 'that was in peace time. I'll talk to the Colonel tomorrow – and phone you at once.'

Another week passed so I called Henry at Wellington Barracks.

'It didn't work, did it?' I asked.

'I'm terribly embarrassed,' said Henry. 'No, it didn't.'

Goldwyn's representative called me daily.

'Look, Dave, I've got about thirty offers for you on my desk – shall I forward them to Mr. Goldwyn?'

I was in no mood to be tampered with by the end of November when David Kelburn, now a full lieutenant just back from a North Atlantic convoy, told me the naval facts of life.

'Of course you can get into the Navy tomorrow if you want to – as a stoker – but you want to be an officer, don't you? ... Well, that means standing in line with thousands of people who know about the sea ... little things like navigation. Go back to your old regiment.'

'No,' I said firmly. 'I'm going to change my butcher. I don't want a lot of childish black marks hanging over me today.'

We were having a late supper on the balcony of the Café de Paris ... I stared gloomily down on the dancers. Most of the young men were in uniform, the cavalry men with colourful stripes on their pants and chain-mail on their shoulders and the exotic Rifle Brigade and 60th who wore green patrols with black patent leather cross belts and silver buckles, the newly commissioned, proud but selfconscious in drab khaki. Many R.A.F. and naval officers were also present.

Suddenly, the orchestra leader stopped the music and Poulsen, the owner, stepped forward ... 'Ladies and gentlemen, in case anyone is interested, the air raid warning just sounded.' Such was the effect of the 'phoney war' that this announcement was greeted with cheers, hunting cries and cat-calls ... in ten seconds it was forgotten.

Less than a year later, at the height of the blitz, a bomb shrieked through the roof and exploded on the dance floor, killing Poulsen, nearly all the orchestra and a tragic percentage of the dancers.

David got up to speak to some friends and I was left looking jealously at a table of R.A.F. pilots and their girls immediately below me. Although I was sitting unobtrusively in the balcony, they noticed me and raised their glasses, perhaps mockingly, perhaps not, but I was so selfconscious about the blaring publicity of my arrival in the country that I preferred not to speculate. One girl had her back to me. She too, was in the powder-blue uniform of the R.A.F. She turned and looked up. Long blonde hair fell away and I found myself gazing into a face of such beauty and such sweetness that I just stared blankly back.

Her complexion was so perfect that the inevitable description, 'English Rose', would have been an insult. Her eyes were the merriest and the bluest I had even seen. She looked at me for a long moment and when she got up to dance, I saw that she was tall with a divinely willowy figure.

I had a funny feeling that I would never forget her and in my mind, she became marked down as 'the W.A.A.F.'.*

I was shaken out of my musings by a rude voice behind my chair. I turned to see a beefy young man in army uniform. He was swaying slightly.

'When are you going to win the war single-handed?' he asked.

A girl was plucking ineffectually at his sleeve. To avoid him, I looked again down on the scene below. A hefty shove in the back nearly embedded my front teeth in the table top.

'I'm talking to *you* Niven,' said the young man.

'Please, Sidney,' said the girl. 'You promised not to.'

*Women's Auxiliary Air Force.

'Piss off, Janet,' said Sidney, loudly.

Heads were turning and I could see even more unpleasant publicity looming ahead. Luckily, David arrived with some naval reinforcements and Janet led a glowering Sidney back to his table.

'I don't know why you rush it,' said David, 'the bloody war will probably last a hundred years anyway ... everybody's waiting to get into uniform – you're not the only one.'

'My name's Jimmy Bosvile.' I looked up and saw, in the darkness of the night club, what I took to be a small wiry, elderly subaltern, wearing khaki with black buttons.

'I was with an air commodore this morning who was talking about your visit to his office the other day ... how splendid! I wish I'd been there.'

Bosvile sat down and I filled his glass.

'Having trouble finding a home are you?' he said. 'Why don't you come to the Rifle Brigade?'

'You couldn't get me in to the ladies' lavatory in Leicester Square,' I said, sourly.

He laughed. 'I happen to command the Second Battalion.'

Only then did I notice that one of the pips on his shoulder was a crown ... a lieutenant colonel.

So it was arranged. I told him very briefly of my previous military history and he said, 'You'll be commissioned as a second lieutenant, but put your two pips up anyway. Mark Kerr is my adjutant, he'll write and tell you what you'll need in the way of kit ... When you've got it together, come down to Tidworth. I'll expect you in about three weeks.' He smiled and we shook hands.

The Rifle Brigade! Probably the most famous of all the elite light infantry regiments in the British Army ... Army again ... oh! well ... the die was now cast. I had achieved what I had set out to do several weeks before in California... I had a strange feeling of anti-climax.

Philip Astley was himself waiting to be called up in some capacity. Some ten years older than me, he was doubtful what jobs could be found for him. 'Ever been to a war cemetery?' he asked, 'it doesn't matter what war or which army ... the average age on those crosses is about twenty ... it'll be the same this time.'

When instructions arrived, I visited a recommended tailor. While he was measuring me for my uniform, I asked him, 'How's business in these days of drastic clothing rationing?'

'Very slow, sir, very slow indeed ... of course, it'll pick up nicely once we start having heavy casualties.'

I decided to visit my club. My brother and Brian Franks and others had insisted that I join during my last visit to England. My name had been put down and some months later, I had been duly elected to Boodle's.

Mr. White, Mr. Boodle and Mr. Brooks all kept coffee houses in St. James's Street in the days of the Prince Regent. The horse racing, gambling 'bloods' had frequented White's, the politicians – Brooks's, and Boodle's had been the haunt of the landed gentry. Upon the demise of the owners, these coffee shops became clubs.

It is arguable which, today, has the most attractive interior but Boodle's, with its cream-coloured columns and bow windows certainly has the most beautiful face.

Davy, the hall porter, showed me round the premises at eleven o'clock one morning. The perfect club servant, he had spent his whole life in Boodle's since he had started there as a page.

'Of course, some of my older members are a little awkward nowadays, sir ... they don't take to the rationing at all, sir ... luckily Chef can still put on a good table because so many of my members bring game from home ...'

He prattled on as he showed me the beautifully proportioned rooms. 'Of course, the Scarlet Pimpernel, he was a member, sir, and all his gang too ... very exciting times those must have been, sir.'

He showed me a secluded corner of the main room. Large, leather chairs, discreetly separated one from the other, were placed beneath portraits of former members, Prime Ministers, Dukes and Masters of Foxhounds. 'In this corner, some say Beau Brummel used to sit looking out into the street though personally I fancy he belonged to Whites ... this is the silence corner, sir ... in here my members speak only to the waiters, never to each other.

'Welcome to the club, sir, we've never had a movie star in Boodle's before.' He withdrew.

No other members were about at that hour so I settled

225

myself in the silence corner with a weekly magazine and rang the bell. The waiter brought me my glass and tidied up an ashtray: without looking up he whispered,

'I took my wife to see *Bachelor Mother* last night, sir ... you're her favourite fan. Lovely pictures of you and Miss Rogers in all the papers today, sir.'

I had seen them. The film had just gone on general release and once more, I was staring out of the movie pages from enormous advertisements.

From the silence corner, I had an interesting view of the passers-by in St. James's Street. Always fascinated by the expressions of people who do not know they are being observed, I was too occupied to realise that I was myself being examined, with some distaste, by an elderly gentleman with a white walrus moustache. He stood right over me and flapped at me with a newspaper, a sort of fly-removing underhand flick.

'Hhhrrrump!' he said. I looked up at him.

'Hhhrrrump!' he went again and flicked once more.

I wondered if he wanted me to throw him a fish.

He 'hhhrrrumped' and flicked at me for quite a while and finally subsided angrily into a leather chair directly facing mine. There he breathed heavily, and furious, intolerant, upper-class eyes stared out at me malevolently from beneath cotton wool eyebrows.

I tried to concentrate on my magazine but the tension between us was oppressive. At last, he appeared to relax somewhat. He sat back and opened his newspaper.

Suddenly, he sat bolt upright as though he had sat on a nail. He stared appalled at the paper in front of him, then very slowly, like eighteen inch guns in a warship, his horrified gaze zeroed in on me. His eyes never left my face as he rang the bell beside his chair.

'Bring me a list of members,' he commanded with the voice of doom.

'Very good, m'lord.'

Those terrible orbs bored into me till the members' list was brought to him on a silver tray. Before he opened it he took one last look at his paper, then his fingers travelled up and down the pages. The waiter hovered, nervously. Finally, the old man closed the list with a snap, looked at me for fully a minute, then let out a long moaning sound of deep despair – treachery! treachery! it said.

He turned to the waiter and trying to keep his voice steady, said bravely, 'Double brandy – quick!'

'I enjoyed that very much,' said a naval lieutenant-commander, with a pleasant ruddy face and a broad smile. 'That's our oldest member. He hates people sitting in his chair.'

I had moved out of silence corner in a hurry and a few members were now filtering in. Over drinks and luncheon he told me he was in Naval Intelligence 'probably stuck in the Admiralty for the duration'. Ian Fleming was his name and we laughed together at the same things for years to come.

While I was gathering my necessaries together for a second military career, I found Trubshawe.

He was still living at Barton, waiting, like so many others, to be called up, but his marriage to Margie was foundering and he was being comforted increasingly by the solicitous Mrs. Tower.

Ditchley Park, in Oxfordshire, was the beautiful home of Nancy and Ronnie Tree.

Nancy was a cousin of Norah Flynn and Ronnie had lately distinguished himself by being one of the small band of rebel Conservative M.P.s who had voted with Winston Churchill against Chamberlain at the time of Munich. They invited me for the weekend and in the lovely house, decorated with sublime taste by Nancy, I was to spend some of my happiest times.

For some reason I returned on Sunday afternoon instead of Monday morning. Philip had also gone away so I was surprised when I let myself into the flat to find myself greeted by a minute Yorkshire terrier. Further shocks awaited me when I heard strange cries coming from the bedroom. I tipped down the passage and peered round the open door.

There, stark naked and strapped to the foot of my bed was a pillar of High Society. Thrashing him with great concentration with a birch, was a large-red-haired lady wearing a black bra, black gauntlets and black thigh boots. . . .

'Mercy, mistress.'

'Mercy, mistress,' he squealed as the birch rose and fell.

227

The little dog sniffed at his heels. Nobody saw me so I left quietly and went to a movie. When I came back later, there was no trace of the activity except for a small puddle in the drawing room. Philip promised to reduce my rent if he lent my room to anyone in the future.

Being the owner of a well-known movie face has opened all sorts of doors. It has also closed a few, but I have had the chance to meet people whom I would only have read about if I had been a successful bank clerk or a well-to-do butcher.

The last weekend before I went to Tidworth, I was invited to the home in Kent of Sir Adrian and Lady Baillie, Leeds Castle. Here, I was to see some of the big wheels of Government at play. David Margesson was Chief Whip of the Conservative party and later, Secretary of State for War. Geoffrey Lloyd was Minister of Transport and 'Crinks' Johnson was Head of the Liberal party.

Individually charming and for all I knew, performing their tasks with the greatest ability, as a group they depressed me.

I had a feeling that they had no right to eat and drink and dress for dinner, to make small talk and gossip like ordinary people. I was quite unreasonably shocked that they were not locked in their offices for the weekend, working tirelessly to find ways to finish the war before it got properly started.

For £190 I bought a Hillman Minx. With the petrol ration of a few gallons a month, its tiny consumption would at least allow me some freedom.

I spent my last night in London at the Café de Paris, hoping to see the W.A.A.F. again, but she did not show up. The next afternoon, I put on my new uniform, threw my baggage onto the back seat of the Hillman and headed out on the Great West Road.

It was a cold, wet, windy and altogether miserable winter's evening when I stopped the car on a hilltop on Salisbury Plain. Woodpigeons were homing into the dark isolated clumps of firs, the sodden turf on either side of the road had been chewed up by tanks. Below me lay Tidworth ... acres and acres of Victorian Barrack squares in all their red-brick horror. Grey slate roofs glistened in the drizzle. A band of blue smoke hung above the place and the sound of bugles rose.

With every mile that Tidworth had come nearer, my

228

depression had increased. 'What have you done?' I asked myself. 'Nobody asked you to come – they even told you not to ... you hate the Army ... you certainly are not very brave and you don't want to get hurt ... you've thrown away a wonderful life and career in Hollywood ... you're going to miss all that, you know ... why did you do it? ... are you sure it was not just to show off?'

I put my head on the steering wheel and warm tears of self-pity pricked my eyeballs. After a while, I drove downhill.

The Second Battalion was a motor training battalion. I was, by at least eight years, the oldest of the subalterns under training and being an ex-regular but knowing less than the others, a bit of a freak. It didn't take long to catch up. All too soon, I realised that in the intervening years, there had been pitifully few innovations. We now formed threes instead of fours; the Lewis light automatic had been replaced by the Bren; a few small Bren-carriers with tracks had been added, and instead of marching into battle, we were now driven there in trucks. Once there, we were required to perform in much the same way as before.

Jimmy Bosvile was an excellent Commanding Officer. Dick Southby, my Company Commander, was first class as was Mark Kerr, the Adjutant.

The officers came from all corners of the British Isles, the men recruited almost exclusively from London with a preponderance from the East End.

Conscripts, particularly cockney ones, were, I soon discovered, very different from the professional peacetime Jocks of the Highland Light Infantry and it took me a while to get used to the grumbling of bored soldiers who resented being pulled out of good jobs and warm homes to train in acute discomfort for a war they didn't believe would ever come to anything.

Jimmy Bosvile made it clear that I was earmarked for the First Battalion which was already on the Belgian border, and in the meanwhile, I settled down to a deadening routine of teaching men to drive trucks and to march and march and march. . . .

A tall flaxen-haired Danish model, a nymphomaniac of heroic proportions, came down from London most weekends and I installed her in a cottage in a nearby village. The Great

Dane did not pack a prodigious intellectual punch but her bed, though every bit as tiring, was a welcome change from spending cold frustrating nights chasing non-existent German parachutists all over Salisbury Plain. I introduced her to a rather dubious Jimmy Bosvile . . . he was convinced she was a spy.

A few days' leave came my way in February and I spent them at Ditchley.

Winston Churchill was there with Mrs. Churchill. Also Brendan Bracken, his trusted lieutenant, and Anthony Eden.

I arrived in uniform just in time for dinner – the meal had, in fact, already been announced and a move was being made in the direction of the dining room. Nancy Tree took me by the hand. 'Come and sit next to me,' she said, 'it's too late for introductions.'

We were twenty in number and just as we were about to sit down, Churchill spotted me from the far end of the table. I had heard before that he was an ardent movie-goer but I was unprepared for what was to come. He marched the whole length of the dining room and shook me by the hand.

'Young man,' he growled, 'you did a very fine thing to give up a most promising career to fight for your country.'

I was conscious that the great and the near-great in the room had remained standing and were listening with interest.

I stammered some inane reply and Churchill continued with a twinkle, 'Mark you, had you not done so – it would have been despicable!' He marched back to his seat.

After dinner Churchill talked and expounded on every subject under the sun. Eden took issue with him on several occasions but Bracken, always so opinionated on his own, was very subdued in the presence of the Champion.

After church on Sunday, Churchill requisitioned me for a walk round the walled garden.

He talked at great length about vegetables and the joy of growing one's own. He made it clear that before long, rationing would become so severe that 'every square inch of our island will be pressed into service'. He questioned me about the problems of a junior officer in the Army and listened most attentively to my answers. It saddens me greatly that I had the enormous good fortune to have several

230

of these 'garden tours' with this unique human being and that I remember so little of what he actually said.

That first weekend he extolled the virtues of Deanna Durbin, 'a formidable talent', and whenever he spoke of Hitler, he referred to him either as 'Corporal Hitler' or as 'Herr Schickelgruber'.

Ronnie Tree asked me if I could arrange an occasional private showing of a movie for Churchill. 'He loves films but he doesn't want to go out in public to see them for obvious reasons.'

The next morning I got busy and on the last evening of my leave, I booked a projection room in Soho and obtained a copy of the latest Deanna Durbin musical. I installed a bar in the projection room and gave a small dinner in the private room of a nearby restaurant before the showing.

The Trees and Eden came to dinner. Churchill was detained at the Admiralty but he joined us for the show. When he arrived, he accepted a large liqueur brandy, lit a cigar and settled happily down in his seat. Half way through the film, whispering started at the back and I saw that Churchill was leaving. I followed him out and he thanked me kindly for my efforts but said that 'something important' had come up and he must return to the Admiralty.

The next day the headlines were ecstatic. Churchill had given the order for H.M.S. *Cossack* to enter the Josling Fjord 'to board with cutlasses' the German naval auxiliary *Altmark* and free three hundred British prisoners – seamen of merchant ships sunk by the *Graf Spee*.

The phoney war continued and the deadening boredom of the training battalion melted into that which I had found so intolerable in the Citadel Barracks, Dover ... I felt I had never been away.

New battalions were being formed but I still waited for my posting to the First Battalion in France. Suddenly at the beginning of May, all hell broke loose. Norway fell, Holland and Belgium were invaded and Churchill became Prime Minister.

By the end of the month, our First Battalion were fighting desperately in Calais with their backs to the Channel, as a rearguard, protecting the evacuation from Dunkirk. I was ordered to standby to move there with two hundred replacements. Events moved too quickly. By June 4th the last troops had left Dunkirk, and our entire gallant First Battalion was wiped out – all killed or taken prisoner.

My brother decided that this was the moment to get married to a beautiful South African from Durban, Doreen Platt.

After their three-day honeymoon ended, he was sent out to the Eighth Army in the desert and did not see his wife again till he came back in one piece six years later. Miraculously, the marriage also survived.

I was shown an interesting document by Mark Kerr, calling for volunteers for a new 'elite force' of a highly secret nature. There followed qualifications about age and questions about liability to air- and sea-sickness.

'I think it must be parachuting,' said Mark. 'I heard rumours that they are forming something like that.'

'Jesus!' I said. 'I don't want any part of *that*.' But the Tidworth boredom prevailed and 'anything to make a change', I put my name down.

It turned out to be something equally alarming ... the beginning of the Commandos.

I was accepted and found myself being interviewed by Colonel Dudley Clarke at the War Office.

He told me the whole conception of the quick cut and thrust of raids on the enemy coastline. He had some special ideas, he said, which he might disclose later. In the meanwhile, I was to report to a prohibited area in Scotland – Lochailort Castle in the Western Highlands for special training with the other volunteers.

Before leaving, I made a quick but fruitless reconnaissance of the Café de Paris in the hopes of seeing 'the W.A.A.F.' who I could not get out of my mind, and then fulfilled a noisy, bruising late-night rendezvous with the Great Dane.

Volunteers usually fall into two groups. There are the genuinely courageous who are itching to get at the throat of the enemy, and the restless who will volunteer for anything in order to escape from the boredom of what they are presently doing.

There were a few in my category but most of the people I was thrown together with were made of sterner stuff.

232

Bill Stirling, Brian Mayfield and the Everest climber, Jim Gavin, were the founder members of the group. They were lately recovered from being depth-charged almost to death while returning in a submarine from some secret operation on the coast of Norway. Other instructors were David Stirling,* who later collected a record three D.S.O.s for desert raids deep behind the enemy lines, 'Mad Mike' Calvert, the demolition expert; Lord Lovat, who became the great Commando leader of the Dieppe Raid and the Normandy landings, where he also lost half his stomach; Colonel Newman who collected a Victoria Cross when he raided St. Nazaire and blew up the dock gates; the highly decorated Freddie Chapman who spent three and a half years behind the Japanese lines in the Malayan jungle; and two very formidable Shanghai police, Mr. Sykes and Mr. Fairbairn, who concentrated on teaching us a dozen different ways of killing people without making any noise.

Volunteers of all ranks came from every conceivable outfit and were a tough adventurous group prepared for any hardship. Mixed with us, for a while, were the semi-mutinous remains of the independent companies, defeated in Norway and now awaiting either absorption into the Commandos or disbandment. The Regimental Sergeant Major of this rugged conglomeration was a huge man, brought by Brian Mayfield and Bill Stirling from their parent regiment, the Scots Guards. The first morning I was at Lochailort, this splendid creature passed me, ramrod straight and moustache bristling. He let fly a tremendous salute which I acknowledged. He replied to this with an unmistakable and very loud Bronx cheer or common raspberry.

I spun round as if shot and shouted after him,
'Sergeant Major!'
'SAH!'
'Come back here!'
'SAH!'
He came back, halted and snapped off another salute.
'Did you make that rude noise?'
'YESSIR!'
'Why, may I ask?'

* The younger brother of Bill.

'Because you look such a cunt in a Rifle Brigade hat –
SAH!'

Only then did I catch on – it was John Royal of Green
Beer fame!'

While I gaped at him he said,

'I heard you were coming ... I have a room in a crofter's
cottage, name of Lachlan, just behind the kirk in the village
– see you there this evening ... SAH!'

Another Scots Guards salute and he was gone.

John's cottage was a godsend. Every evening, I repaired
there and tried to forget my aching, bruised body and my
'fleabag bed' on the hard wooden floor of a loft, shared with
forty or fifty others.

John, after his problems in India, had found it impossible
to obtain a commission so he had joined the Scots Guards as
a guardsman and within a few months had risen to his
present dizzy height. Later he became a parachutist and at
last got back his commission as a glider pilot. He was killed
at Arnhem.

After two months running up and down the mountains of
the Western Highlands, crawling up streams at night, and
swimming in the loch with full equipment, I was unbearably
fit. I spoke to Bill Stirling about my problem and he, most
understandingly, allowed me forty-eight hours' leave in
London to rectify the situation.

I visited the little village sweet shop which doubled as post
office and sent a telegram to the Great Dane.

ARRIVING WEDNESDAY MORNING WILL COME
STRAIGHT TO FLAT WITH SECRET WEAPON.

The Great Dane lived in Swan Court and I went there as
soon as the night train from Glasgow had deposited me in
London.

I was about to ring the bell when I was tapped on the
shoulder. A major and two sergeants of the Military Police
had materialized from nowhere.

'Come with us, please,' said the major.

'Why? What's the matter?'

'I couldn't say – my superior wants to see you.'

I was taken in a military car to a building in St. James's
Street almost opposite Boodle's and shown into an office
where sat a man in a blue suit. He didn't look very friendly.

'M.I.5 would like to ask you one little question,' he said grimly. 'You are a member of the most secret outfit in the British Army: you are in training in a Prohibited Area; you have sent a message in code to an enemy alien: WHY?'

I said, 'Sir ... that's not code – that's fucking.'

I explained the circumstances and finally persuaded him that all was well. He melted a little but said that he would investigate the whole matter further. The upshot of it was that although I spent my holiday as planned with his daughter, the Great Dane's father was discovered to be working in the Ministry of Supply in a department closely connected with the organisation of convoys at sea. He was removed.

By September, I was sent back to Colonel Dudley Clarke who told me that I had been promoted to Captain and was now the liaison officer between M.O.9 – the War Office department which was responsible for the Commandos and their operations – and the units themselves. When at the War Office, I shared a desk with a portly amiable captain who coped tirelessly and uncomplainingly with the mountainous paper work – Quintin Hogg – now Lord Chancellor of Great Britain. The rest of the time, I was on the move.

A weekend leave at Ditchley provided me with a second tour of the walled garden with Winston Churchill, now Prime Minister.

He asked me what I was doing at the moment so, as we walked, I filled him in on the exciting prospects of the Commandos.

He stopped by a greenhouse and said, 'Your security is very lax ... you shouldn't be telling me this.' He was always a superb actor but to this day I don't know whether or not he was joking.

The first big raid was on Guernsey. We trained in the Isle of Wight. R.A.F. crash boats were used because landing craft had not yet been built.

It was a success and a few bemused prisoners were taken out of their beds. One party made a landing by mistake on Sark which had no Germans on it at all. They were invited to the nearest pub by the locals.

The Battle of Britain was now in full swing as Goering tried to break the back of the R.A.F. as a prelude to invasion.

As the battles over London and the south and east coasts raged, friends suddenly disappeared. Billy Fiske, the first American killed in World War II, died flying a Spitfire with 601 Squadron. The phoney war was over with a vengeance.

Dudley Clarke switched the role of Commandos from offence to defence and we trained to be overrun by the invaders and then to form the nucleus of an underground movement.

London was being heavily bombed and moves were made to take the minds of the civilians off their increasing discomfort. At the National Gallery, for instance, as an inducement to relax and forget what was happening over one's head, eminent musicians gave free lunch-time concerts.

I took advantage of this and one day, I walked there from the War Office and wandered round a couple of galleries. From a third, I heard a cello being played by an expert. I watched her complete concentration and bathed myself in the haunting sounds for several minutes before I realised that a few feet away, and totally engrossed, stood – 'the W.A.A.F.'

Almost guiltily, I stared at her. At close quarters and under the overhead lighting of the gallery she was even more beautiful than I had remembered and so sweet looking and gentle.

When the music ended she did not move: she stood quite still, lost in the beauty of what she had heard. People applauded and the cellist picked up her things and left. Still the W.A.A.F. did not move. When there was only two of us left in the gallery, she looked up and noticed me.

'Hello,' she said, 'wasn't that wonderful?'

I persuaded her to have a sandwich with me at a nearby coffee shop ... we were both on the point of being late back to work.

I discovered her name, the fact that she was the cypher clerk at the R.A.F. Reconnaissance Squadron at Heston just outside London and that she was billeted on a family friend who lived in the middle of Regent's Park.

There was never a shadow of doubt in my mind that this was the one, but with the whole world flying apart at the seams, there was no time for the niceties of a prolonged courtship. That night I called at the house in Regent's Park

236

and passed in a note saying that I was outside the door, was considering buying the Park from the King and would like some advice on the dredging of the lake.

She appeared giggling deliciously and invited me in.

Two days later I was invited to luncheon to meet her mother and by the end of the week, I found myself shaking and sweating and being introduced to her father who lived apart. My mission was to persuade him to allow his daughter to become my wife.

Bill Rollo was an angel. Nobody has ever been able to say a word against him and this despite the fact that he was a famous divorce lawyer.

When I met him he was, though over fifty, also in the uniform of the R.A.F. ... on his chest an impressive row of ribbons from World War I.

He worked all day at his law office and did night duty in a special war room where on a wall map, the Prime Minister could see at a glance the latest dispositions of flotillas, brigades and squadrons.

He protested mightily: 'But, Primmie darling, you *can't* put me in this position because I don't know how to behave!'

'Don't be nervous, papa,' said she, 'leave everything to us.'

He handed me an enormous drink and helped himself liberally. 'Oh, God!' he said, 'this is agony, isn't it? I ought to ask you all sorts of questions ... do you have any prospects? ... well, that's bloody silly for a start because the air raid warning has just gone.'

It was the night of a particularly heavy 'blitz' and bombs were soon raining down. It had been arranged that we would go out to dinner but there was so much shrapnel flying about that we decided against it.

'I can't think why you want to marry her,' said Bill, 'she can't cook and she can't sew.'

'You're a big help,' said his daughter.

We opened some wine, some cans of beans and some cheese and as a particularly heavy bombardment made the high old building shudder and sway, with the three of us huddling under the kitchen table, Bill Rollo gave his consent.

War is a great accelerator of events so ten days later, we were married in the tiny Norman church of Huish village at the foot of the Wiltshire Downs. Trubshawe, now in the uniform of the Royal Sussex Regiment, was best man, and friends from far and near came by train, by bicycle or by blowing their petrol rations for a month – some came on horseback.

Primmie looked like a porcelain figure in a simple pale blue dress. The Battle of Britain on that cloudless September day, was raging in the skies above it – it was no time for veil and orange blossom. She carried a bouquet of pink flowers picked from her parents' garden a hundred yards away. Half way through the service, as we were singing her favourite anthem, 'Sheep may safely graze', a small flock, as though divinely summoned, wandered in from the Downs and stood chewing benignly round the font.

Our first days of honeymoon were spent finding a place for Primmie to set up a home.

We had no money apart from my army pay so we were lucky to find a fourteenth-century, unheated, thatched cottage between Dorney and Slough. Primmie had left the R.A.F. in order to get married but she was determined to contribute to the war effort so she bicycled to Slough every morning at seven o'clock and worked at Hawker's factory, building Hurricane fighters. She took in an elderly refugee from the London bombing who had just lost her husband and her home near the docks. Mrs. Wisden was a little birdlike cockney who wore pince-nez. She kept 'Halfway Cottage' tidy and cooked – after a fashion – but behaved rather strangely during air raid alerts. Hawker's being an obvious target for the Luftwaffe, these were frequent. Thanks to a permanent smoke screen from smudge pots, the factory itself remained untouched but the whole neighbourhood became pitted with bomb craters to Mrs. Wisden's apparent satisfaction. The moment the banshee wailings of the sirens started, she would rip down the blackout curtains, turn on all the lights and rush out into the garden, tearing at her blouse.

'Let me 'ave it, 'Itler!' she would scream, 'rite through me bleeding' chest ... I want to join my 'Arry ... Roll on death!'

The Commandos were being prepared for offensive operations but these were held up while landing craft were designed and built. In the meanwhile, the danger of our own invasion by the German Army, poised across the Channel,

238

was very real. A new and highly secret outfit within the Special Services was formed to help deal with this possibility and I was ordered to join it in Richmond Park. Before I went, I did something for which, in my opinion, the military has never adequately rewarded me. I suggested to my new uncle by marriage, Robert Laycock, that he should join the Commandos.

He was then a captain in the Royal Horse Guards and had just received a posting to India to become gas officer of a division and was due to embark in a few days' time. He came to the War Office and I introduced him to Dudley Clarke who immediately decided that this was just the man he wanted.

Bob and I paced the stone corridors of that dreary old building while Clarke dashed about, pulling strings as a result of which somebody else went to India and Bob formed No. 8 Commando, embarking on a career of legendary gallantry which included his famous efforts to blow up Field Marshal Rommel in the desert some 200 miles behind the German lines in Libya. It culminated, five years later, in his becoming Chief of Combined Operations with the rank of major-general.

Richmond Park was the headquarters of 'Phantom' – the brainchild of 'Hoppy'.

Colonel Hopkinson had realised painfully during the retreat to Dunkirk that if a general fighting a battle is not receiving a steady flow of reliable information from the front, he cannot contribute very much towards the outcome. In the heat of contact, normal communications frequently break down, radio transmitters get destroyed and dispatch riders get killed.

'Phantom' was composed of a number of highly mobile squadrons of 'officer patrols'. These were deployed among the forward units, equipped with radios, endowed with expert dispatch riders and as a last resort, a basket of carrier pigeons. The commanding officer of 'Phantom' stayed at the army commander's right hand and when the situation at a certain point on the map needed clarifying, a message went direct to the nearest 'Phantom' Squadron to find out exactly what was going on. In practice the answer usually came back explaining that the situation was unclear because the place was full of Germans.

After a brief period of intensive training, I was promoted to Major and for over three years I had the great honour to command 'A' Squadron.

'Hoppy' was a short, square officer with a fertile imagination and a great gift for extracting the maximum of loyalty and hard work from all ranks. Before he was killed in action in Italy, he built up a unit that again and again proved its worth in the reconquest of the Continent.

Hugh Kindersley, a handsome giant from the Scots Guards, was second-in-command and the officers and men came from every unit in the British Army.

During the threat of sea-borne invasion, the 'Phantom' squadrons were distributed along the southern and eastern coasts where, apart from our primary function, we also made ourselves ready to go underground and a large stock of disguises was earmarked for distribution if the invasion was successful. I, personally, was ready to re-emerge dressed as a parson.

For a start 'A' Squadron was attached to 5 Corps in the danger area behind Poole Harbour. The Corps Commander was a dynamic little man who demanded a fearsome standard of mental alertness and physical fitness. Just inside his headquarters was a large notice board ...

ARE YOU 100% FIT?
ARE YOU 100% EFFICIENT?
DO YOU HAVE 100% BINGE?

We never discovered what he meant by 'BINGE' because nobody dared to ask him. His name was General Bernard Montgomery.

'A' Squadron was my pride and joy. The second-in-command was a sardonic Irish newspaper man and the patrol officers included a Cameron Highlander, a Frenchman, a Lancastrian, a weight lifter, the assistant Bursar at Eton College, an amateur steeplechase jockey and an interior decorator who frequently called me 'dear' instead of 'sir'.

The Squadron Sergeant-Major was a Scots guardsman and the seventy other ranks were made up of bank clerks, burglars, shop assistants milkmen, garage mechanics, school-masters, painters, bookmakers, stockbrokers and labourers.

A rugged corporal told me he was 'a lion tamer in usual

life' and of the two men who cooked for and catered to the officers, one came from the Royal Household at Buckingham Palace while the other, a Norfolk man, said he 'liked a bit of poaching better than anything'. In action, of course, these two were 'runners' at Squadron Headquarters and once when General Montgomery visited us unexpectedly, I was waiting under his eagle eye for an important message to be delivered when I was appalled to see my 'runner' approaching with the message in one hand and a pheasant in the other.

In the autumn of '41, the Trees invited Primmie and me to spend my week's leave in the comfort of Ditchley. Walter Monckton, Director General of the Ministry of Information, was there, also a charming American, David Bruce. As the Germans had radio beams from Norway and France pinpointing Chequers, the Prime Minister's country retreat was considered a bad risk so Ronnie and Nancy made a large part of Ditchley available to Winston Churchill and his staff. It was fascinating to rub shoulders with the greats, with Sir Charles Portal, the Commander in Chief of the R.A.F., and Sholto Douglas, Chief of Fighter Command.

Churchill bade me take another walk in the walled garden. Things were looking grim – the war in the desert was at its lowest ebb with Rommel snapping at the gates of Alexandria and after their spectacular success in Crete, the possibility of an enemy airborne invasion of the U.K. had now superseded the threat of a conventional one. Food was getting more and more scarce and a glance at the map sent cold shivers down one's back.

The whole of Europe was under German domination and in Russia, Von Rundstedt had just captured 600,000 prisoners at Kiev and Von Bock another 600,000 at Vyazma ... Leningrad was besieged and the road to Moscow appeared wide open.

'Do you think, sir,' I asked, 'that the Americans will ever come into the war?'

He fixed me with that rather intimidating gaze and unloosed the famous jaw-jutting bulldog growl.

'Mark my words – something cataclysmic will occur!'

Four weeks later the Japanese attacked Pearl Habour.

Months later, when we were once more enjoying the

241

delights of a short leave at Ditchley, I asked in the walled garden if the Prime Minister remembered what he had said so long ago. His reply gave me goose pimples.

'Certainly I remember.'

'What made you say it, sir?'

'Because, young man, I study history.'

When Primmie became pregnant in the spring of 1942, she stopped building fighter planes, left Mrs. Wisden baring her bosoms in the garden at the first sign of a German bomber and followed 'A' Squadron wherever it went, living in a succession of farms, stables and vicarages. We were wonderfully in love and spent a lot of time praying that Phantom would not be sent to the African desert, or the Malayan jungle.

In mid-August, the ambitious raid on Dieppe was carried out. About 8,000 men, mainly Canadians were employed. Commandos under Lord Lovat were also involved and a specially trained force from Phantom.

Though the raid taught many invaluable lessons that saved devastating loss of life later on the Normandy beaches, the cost was appalling with almost two-thirds of the attacking force wiped out.

Writing and re-writing letters I had to send to the wives and girl friends of the men lost from 'A' Squadron, I kept thinking of a scene from *Dawn Patrol* when the Commanding Officer was going through the same agonising ritual. The adjutant watched him for a while and then said, gently, 'It doesn't matter how you word it, sir, it'll break her heart just the same.'

By autumn, Primmie was less mobile so she moved to London during the height of the blitz and calmly waited for the arrival of her baby.

I thought perhaps Philip Astley might let her stay in his comfortable flat and went to see him. The building had been demolished by a direct hit. Fortunately, Philip had been out at the time.

By a great piece of good luck, 'Hoppy' had recalled 'A' Squadron to Richmond to refit with new equipment so I was well within reach when Primmie was whisked off in the middle of a December night and admitted to the Royal

Northern Hospital in Camden Town in North London. 'Hoppy' gave me permission to spend the nights in the hospital so, every evening after work, I borrowed a dispatch rider's motor cycle and rode through the black-out across the whole of London to be with Primmie and her little boy. They were unattractive trips. Hitler's full fury was raining down on the city and shrapnel from the anti-aircraft batteries was also falling like lethal confetti. I wore a steel helmet and too often aided by the light of the fires, chugged my way past bomb craters and debris, peering ahead at the glow-worm reflection from my dimmed-out headlight. Happily the motor cycle made so much noise that I could not hear the express train whistle of falling bombs.

I slept on the floor beside Primmie's bed and marvelled at her serenity – she was totally unafraid. Camden Town, a working class district, for some reason had become a prime target for the German bombers ... the devastation around the hospital was awful. The bombing started nightly, as soon as darkness fell, and continued till dawn. More than once, on hearing a bomb screaming down in his direction, the brave major on the floor had to steel himself against taking cover under his wife's bed.

A few days after Primmie and the baby left for Dorney, the inevitable happened – the hospital received a direct hit.

During 1943, the soldier's oldest enemy – boredom – attacked Phantom. It was quite evident to us that we were being prepared for the final assault on the continent of Europe, but like footballers, we were becoming overtrained, so 'Hoppy' sent his squadrons whizzing all over England.

At one moment, 'A' Squadron found itself isolated outside the walls of Dartmoor Prison.

'Keep the men interested,' ordered 'Hoppy' by radio. 'Think of novel employment for them – turn night into day – make front-line conditions.'

Obediently, I arranged three days on the moors of intensive manoeuvres and, at the last minute, to simulate what might easily lie ahead of us, I cancelled the ration trucks.

Naturally, at the end of seventy-two hours on a windswept escarpment, covered with nothing but heather, ferns and wild pony shit, 'A' Squadron, forced to 'live off the land', were in a sorry condition. All, that is, except their gallant commander who had taken certain precautions and Squadron Sergeant Major Lonsdale of the Scots Guards.

'How is it possible?' I asked him. 'I am the only one who knew that the squadron would have no food or water for three days.'

'Sorr,' he replied, 'I happened to have aboot my person one large fruit cake.'

The naval commander of a flotilla of motor torpedo boats in Darmouth contacted me.

'We are made of three-ply,' he said, 'and we are fitted with last-war 2-pounders. The German E boats have twin Oerlikens operated electrically from armour-plated bridges and we are supposed to protect the convoys from the bastards – do you have any anti-tank weapons? If so, please come and help us.'

'A' Squadon spent many miserable seasick hours as a result of my quixotic acceptance of this dangerous invitation.

'Hoppy' finally gathered all the squadrons into Richmond Park and told me to arrange a concert. I went to beg the help of the Crazy Gang at the Victoria Palace.

Bud Flanagan's response was typical. 'Leave it to us,' he said, 'just provide the transport and we'll provide the show but you be Master of Ceremonies and give us some grub after.'

The concert took place at midnight, in the big movie house on Richmond Hill. It was a classic show business answer to an S.O.S. Flanagan and Allen showed up, also Nervo and Knox, Naughton and Gold, Debroy Somers and his Band, Teddy Brown and his xylophone, Sid Field, Zoe Gail, Frances Day, Naunton Wayne, Arthur Riscoe and Leslie Henson.

The show lasted for four hours and was wildly appreciated. Civilian morale on a small beleaguered island was also in constant need of bolstering and during the time I spent in the Home Forces, I was used for all sorts of capers. I was given four weeks 'special duty' and with a radio transmitter in my dressing room from which I controlled 'A' Squadron, I played a part in a film about the Spitfire, backed by the R.A.F. – *The First of the Few* with Leslie Howard.

Two years later, I collected a few more weeks of 'special

duty' and played in an Army-backed film, directed by Carol Reed, written by Eric Ambler and Peter Ustinov – *The Way Ahead* – which was not only a huge public success but for ten years after the war was used as a training film at Sandhurst.

These short bursts of escapism were a bonanza and I was only too happy to sample the first marvellous fruits of a happy married life.

With my Major's pay, Primmie had now left the numbing damp of 'Halfway Cottage' for the roaring draughts of a phoney Tudor villa nearer the centre of the village of Dorney.

It was always full of friends, bringing their own food and drink of course. Larry Olivier did the carving, having been brought up in a low budget parsonage he could make a chicken do for ten people. He and Vivien lived nearby as did Johnny and Mary Mills, Rex Harrison and Lilli Palmer. Noël Coward was a frequent and greatly cherished visitor and all of them looked after Primmie while I was away and gave her a wonderful introduction into the strange, half-mad world of show business.

Del Giudice, the Italian dynamo who produced the pictures that took Arthur Rank out of his flour bags and put him at the top of the film world, was another neighbour. A popular guest at Del Giudice's house was the then Minister of Labour and later, one of the greatest Foreign Secretaries that Britain has ever known – Ernest Bevin.

I discussed with him the problem of my soldiers' boredom.

'Make 'em use their noggins,' he said, 'they're all intelligent fellers . . . get a few debates going – but don't take sides yourself or you'll be in a bloody mess.'

The discussion periods I organised as a result of Bevin's advice were a huge success. The liveliest one was sparked off by a leading article which had appeared in the *Daily Mirror*, '. . . the accepted tip for Army leadership would, in plain truth, be this: All who aspire to mislead others in war should be brass-buttoned boneheads, socially prejudiced, arrogant and fussy. A tendency to heart disease, apoplexy, diabetes and high blood pressure is desirable in the highest posts . . .'

One thing stuck out a mile during these debates – the vast majority of men who had been called up to fight for their country held the Conservative party entirely responsible for the disruption of their lives and in no circumstances would they vote for it next time there was an election – Churchill or no Churchill.

Weekends at Ditchley afforded close-ups of other members of the Cabinet: Anthony Eden was unfailingly kind and charming, but, somehow, left me with the impression that he was floating in the air far above me. Duff Cooper, a much tougher, much more down-to-earth character, was given to bursts of ungovernable fury during which his face would congest and turn an alarming magenta colour. The smallest thing could set him off and Trees' two sons would come rushing to find me ... 'Come quick ... Duff's doing a turkey cock in the library!'

I got on famously with him once he realised we had one big thing in common – we both loved America and Americans. His wife, the legendary Lady Diana, was, of course, sublime.

My fast-becoming-forgotten movie face was occasionally pressed into service and I was sent to make impassioned speeches in factories in the Midlands during 'Tanks for Russia Week'. I was also sent to Glasgow to head a drive to get more volunteers for the Women's Army – the A.T.S. There, for a week, I appeared in fog-filled movie houses all over the city and harangued the paying customers whom I could barely see in the gloom.

By the beginning of 1944, the Americans were pouring into Britain and many old Hollywoood friends appeared at Dorney. Bob Coote materialised in the Royal Canadian Air Force. Clark Gable, whose adored wife, Carole Lombard, had been killed in an air disaster, appeared as a major in a bombing squadron and Jimmy Stewart showed up – a colonel in the same line of business. John Ford and Douglas Fairbanks Jr were in the U.S. Navy. Willie Wyler and John Huston were with Combat Photographic Units. Garson Kanin was doing something very mysterious in the Army and joy of joys, John McClain arrived, a lieutenant in the U.S. Navy attached to the O.S.S.

Dorney features so often in this account that I feel I should explain that I was in other places too. At the end of a war one forgets, thank God, the numbing patches of boredom and frustration and remembers only the fright and the fun. I am chiefly concerned with the fun and Dorney, with Primmie, was where my fun lay.

The Free French frequently cooked their rations in our kitchen, among them Claude Dauphin and Jean Pierre Aumont. These two gave a party for us in London and Joseph Kessel ate a champagne glass, stem and all.

Guy Gibson, the master bomber, spent a weekend with us just after he had been awarded the Victoria Cross for blowing up the Eder and Mohne dams. He was in a rare state of excitement because Winston Churchill had invited him to dinner at 10 Downing Street on the Monday. Guy made a date with us for luncheon at one o'clock on the following day so he could report everything the great man said.

Primmie and I were at the Berkeley sharp at one – no Gibson. Two o'clock – no Gibson. We were just finishing our ersatz coffee around three o'clock when he came tottering in looking ghastly, eyes like dog's balls.

'How was it?' we asked.

'Marvellous – fabulous!' he croaked. 'God! I'm tired – that was the best yet!'

'What did he say?'

'Who?' said Gibson.

'Churchill,' I said with a touch of asperity.

Gibson looked stricken – Then he clutched his head.

'Jesus Christ! – I *forgot*!'

A month later on his one hundred and twentieth bombing mission, he was shot down.

By the early spring of 1944, it was obvious that the Second Front would soon be opened on the Continent. Training increased in tempo and there were so many American troops in Britain that only the barrage balloons kept the island from sinking beneath the waves under their weight.

Out of the blue, I was ordered to report to General Sir Frederick Morgan at a highly camouflaged headquarters in a wood near Sunningdale. Morgan, although I did not know it, had for months been drawing up the invasion plans that would soon be put to effect in Normandy. He came straight to the point.

'You've lived in America for some years?'

'Yes, sir.'

'Do you like Americans?'

'Very much, sir.'

'Good, because you're going to be seeing a great deal of them ... I'm taking you out of Phantom and promoting you to Lieutenant Colonel ... from now on you will be under the direct order of General Barker – an American.'

He told me where to go and I found General Ray Barker in a Nissen hut under the trees. He, it transpired, had been working with Morgan on the overall invasion plan.

'One thing we dread is a repetition of what happened between the British and the French in the last war,' he said. 'Sir John French and General Lanrezac were commanding adjoining armies. They didn't speak each other's language; they detested each other and tried to win private feuds to impress Field Marshal Joffre.

'Their feeling percolated down to the troops. The Germans repeatedly attacked this weak link in the chain and very nearly won the war as a result.'

General Barker was the finest type of contemporary American ... quiet, courteous and full of humour but underneath his evident compassion and gentleness, one could detect the steel ... I listened attentively as he went on ...

'When we land on the Continent, there will be Americans, British and Canadians to start with. Later there will be Poles and French. I am charged by General Eisenhower with seeing that this time, there are no weak links in the chain. Misunderstandings and rumours are bound to arise but they will have to be dealt with promptly at all levels from friction between army commanders, right down to arguments about what programmes should be beamed to the troops by the B.B.C. and the American Forces Network. After we invade you will be in the field doing odd jobs for me and from now on you take orders only from me.'

'A' Squadron gave me a silver tankard and I handed over to John Hannay, my second-in-command for the past two years. It was a big wrench but my love of change soon dispelled my disappointment and under the highly efficient John the squadron prospered.

A celebration luncheon with Ian Fleming at Boodle's revealed that the place was much changed. A direct hit had demolished the back of the building but the beautiful façade and famous ceilings were still intact. Most of the windows were boarded over. Food had become very scarce.

'My members don't take to whale steaks at all,' said Davy mournfully.

We were peering at the daily menu displayed in the darkened hall when the oldest member growled in my ear,

'Can't see the damn thing in this gloom — what's on the card today?'

'Moules marinières, sir,' I said.

'Good God!' he trumpeted, 'the bloody fellers have got us eatin' moles now!'

We held a belated christening party for little David and with the exception of Bob Laycock, all the godparents came to Dorney.

Larry and Vivien produced a Jacobean drinking mug with 'D.W.' engraved on it. I complained about this to Godmother Vivien who said, 'I'm not going to change it so from now on you'll just have to be called "Wiven", that's all.'

Godfather Noël Coward donated a silver cocktail shaker on which was inscribed —

'Because, my Godson dear, I rather
Think you'll turn out like your father.'

The day, however, was made by a retired Nannie — Miss Maple — who at seventy had decided that she could still 'do her bit' so she struggled with little David to enable Primmie to return to work at Hawker's. Some of my methods, however, had upset this redoubtable old lady and she suddenly appeared and announced to the assembled guests.

'It's bad enough when the Colonel takes Master David's olive oil for the salad dressing — but when he steals his concentrated California orange juice for the cocktails — it's going *too far!*'

I was so proud of Primmie, of her flower-like beauty of course, but everyone loved her and the reason was obvious ... She never thought an unkind thought about anyone. She was incapable of saying an unkind word. On the June night before I left for Normandy we clung together miserably. The parting was not made easier by the news that her uncle, Michael Laycock, had just been killed on the beaches and that her brother, Andrew, had been blown up when his destroyer hit a mine. His captain reported that 'blown up' was the correct description because Andrew was on the foredeck when it happened and the next moment the captain, high on the bridge, saw Andrew above his head. Miraculously, he fell in the sea and survived.

I lied to Primmie about leaving after breakfast and at dawn when she had finally fallen asleep, I slipped out of bed, dressed, looked down at her with the little boy asleep in his cot beside her, and tiptoed out of the house.

The *Empire Battleaxe* was a Liberty ship with elements of an American Division. I boarded her at Southampton.

'That's one helluvan encouraging send-off,' observed a G.I. as, over the side, we watched hundreds of wounded being helped or carried ashore from a tank landing craft — boys with shocked faces and staring eyes, in their bandages and hastily applied field dressings, grown old in a few short hours.

Once opposite the Normandy beach, we were ordered into the landing craft and, to the continuous roll of gunfire, ferried ashore. Beach Masters pointed to the white taped paths through the minefields and we went our separate ways.

There is no place in these pages for harrowing blood-soaked descriptions of man's inhumanity to man — all that has been raked over a thousand times by a thousand more competent writers since that June of 1944 so let me say at once that lying in a ditch that first night in Normandy, my most vivid recollection was the sound of the nightingales.

Before the war, eminent lady cellists were employed by the B.B.C. to sit in remote black woods to try and coax these timid little birds into song. The nightingales of Normandy were made of sterner stuff — they all but drowned out the gunfire with their racket.

Between British Second Army and American First there was a small bridge at Carentan. It was in fact the one vital link between our very meagre bridgeheads and, consequently, was shelled by the Germans at close range many times a day.

Several spare Bailey bridges were kept handy so that replacement was speedy and the lifeline kept open, but it was a hazardous crossing and I had to make it frequently. Foxholes were dug on either side of the bridge and once, trapped by the shelling, I was cowering in the bottom of one of them when, after what seemed an eternity, the lethal rain seemed to have let up. I peeked timidly out and couldn't believe my eyes. Like a cock-pheasant in the bracken, a familiar head was sticking out of a foxhole a few yards away – John McClain.

After the barrage, my transport was no longer functioning so my old friend gave me a ride in his command car driven by a very disapproving American sergeant. McClain also pinned on my chest the Iron Cross.

Cherbourg was still in enemy hands and McClain, with a psychological warfare unit, had been bombarding the defenders with a verbal barrage via sound truck. General von Schlieben, in an attempt to shore up the morale of the defenders, had for some days been handing out decorations like Lady Bountiful at a village fête. He had radioed for more Iron Crosses to be delivered by parachute and they had been dropped in error on McClain and his outfit.

My work completed at First Army, McClain suggested a light luncheon at a little inn he had heard about from Captain Bob Low, an ex-*Time* reporter, now working in First Army Intelligence.

'Low says it's in a backwater,' he said, 'no krauts there – nobody – untouched by the war – let's go.'

Quetthou, on the coast about five miles south of Barfleur, was all that Bob Low had predicted and the inn, 'Aux Trois Cents Hommes', was unforgettable. The disapproving sergeant refused to join us and sat outside morosely chewing his 'C' rations, while McClain and I, the first Allied combatants they had seen, were treated like royalty by the three bosomy ladies who ran the place. We were given a sumptuous meal of omelettes, delicious little flat fish and Camembert cheese, washed down by bottles of Bordeaux which they dug up from the cabbage patch where they had been hidden from the Germans.

On the way back, we grew strangely silent as we approached Carentan because it became obvious from the noise that we were going to have to run the gauntlet of the bridge once again.

'Er ... lookit, Sarge,' said McClain. 'Isn't there some way round by the beach so we can cut out that goddam bridge?'

The disapproving one was unbending.

'The way I see it Lieutenant – it's either got your name on it, or it hasn't.'

McClain's reply was really brave.

'Well – it may have your fucking name on it – but it doesn't have mine.'

The Normandy battles raged around Caen and St. Lô longer than had been expected and this frustration of their plans sparked the first differences of opinion between the Allied commanders. Finally, at the end of July, with the British and Canadians containing the bulk of the German armour, the Americans were able to break out on the Western flank and the charge on Paris and Brussels began.

I found 'B' Squadron of Phantom hidden in a wood behind the Orne. Dennis Russell was still in command. Hugh (Tam) Williams, that fine actor, was still in the squadron. They told me that Hugh Kindersley had been badly wounded and 'Tam' and I agreed that if we had known about the German Nebelwerfer – a six-barrelled mortar – we would never have joined the Army in the first place. (After the war, like many others, 'Tam' found his place had been filled while he had been away and that he had been largely forgotten as an actor. He went bankrupt and then emerged triumphant as one of the most successful playwrights that London has seen.)

In a tent far to the rear lived a group of war correspondents typing out pages of self-glorification ... 'as the bullets sang past my head', etc. There were some heroic and exemplary war correspondents, of course – Ernie Pyle, Bob Capa and Chester Wilmot, to name a few – but anyone who says a bullet sings past, hums past, flies, pings or whines past, has never heard one – they go *crack*.

Just before the breakout at Falaise, General Barker recalled me for a few hours to England.

The D.C.3 lumbered off the makeshift runway on a cliff top above the landing beaches. After an alarming dip, it gained height and headed home. Below much of the damage wrought by the disastrous three-day storm at the end of June was still apparent. The 'Mulberry' harbour opposite St. Laurent was completely wrecked and of the 800 landing craft originally smashed ashore, at least half still lay there like beached whales.

An American intelligence colonel sitting on the bucket seat beside me, told me that the storm had reduced the unloading of vital stores and reinforcements to a trickle and for two weeks it had been touch and go whether we could hang on in Normandy.

We landed at Croydon at eight o'clock in the morning. Flying bombs were now being directed into London all day long and driving through the City, the damage was much greater than I expected.

General Barker concluded his business with me with great dispatch, then with his customary thoughtfulness, he said, 'Your plane goes back at seven this evening so go on home and give your wife a surprise.'

I caught the fast train to Reading, got off at Taplow and borrowed the station master's bicycle. I could be in Dorney by one and the five o'clock train back seemed days away.

Land-girls were cutting lettuce and digging potatoes in the fields on either side of the road. They looked up and waved as I pedalled past. My heart was bubbling with excitement. In my mind I rehearsed all sorts of stiff-upper-lip-returning-warrior platitudes. I wished I had a toy for the little boy.

Quietly, I leaned the bicycle against a tree and pushed the back door – it was locked. The front door was locked too. I walked round and round the house ... nobody was home. I opened a back window by breaking a pane and crawled through ... The family was gone and judging by the state of the kitchen had been gone for some days.

Disconsolate and also alarmed, I mounted the bicycle and made enquiries in the village shops.

'Mrs. Niven picked up her ration books a week ago but nobody knows where she went.'

Back at the house, I called Bill Rollo in London at his office but he was out.

I had beer, bread and cheese and pickled onions in the village pub then went home again and waited for Bill to call back. While I was waiting, I mowed the lawn and weeded Primmie's little vegetable garden. At three o'clock Bill called and told me she had decided to evacuate the London area and take little David up to the peace and quiet of Quenby in Leicestershire.

I put through a call to Quenby but there was a three-hour delay. I pleaded with the operator but she was granite.

'We all 'ave our little problems these days don't we, luv?'

I drank the remainder of a bottle of gin in the kitchen and weaved off on the stationmaster's bicycle in time to catch the five o'clock for London and Normandy.

CHAPTER THIRTEEN

By mid-August the Canadians had entered Falaise. The Poles were above Chambois and with the British and Americans in full spate, the bulk of the German Seventh Army was wiped out in the Mortain Pocket. Sixteen of the twenty German generals involved, however, managed to escape to fight another day and this touched off more asperity between the Allied commanders with everyone accusing everyone else of being too slow, too quick or too cautious.

The Americans and Free French entered Paris on the twenty-fifth and the British, Canadians and Poles rushed headlong for the Channel ports and Belgium.

With the Germans in full retreat, conflicting plans were put forward for bringing the war to a speedy conclusion and even louder squabbles now broke out between those super prima donnas, Montgomery, Bradley and Patton. Distorted versions of their differences filtered down to the fighting troops and General Barker's department had a lot of fence-mending to do.

I was ordered to Paris to deliver some important documents to an American colonel. 'Meet him in the bar of the Hotel Crillon', was my highly sophisticated directive and I hastened south, most anxious to see my favourite city in the full orgiastic ecstasy of her liberation.

An American corporal was driving my jeep. We got lost in Neuilly till I realised I was only a stone's throw from Claude's apartment. I bade the corporal wait, and leaving him festooned with flowers in the centre of a singing, kissing, bottle-waving throng, I pushed my way into the building.

My welcome was rapturous but the set-up had changed. 'Monsieur' having been deported to a forced labour camp near Essen. Madame and Claude, in their misery, had buried their hatchets, pooled their resources and Claude had moved in upstairs with the family. They nourished me from the sparse supplies of food and drink, heated water in pails

255

so I could have a hot bath and clucked over me like two hens.

Luckily, I had kept the documents with me because when I descended to keep my rendezvous at the Crillon the jeep and corporal had disappeared, borne off, he assured me later, on the crest of a wave of hysterical grateful citizenry ... Claude saved the day.

'It's nothing – you take Madame's bicycle ... I come with you!'

From some long-forgotten celebration, Madame produced two small Union Jacks and with Claude at my side, bells ringing, and flags fluttering bravely from the handle-bars, we free-wheeled down the whole length of the Champs Elyseés to the admiring plaudits of the crowd. Mounted on a woman's bicycle, I was probably the first British soldier the French of Paris had seen for five years.

The Guards Armoured Division entered Brussels on September 3rd. Antwerp was freed the next day. The reaction of the French of Paris to their liberation was that of an undertakers' convention compared to the behaviour of the Belgians. The tired faces of the soldiers glowed – it made everything seem worthwhile.

That autumn has been described by the war historians as a 'lull' – the soldiers didn't notice it – particularly the British airborne troops who had to fight for their lives at Arnhem, the Canadians struggling on the Leopold Canal or the Americans at Aachen.

'A' Squadron Phantom, with John Hannay at the helm, was living in great discomfort in flat, water-logged fields near Geldrop. I spent some days with them en route to a chore in Nimegen near the Meuse where I ran across Tony Bushell, Olivier's production manager in usual life, and now a company commander with the Welsh Guards. We were reminiscing in the tank park when the earth shook under an appalling explosion. Instinctively, I dived for cover. I looked out to see Bushell roaring with laughter.

'What the hell was that?' I asked.

'Oh, that's an old friend,' said Bushell. 'They've got a bloody great gun in a railway tunnel across the river. About once an hour they wheel it out and let off a big one – then they pop back in again. We're used to it.'

In early December in Brussels, I found Bobby Sweeney who had been distinguishing himself with the R.A.F. He was on leave.

'They tell me,' said Bobby, 'that the wild duck are really flighting in to the flooded farmland on the Scheldt Estuary, let's go and knock some off.'

A great organiser of comfort, Sweeney conjured up a jeep, guns and ammunition and we set off, accompanied by a carload of Bobbie's Belgian friends. The shooting at dusk was spectacular. On the other side of the river it must have been equally good because we could hear the Germans taking full advantage of it.

The Belgian group returned to Brussels after dark but 'the Comfort King' had a better idea.

'Nothing in the world like wild duck cooked absolutely fresh ... much better than after they've been hung,' he said. 'One of the best restaurants in Europe is the "Panier d'Or" in Bruges. The Canadians have probably taken the place by now – let's go in there and if the "Panier d'Or" is still standing, we'll get 'em to cook for us.'

At the outskirts of the beautiful little seventh-century Flemish town, the Military Police told us that the Germans had indeed been pushed out several hours before. In the centre of the town there was very little damage and we found the 'Panier d'Or' intact.

Bobby was right about the duck – they were sensational but we both underestimated the hospitality of the owner and his family.

They plied us for hours with every known kind of drink and before we staggered out, they produced their 'Livre d'Or' for our signatures. A special page was prepared and after five years of German names, the two first Allied ones were scrawled with a flourish. Outside, a full moon was riding in the cold winter sky. The town, with not a chink of light showing, was unnaturally quiet – not a cat was stirring – it was eerie.

We started up the jeep and clattered through the deserted streets and back over the bridge to the main road. A Canadian patrol stopped us and told us the facts of life. During our long meal, the enemy had started a vicious counter-attack and the Canadians had pulled back through

257

the town. Half an hour after we left the 'Panier d'Or', the centre of Bruges was once more swarming with Germans.

In the middle of December, I was passing through Spa, American First Army Headquarters in the Ardennes. I spent the day with Bob Low and he showed me the map room of the Intelligence Section.

'What happens here?' I asked.

'You mean here in Spa?'

'Yes.'

After all these years I can quote what he said, word for word – it was impossible to forget. He pointed out of the window.

'You see the trees on the top of those hills?'

'Yes.'

'Well, the other side of those hills, there is a forest and in that forest they are now forming the Sixth Panzer Army and any day now the Sixth Panzer Army is going to come right through this room and out the other side, cross the Meuse, then swing right and go north to Antwerp.'

'Have you told anyone?' I laughed.

'We've been telling them for days,' said Low. 'Every day we have to give three appreciations of what we *think* may happen – that has been our number one appreciation.'

The next day I went down through the fog-shrouded Forest of the Ardennes to Marche. Within hours the last great German offensive of the war erupted. Ahead of it, Skorzeny's Trojan Horse Brigade, American-speaking and wearing American uniforms, infiltrated everywhere with captured American tanks and half-tracks. Sabotaging as they went, they rushed for the Meuse. The rumours of Skorzeny's men flew wildly. In my British uniform and jeep with 21st Army Group markings, I had some anxious moments at the hands of understandably trigger-happy G.I.'s. Identification papers mean nothing – 'Hands above your head, Buddy – all right – so who won the World Series in 1940?'

'I haven't the faintest idea but I do know I made a picture with Ginger Rogers in 1938.'

'O.K. beat it, Dave, but watch your step for Crissake.'

Time and again I was stopped, and, thanks entirely to Sam Goldwyn, survived.

At the end of February, the British Army was fighting

bloody battles in the Reichwald where a sudden thaw had turned the frozen forest floor into a quagmire. Great battles were in progress for the Roehr and the Maas. During the first week of March, U.S. First Army reached the Rhine at Cologne and two days later U.S. Third Army did likewise at the junction of the Moselle, 9th U.S. Armoured Division that week made their miraculous discovery that the Ludendorf Railway Bridge at Remagen had not been blown, and secured the first small bridgehead across the Rhine, a bridgehead that cried out for exploitation. Montgomery was all set to cross in strength further down and surge across the Ruhr plain, but first a big build-up, he felt, was necessary. This stoked up all the old friction between Montgomery's dedication to 'tidy battles,' and the American genius for improvisation. The super prima donnas were at it in earnest this time and the heights, or rather the depths of idiocy were surely reached when, according to military historians, Patton telephoned Bradley and said,

'I want the world to know Third Army made it before Monty starts across.'

I crossed the Rhine at Wessel and I had never seen such destruction – the smoking town had ceased to exist. At Munster nothing was left standing except a bronze statue of a horse. In the open country between Hanover and Osnabrück, both of which were totally ruined, was a huge hastily erected prisoner-of-war cage. There must have been a hundred thousand men already inside when the American Unit I was then with passed them. The first warming rays of the sun were just touching the prisoners. It had rained heavily during the night and now a cloud of steam was rising from this dejected field-grey mass of humanity.

The Burgomaster of Hanover said that at least 60,000 corpses were still under the rubble of his city. Bremen was no better.

Hitler had started the whole horrible shambles but looking at the places where his chickens had come home to roost, I watched the miserable survivors picking around in the ruins of their towns and was unable to raise a glimmer of a gloat.

In a siding near Liebenau, I came across a freight train, its flat cars loaded with V.2 rockets destined for London. In the woods nearby, was a slave labour camp where they had been made. The notices in the camp were in Italian, French, Czech, Polish, Dutch, Yugoslav, Russian and Ukrainian. The liberated workers were wandering dazedly all over the place, asking how to get home, mingling with the dead-eyed prisoners from the concentration camps, gaunt and shuffling, conspicuous in their black and white stripes.

By May 8th, the war in Europe was officially over, but people were still being killed and Hitler's werewolves were still hopefully stretching piano wire at head height from trees on either side of the roads. To avoid decapitation, the wiser jeeps now carried sharpened iron stanchions welded to their radiators. The routes west out of Germany were becoming clogged with an estimated eight million homeward-bound displaced persons pushing their pathetic belongings on bicycles or dragging them in little home-made carts. One became hardened to the sight of people lying under trees or in ditches too exhausted or too hungry to take another step.

On a country road near Brunswick, I drove through an attractive red-roofed village on the outskirts of which was a large manor house. Two tow-headed little boys were playing in the garden. A mile or so away, I passed a farm wagon headed for the village. I glanced casually at the two men sitting up behind the horse. Both wore typical farmer head-gear and sacks were thrown over their shoulders protecting them from a light drizzle. We were just past them when something made me slam on the brakes and back up. I was right, the man who was not driving was wearing field boots. I slipped out from behind the wheel, pulled my revolver from its holster and told the corporal to cover me with his Tommy gun.

I gestured to the men to put their hands over their heads and told them in fumbling German to produce their papers.

'I speak English,' said the one with the field boots, 'this man has papers – I have none.'

'Who are you?' I asked.

He told me his name and rank – 'General.'

'We are not armed,' he added, as I hesitated.

Sandhurst did it – I saluted, then motioned to them to lower their hands.

'Where are you coming from, sir?'

He looked down at me. I had never seen such utter

weariness, such blank despair on a human face before. He passed a hand over the stubble of his chin.

'Berlin,' he said quietly.

'Where are you going, sir?'

He looked ahead down the road towards the village and closed his eyes.

'Home,' he said almost to himself, 'it's not far now ... only ... one more kilometre.'

I didn't say anything. He opened his eyes again and we stared at each other. We were quite still for a long time. Then I said,

'Go ahead, sir,' and added ridiculously ... 'please cover up your bloody boots.'

Almost as though in pain, he closed his eyes and raised his head, then with sobbing intake of breath, covered his face with both hands and they drove on.

On 13th May, Churchill spoke from London and the whole world listened – or did it?

'... we have yet to make sure that the simple and honourable purposes for which we entered the war are not brushed aside or overlooked in the months following our success, and that the words "freedom", "democracy" and "liberation" are not distorted from their true meaning as we have understood them. There would be little use in punishing the Hitlerites for their crimes if law and justice did not rule, and if totalitarian or police governments were to take the place of the German invaders ...'

I cannot claim to have exerted much pressure on the squabbling field marshals and generals but way down the scale, attached to various units, I must have done what General Barker wanted. At any rate, in September, he pinned the American Legion of Merit on me and the British Army gave me –

1 suit, worsted grey
1 hat, Homburg, brown
2 shirts, poplin, with collars
1 tie, striped
1 Pair shoes, walking, black –
and above all my FREEDOM.

Such was the stringency of the clothing rationing that Major General Robert Laycock, D.S.O., Chief of Combined

Operations, asked me if I could spare him my discarded khaki shirts.

It was an unbelievable feeling to be free again. Primmie was due to have the second baby in November so we took little David and treated ourselves to a holiday of luxury at the Ferryboat Inn on the Helford River. Then I cabled Goldwyn to the effect that I was 'available'.

Goldwyn generously replied that he was giving me a new five-year contract at a mouth-watering figure and that in the meanwhile, he was loaning me out to Michael Powell and Emeric Pressburger to star in *A Matter of Life and Death* (*Stairway to Heaven* in the U.S.)

This was a huge relief because although I had been disguising it from Primmie, I was extremely nervous about my future. Six months is too long for an actor to be out of business – six years is almost certain disaster.

A whole new breed of stars had taken over the movie audiences and at thirty-five I had good reason to be worried. I was also highly apprehensive lest I had forgotten how to do it.

Powell and Pressburger wrote a brilliant screenplay. Kim Hunter played the girl and my old friend, Raymond Massey, the 'heavy'. Jack Cardiff's fantastic colour photography helped enormously to make this picture a big success on both sides of the Atlantic and in Britain it was chosen as the first Royal Command Film.

After Primmie produced Jamie, we set about planning our new life. Although she had never seen California, I had described it all to her so carefully that she knew exactly what she wanted – 'an old house, falling down, that we can do over, a big rambling garden for the children and dogs, and a view of the mountains or the ocean.'

She was wildly excited at the prospect of going, but nervous about the people she would meet.

'I'm not nearly beautiful enough,' she would say. 'I'll be lost in all that glamour.'

She started buying old furniture, Regency mostly, for the house she could visualise. Vivien Leigh, a great expert, spent hours with her foraging around in the antique shops of Windsor, Amersham and Beaconsfield.

262

The problem of obtaining transportation to the U.S. appeared insurmountable; with over two million American servicemen champing at the bit to get home, there was obviously no room for a family of foreigners. General Barker came to the rescue and told me that he had secured a berth for me, alone with the 101 Airborne Division leaving in a week's time in the *Queen Mary* but Primmie and the children would have to wait at least three months. We decided that I should go on ahead to take up my contract and find, if possible, our dream house.

I gave myself a farewell party for two hundred at Claridge's. So that nobody could be wrongly dressed, Primmie borrowed a tiara and a ball gown and I wore an open-necked shirt and my trousers, worsted, grey.

All the guests had one thing in common; at some time in our lives they had been specially nice to us. It was a funny mixture – duchesses, policemen, actors, generals, privates, hospital nurses, taxi drivers, country squires and Mrs. Wisden.

I took a sadistic delight in standing at the door and personally winkling out the gatecrashers.

'Please go away ... you've never been nice to me in your life.'

The evening cost a fortune but no matter – great days were ahead – we could save money later.

Next morning, I went to collect my sailing permit.

'Sorry, old man,' said the official, 'can't give you that till you show us your income tax clearance from the Inland Revenue.'

Off I went to another dreary government office. Thick white tea cups with G.R. on them littered the untidy desks.

The man who interviewed me was a thin, self-important civil servant with a particularly active Adam's apple. He produced a file.

'Now, let's see, you want to leave the Old Country do you – emigrating are you?'

'No, I'm going back where I came from ... to the United States. I have a contract to work there.'

He turned the pages of a file.

'Now let me see ... in 1939 you left the United States and came back to this country. Why was that?'

'To join up . . . for the war.'

'Yes, we all know that, we read the papers at the time but nobody *asked* you to come, did they? It's not as if you were called up, is it? You paid your own way, didn't you?'

'Yes.'

'Well, then, obviously you came here intending to reside again in Great Britain, so that confirmed you a resident of Great Britain for tax purposes and we are back-taxing you on your world earnings from the time you left here in 1934.'

The *Queen Mary* was sailing in two days' time and I had to have that sailing permit.

He was very generous. On condition that I did not come back during that time, he allowed me to pay over the next three years but it still cost me several thousand pounds for the privilege of spending six years in the British Army.

The *Queen Mary* carried fifteen thousand troops. We were packed like sardines. It didn't matter. We ate in shifts, slept in shifts and lay about in shifts. The teak rails of the upper decks bore the carved initials of countless G.I.s who had made the journey to Europe – how many, I wondered, were left behind for ever.

On the night I landed in New York, my old employers at '21' gave a large cocktail party for me in the upstairs room of their establishment and I spent the evening with John Huston.

Next day I shopped for some badly needed clothes and took a sleeper on the transcontinental train for California. I was feeling very tired and rather odd so the trip would rest me up, I thought. David Selznick was on the train and he brought me up to date on who was who now in Hollywood and what was going on. David was a friend who never minced words, however ominous.

'It's going to be tough for you,' he said. 'It's a whole new ball game now – a lot of new stars and new directors have come up while you've been away – you're lucky to have Goldwyn behind you.'

At Chicago, a telegram was delivered from Eddie Goulding saying that he was giving me a welcome home bachelor party of a hundred at Romanoff's on the night of my arrival. Another came from Goldwyn saying there was to be a big press luncheon the same day. I looked forward to it all but I also dreaded it ... I really was very tired and coughed a lot.

WELCOME HOME DAVID!!

A big banner was strung across the main gate of the studio. Stage 8 had been transformed into a restaurant and several hundred studio employees and members of the press listened to speeches of welcome by Goldwyn, Hedda Hopper, the head prop man, Dave Chasen and others. The room was spinning, I was sweating and I had a terrible headache. I wondered how I was going to get through it. I might have been Hollywood's first recruit but I was being treated as if I had won the war single-handed.

After luncheon, 'Willie' Bruce said, 'I'm taking you home, putting you to bed and getting you a doctor – you look awful.'

'I can't let Goulding down,' I said. 'He's asked a hundred people tonight.'

'Nonsense,' said Willie, 'if the doctor says you can go – all right – otherwise, bed.'

The doctor took my temperature – it was 104° – and told me I had bronchial pneumonia. Goulding was marvellous when he was told. He came to see me and insisted on going through with the party without me.

'I'll have a direct line to your room and an amplifier. You'll be able to hear what's going on and you can talk to old pals on the phone.'

Among the hundred bachelors, Goulding rounded up most of my actor friends including Clark Gable, Doug Jr., Flynn, Gary Cooper and 'Ty' Power. Also, I noticed from the book of photographs he sent me later of the proceedings, an impressive body of the Hollywood super-brass had also dusted off their dinner jackets including Goldwyn, Selznick, Pandro Berman, Eddie Mannix, Billy Wilder, Howard Hawks, Mervyn Le Roy, Hal Wallis and even Harry Cohn.

There was a pipe band. My name was carved in a huge block of ice and the whole place was festooned with American and British flags.

It was extremely generous of Goulding, highly flattering and completely unwarranted.

I convalesced in the desert at Palm Springs and, as soon as I was well enough, Goldwyn put me to work. He loaned me to Paramount to do a picture with, of all people, Loretta Young.

Primmie cabled that she hoped to get passage soon and I went, frantically, house hunting.

The Fairbanks's found it for me, right next door to theirs, exactly what she had always said she wanted – old and rambling with a big garden and a view of both the Santa Monica Mountains and the ocean. The basement had about three feet of water in it when the agent showed it so I was able to buy it very cheaply. Vicki Baum, author of *Grand Hotel*, had built it forty years before.

'The Pink House', as it was known for obvious reasons, became of tremendous importance to me. It was the first home I had ever owned, and with my adored family, I longed to settle down at last. I seemed to have been running and running all my life.

I decided to give the place to Primmie as a surprise when she arrived, then let her do it over and, with her wonderful taste, decorate it in her own good time – in the meanwhile, I rented a big Spanish-style monstrosity in Beverly Hills.

The picture at Paramount finished just in time for me to fly East to meet my family. They had taken eighteen days in terrible gales to cross the Atlantic in an old Liberty ship. They finally docked in Portland, Maine.

Primmie looked radiant as she came running down the gangplank. Little David was full of chat and questions. As a typical war baby, he noticed the skeleton of a house being built,

'Look, Daddy,' he said, 'a bomb.'

Jamie, now five months old, slept all the time in a carrying cot. The handle broke in New York and I dumped him on his head in the middle of Penn Station, which may account for the fact that he became an extremely efficient merchant banker.

Primmie fell in love with California on sight and was over the moon when she saw the 'Pink House'.

'The furniture will be perfect in it,' she cried, her eyes shining like a little girl's. 'I'm going to make it *so* beautiful for you! You're going to be *so* proud!'

It was decided that she would do the house herself without telling me anything and then, one day, when it was all finished she would let me carry her through the door.

She had brought 'Pinkie' with her – a fresh-faced English girl who had spent the war in an anti-aircraft battery in London. 'Pinkie' adored the children and soon made the Spanish dungeon shine like a new pin.

Goldwyn loaned me to Universal to make an historical film with Ginger Rogers. Ginger was to play Dolly Madison and I was to portray Aaron Burr – the two most unlikely bits of casting of the century. The script was gibberish, but I was far too happy and the prospect of, at long last, settling down with my family in my own home was too good to be ruined by renewed quarrels with Goldwyn and by suspensions which I could ill afford.

Larry Olivier had left behind a large black Packard when he had last been in California. I bought it by cable, left Pinkie in charge of the children and with Clark Gable, Rex Harrison, Ida Lupino and Nigel Bruce, we set off in convoy for a week's golf at Pebble Beach ... They were golden days and Primmie showed me a letter she wrote to Bill Rollo saying that she never imagined she could be so happy. We came back on a Sunday because I had to do wardrobe tests the next morning.

'Ty' Power and Annabella gave a small party for Primmie that evening. John McClain had just arrived from New York and all my closest friends were there. As I looked around at them and at Primmie's radiant face, I wondered how it was possible for one man to have so much.

Nearly everyone was working the next day which meant being up by five or six o'clock so we had an early barbecue round the pool. 'Ty' cooked.

Afterwards, we went indoors and played some games. Someone suggested 'Sardines' – an old children's game, played in the dark. I was hiding under a bed upstairs when I heard 'Ty' calling me.

'Come down, quick, Primmie's had a fall!'

I rushed down.

In the dark she had opened a door thinking it was a coat closet –it was the door to the cellar and she had fallen down a dozen steps. She was lying unconscious on the floor.

We dabbed her head with water and she started moaning and moving a little.

Within twenty minutes the doctor arrived and within another half hour, she was tucked in bed in hospital.

'She's very concussed,' the doctor told me after his examination, 'but it's nothing to worry about. She'll have to stay absolutely quiet and in the dark for a few days – she'll be fine.'

I went back to Ty's house and told everyone the good news. Then I went to the Spanish house and Pinkie helped me pack up a few things Primmie might need, a couple of nighties, a toothbrush, some perfume.

Back at the hospital, they repeated that she was fine, and said there was no good I could do by staying and to go on home: if I wanted to, to drop by before I went to work in the morning.

I was back about six the next day. They let me see her. She looked beautiful but very pale. Her eyes were still closed.

'She's had a good night,' said the nurse.

All during the day I called from the studio.

'Nothing to worry about – it's a bad concussion – all she needs is complete rest and quiet.'

After work I went back to the hospital. They were most reassuring. I sat with her for a long time holding her hand. She was very still.

Suddenly, she opened her eyes, looked right at me, smiled a tiny smile and gave my hand a little reassuring squeeze. It was the first time she had recognised me. The matron said, 'Why don't you go on home and get some sleep yourself, there's nothing you can do. We'll call you at once, of course, if there is any change . . . go on home and don't worry.'

Bob Coote was in the house when I got back waiting for news. I told him everything was going along well, that no one was worried, and we raided the ice box for a snack.

About eleven o'clock, the phone rang. It was the doctor.

'I think you'd better come down,' he said . . . 'there are certain symptoms we don't like. I've alerted the best brain surgeon there is . . . we may have to operate.'

Bob came with me. An hour later, they started the operation. Two hours passed before the doctors came down.

I knew.

I knew as soon as I saw them come out of the elevator.

I knew by the way they walked.

I knew by the way they stood murmuring together without looking at me as I waited across the hall.

She was only twenty-five.

CHAPTER FOURTEEN

SOMEHOW the dreadful days dragged by – somehow into weeks and months.

Friends tried valiantly to cushion the despair and I was infinitely lucky to have them.

Ronnie and Benita Colman took me into their home for I never again set foot in the Spanish monstrosity; then Douglas and Mary Lee Fairbanks gave me sanctuary. Joan Crawford took the children, with a stunned Pinkie, till they were settled on the Colmans' ranch at Montecito. Everyone tried to help, but there comes a time when friends must be allowed to get on with their own lives, so I went back to work at Universal and occupying myself with such a disaster was some sort of relief from the alternative. Even so, after work I walked for hours alone on the darkened beach, hoping, perhaps, that a merciful tidal wave might sweep out of the Pacific. Then I went to bed to toss in torment till dawn when exhaustion took over. A couple of hours of deep sleep would be brutally ended by an alarm clock and smashing down once more came the awful realisation that it had not been a dream.

Work on the Pink House continued. Not because I wanted to transform it into a shrine: it held no memories: we had never lived in it ... so work went on. After a while, with the rest of the house still gutted, one room, the cook's, and the kitchen, were finished.

With a few belongings, I moved in among the cement and sawdust, coils of wire, unattached radiators and toilets, buckets of paint ... utter desolation that seemed somehow symbolic.

The so carefully collected furniture and china arrived from England but somewhere the container had been dropped and most of the contents were smashed beyond repair.

I had with me, for comfort, in the cook's room, a little case full of Primmie's most private things, childhood treasures, some photographs of our wedding and of the children's christenings, my letters written during the war and her tiny cache of inexpensive jewellery. While I was away at work one day, the case was stolen.

That night I nearly gave up.

The Pink House was finally finished and upstairs, a white carpet was laid.

That day, Rex and Lilli Palmer gave me a Boxer puppy to keep me company. Within an hour, 'Phantom' had permanently changed the colour of the carpet.

On Sundays, the house was full of people from morning till night. Every week Gable arrived accompanied by some gorgeous creature while Lana Turner, Anita Colby, Rita Hayworth, Deborah Kerr, Ava Gardner, Ida Lupino and Patricia Medina set an unassailable standard of beauty and fun. Bob Laycock was stunned when he saw them. In his capacity as Chief of British Combined Operations, he came to California as the guest of the American Pacific Fleet at San Diego and stayed with me for several days. It cheered me a lot to think that he took back to Bill and Kathleen Rollo good reports of their grandchildren.

Like the understanding Gable who had been through a similar family tragedy himself, John McClain was a staunch and thoughtful friend. One day he said, ' "Betty" Bacall is giving Bogart a surprise party tonight – it's time you got out of your house.'

I didn't really want to go but the alternative was still something I flinched from. Pinkie would relentlessly keep the children up till I came home from work so they could have a half hour's 'play' with their father. It was torture for me and I dreaded seeing their gay, shining, trusting little faces.

After they had gone off to bed it was worse – a lonely meal and then pacing about the house like a caged lion till bedtime. By now, I was making an important picture for Goldwyn playing the Bishop in *The Bishop's Wife* with Loretta as the wife and Cary Grant as the Angel, so I was faced with getting up at six o'clock.

McClain, however, brushed aside all protests and I found myself with forty others hidden in different parts of Bogart's house as a surprise for his birthday.

'Betty' Bacall was the perfect mate for Bogie ... beautiful, fair, warm, talented and highly intelligent, she gave as good as she got in the strong personality department. Women and men love her with equal devotion.

Someone had been delegated by Betty to keep Bogie busy at the studio to give us all time to arrive and hide. When Bogie finally appeared, it was apparent how his busy time at the studio had been spent. He was loudly abusive and cries of 'who needs these bums!' and 'get the bastards outta here!' reverberated from the front door. For a few nervous minutes it was touch and go whether he would throw all forty of us out into the street, but Betty placated him, or rather, answered him loudly in the same vein and the party became a success after all.

Bogart was quite alarming to meet for the first time with his sardonic humour and his snarl that passed for a smile. It took a little while to realise that he had perfected an elaborate camouflage to cover up one of the kindest and most generous of hearts. Even so, he was no soft touch and before you were allowed to peek beneath the surface and catch a glimpse of the real man, you had to prove yourself. Above all, you had to demonstrate conclusively to his satisfaction that you were no phoney.

My test came soon. He asked me if I liked to sail.

'Done it all my life,' I said, blithely, 'in fact I once represented my country in eight metres.'

Bogie looked at me reflectively and sucked his teeth.

'Okay, come aboard *Santana* Sunday.'

Women were only infrequently made welcome aboard *Santana* so Betty was not there when I boarded the sixty-five-foot ketch at Balboa.

Tough and often argumentative ashore, I expected Bogie to be a veritable Captain Bligh afloat. Far from it, he was easy going, perfectly relaxed and highly efficient. I was lulled into a sense of false security and had no idea that this had been earmarked as the day of my entrance exam.

We were sailing along in a good stiff breeze; Bogie was at the helm, I was beside him, the solitary crew – a Dane he called Dum Bum – was forward keeping a sharp lookout because the stiff breeze was doing nothing to dispel a thick mist.

'Tuna boats ahead,' yelled Dum Bum suddenly.

Sure enough we were running fast towards a dozen big

271

drifters, each with its net trailing out astern. It was a tricky situation that called for immediate action and because of the direction of the wind, there were only three solutions: one was correct, the second risky, and the third would have led to losing the mast.

Dum Bum was looking apprehensively at Bogie and I was just thinking to myself that he was leaving things dangerously late when he let go of the wheel, gave me a wolfish grin and said – 'Take over, Big Shot – I'm going to the can.'

He disappeared below.

Luckily, I knew what I was doing. I yelled a few orders which Dum Bum instantly obeyed, spun the wheel and the danger was past.

Christmas alone with the children was something I had dreaded. Although they never ceased asking others when their mother was coming back, some extraordinary radar system prevented them from ever mentioning her to me. I knew one day they would ask me the direct question so until then I resolved not to broach the subject.

On Christmas Eve, with the lighted tree in the window behind me and a mountain of gaily wrapped presents from kind and even anxious friends beneath it, I was sitting on the patio steps swept suddenly by a wave of despair. A little arm went round my neck: they both stood there hand-in-hand.

'Are you very lonely?' asked the eldest and when I just nodded, he said, 'Mummy's never coming back, is she?'

'No she's not,' I said.

'Has she gone up to Heaven?'

'Yes, that's right ... she's gone to Heaven.'

The evening star was very bright over the distant ocean. He looked up.

'I can see Mummy's eye,' he said.

The Bishop's Wife turned out well. It, too, was chosen for the Royal Command Film in London and Goldwyn, loaning me out all over town, kept me blessedly busy. I made pictures with Barbara Stanwyck and Jane Wyman. I played all sorts of roles, including a world-famous pianist. During my big concert scene an expert played the piano with his arms through my tail coat while I rolled my eyes and looked soulful.

272

When a man is deeply unhappy, he brings out the very gentlest instincts in the very nicest women. They want to wrap him up, take him home and look after him. They give all of themselves but he, in turn, can give in only one direction and, inoculated by his unhappiness, rides rough-shod far and wide.

This happened to me in full measure and I also believe at the same time I went a little mad. I began to resent and avoid the married friends who had showered me with kindness and protection when I had so badly needed it. Perhaps I was jealous of their happiness. Perhaps I was ashamed that they had seen me at my weakest and most vulnerable. This phase lasted several months, and, bewildered and hurt, some wonderful people must have found my coldness most difficult to understand.

The Pink House in the spring was a dream place for the children. They took swimming lessons in the pool. Peach trees, avocados, pomegranates, cherries, oranges, limes, lemons and guavas were in full blossom. Phantom dashed about the lawn chasing humming birds, the bantams crowed and the rabbits bred in great profusion. I planted a hundred rose bushes and at last, I, too, began to feel roots going down and some happiness seeping back up again. The boys were settling down marvellously, and some pattern for the future seemed to be emerging. I was, therefore, appalled when Goldwyn called me in and told me he had loaned me to Alexander Korda to make *Bonnie Prince Charlie* in England.

'You'll be away at least eight months,' he said.

I begged him not to send me and pointed out that not only would it disrupt the children's lives, it would also make new and hideous problems for me with the Inland Revenue.

He was adamant so I refused to go. Immediately, I was put on suspension.

Knowing that I was up to my ears in debt because of the Pink House, Goldwyn sat back and waited for me to crack. It didn't take long and in the autumn, Pinkie and I packed up two resentful and mystified little boys and started the long trek back to England.

Korda, whose home was the Penthouse at Claridge's, was quite understandably surprised when I spurned the accommodation he had reserved for me in that excellent hostelry. I

273

kept a room there for myself and moved the family into a country hotel near Shepperton Studios.

Bonnie Prince Charlie was one of those huge florid extravaganzas that reek of disaster from the start. There was never a completed screenplay and never at any time during the eight months we were shooting were the writers more than two days ahead of the actors.

We suffered three changes of director with Korda himself, for a time, desperately taking over and at one point I cabled Goldwyn as follows:

I HAVE NOW WORKED EVERY DAY FOR FIVE MONTHS ON THIS PICTURE AND NOBODY CAN TELL ME HOW THE STORY ENDS STOP ADVISE.

He didn't even bother to answer.

I loved Alex Korda, a brilliant, generous dreamer, but with this film he was wallowing around in his own self-created confusion. I felt sorry for him but I felt much sorrier for myself as the Bonnie Prince who would assuredly bear the blame for the impending debacle and for Margaret Leighton and Jack Hawkins gallantly, against appalling odds, trying to infuse some semblance of reality into Flora MacDonald and Lord George Murray.

After nine frustrating months, the Bonnie Prince clanked towards its close. One more week, one more battle, one last mad charge and I would be rid of him. (Whenever we actors really started to breathe down the writers' necks, Korda ordered another battle to delay us for a few more days.)

The director at this point was a robust, hearty and immensely nice ex-naval commander – Anthony Kimmins. No fool, he knew only too well that he was captain of a movie ship heading like an arrow for the rocks, but bravely, he covered up and issued his orders to the several hundred extras as though he were Lord Louis Mountbatten addressing the crew of a badly listing destroyer.

'Now, Bonnie Prince Charlie has just won a great victory! You brave Highlanders have captured the English colours! When he comes out of his tent over there, I want all you Highlanders to give him a big cheer! Let him know you all love him!'

The wild Highlanders, in scruffy red wigs and uncertain kilts, were almost entirely recruited from London's East End. As I came out of the tent for the first 'take', there was scattered cheering. Then, crystal clear in the morning air came a fruity Cockney voice.

'Oi! David . . . we've got their fuckin' flag ! ! !'

The second 'happening' on that most important day came during the charge itself.

I was careering bravely along, skimming over the studio heather at the head of my Highlanders pursuing the fleeing redcoats, when suddenly, claymore in hand, I found myself flying through the air. I still believe Jack Hawkins tripped me. In any event, my sword sank deep into the leg of the redcoat in front of me. It went in with an appalling 'thonk' just behind the knee and pinned him to the ground.

'Cut!' yelled the director (an unnecessary observation). Several women, hairdressers and other camp followers, screamed.

I pulled out the blade, trying not to throw up. The man got up and ran off with a pronounced limp. I chased after him.

'Are you all right? . . . I'm terribly sorry! . . . We'll get a doctor!'

'Wot's the matter, mate?' asked the man.

'Your leg,' I blabbered, 'my sword! . . . It went right in! We'll get a doctor!'

'Oh,' he said, 'thought I felt something . . . not to worry though, David.'

He rolled up the bottom of his trousers. His name was Bob Head. He had lost the original leg at El Alamein.

Happenings go in threes. I was dismissed early that evening and hurried off to get changed so I could go and play with the children. Because of the hours we had been working, I hadn't seen them for days. The gateman stopped me.

'Sorry, David – they just phoned up – they need you for one more shot.'

Furious, I stalked back into Make-up. Sullenly, I sat while the yellow wig was pinned on my resisting head and once more, like a spoilt child whose picnic has been cancelled by bad weather. I glowered my way on to the set, and snarled at the prop man.

'Where the hell's my chair?'

'Over there, David ... there's a lady in it.'

'Then get her out of it!' I snapped.

'Take a look,' whispered Hawkins in my ear. 'Take a look.'

The French have the right word – *coup de foudre* ... I had never seen anything so beautiful in my life – tall, slim, auburn hair, uptilted nose, lovely mouth and the most enormous grey eyes I had even seen.

It really happened the way it does when written by the worst lady novelists ... I goggled. I had difficulty swallowing and I had champagne in my knees.

Ten days later, we were married.

During the whirlwind courtship, there was a lot of activity. First of all, it turned out she was Swedish which posed all sorts of strange problems with the marriage authorities. Also, she didn't speak English too well which helped matters not at all when it came to explaining to them that she had landed in England en route from America to Sweden as the plane had been grounded because of sudden fog at London Airport and a friend on board had invited her to visit a film studio, etcetera.

I had my problems too. I had to complete the *Bonnie Prince*, find gifts for all the crew, present Hjördis to Bill Rollo who adored her on sight and was gay and happy for me through his own sadness; I also had to submit to a series of loathsome meetings with the Inland Revenue because I had returned without being away for three years.

'But I was sent, dammit, by the American company that employs me ... If I had refused, I would have broken my contract.'

'Well, we should read the small print before signing these foreign things, shouldn't we?'

Also, I had to find a ring, track down Trubshawe, who was to be best man again, and make all the arrangements to return quickly to California, where Goldwyn was holding up the start of my next picture.

Small wonder that I had a mini-collapse and when the official at the Chelsea Register Office warned me pompously against the dangers of marrying a foreigner, I could barely croak at him to 'shut up and get on with it'. The number one model of Sweden found herself married to a man with red eyes, a running nose and a fever of 103°.

Audrey Pleydell-Bouverie gave us a wedding party in her little house strategically placed midway between the stables of Buckingham Palace and Watney's brewery, and next day we drove to Southampton to board the *Queen Elizabeth*.

Hjördis still swears that on the way there, I suddenly said, 'Oh! I nearly forgot, there are a couple of little things I have to pick up.'

According to her, I disappeared inside a country hotel and emerged later with two small boys.

On the trip to California, we got to know each other a little better and the little boys adored her.

She loved the Pink House and rose magnificently to the occasion of being pitchforked into the middle of all my old friends. McClain, Coote and Mike Romanoff gave her a 'welcome' party to make it easier and her gaiety and beauty captivated everyone.

Life Magazine had a 'spread' of the ten most beautiful women in Hollywood and Hjördis appeared on the cover. This generated a stampede of producers with offers of contracts but, mercifully, she just laughed and said she was too busy getting to know her husband.

The Pink House came alive under her hand and became everything I had dreamed about as a home. At night, the coyotes hunted in weirdly yelping packs in the canyon below: in the morning, the deer grazed on the hill opposite and the sunsets over the Pacific must have been ordered by the Chamber of Commerce.

Some highly decorative Scandinavian ladies now augmented the weekly gatherings ... Viveca Lindfors and Signe Hasso were often present; also the latest Miss Sweden — Anita Ekberg. The first naked female my sons ever saw was Greta Garbo, swimming happily in our pool.

'Goldwynisms' had been so widely quoted ... '... include me out,' 'a verbal contract is not worth the paper it is written on,' and of a 14th-century sundial, 'What will they think of next?', etc., that for a while I was suspicious that Goldwyn might foster the legend by dreaming up new ones for himself, but I don't believe this was the case. I heard him let loose many of them but I think his mind was so far ahead of what he was saying that he left it to his tongue to take care of

277

thoughts he had left behind. In fact, he had great dignity but when thwarted, he tended to shout loudly.

After three months of my new found happiness, the pleasant routine was shattered. Goldwyn called me to his office and told me he had great news and that I was very lucky.

'I've just loaned you to Alex Korda to make *The Elusive Pimpernel* in England – you'll be away six months.'

Aghast, I told him that I didn't mind what he loaned me out for in Hollywood but that I had no intention of uprooting again so soon. Then the shouting began. He reminded me that he had picked me out of the gutter and given me my first break ... True.

I riposted by saying that with the enormous fees he was charging others for my services, I had already repaid him a thousand times over ... True.

Goldwyn pointed out that it would mean months of suspension if I refused ... True.

I said I looked forward to a good holiday anyway and I had plenty of money in the bank ... UNTRUE.

Goldwyn flicked a switch and said, 'Find out how much money Niven has in the bank.'

Within three minutes a disembodied voice came back, 'One hundred and eleven dollars ...' ... True, unfortunately.

Defeated, I prepared, once more, to make the necessary travel arrangements.

I lived in Hollywood for nearly twenty years without visiting a psychiatrist but my behaviour during the next few weeks was indicative of an unhinged mind and it was a pity I did not 'get help'.

I decided to make life unpleasant for Goldwyn which was tantamount to an eight-year-old with a pea-shooter assaulting Fort Knox. Everyone from Hjördis downwards warned me. My agent was horrified and pointed out that in mogul-controlled Hollywood, one word from Goldwyn could sink me. I knew better, of course, and proceeded very methodically to sink myself.

At the last minute, I refused to fly to London to keep the starting date of Korda's picture and insisted, instead, on being sent by train to New York and by boat – eleven days to Liverpool. Hjördis remained loyal but mystified throughout the trip. Once in London, I cabled Goldwyn reminding him that under the terms of my contract, I had six weeks' holiday each year and unless I was given my holiday at once before *Pimpernel* started, the contract would be broken as there would be no time left between the end of the picture and the end of the year.

'TAKE SIX WEEKS HOLIDAY IMMEDIATELY GOLDWYN' came the answer.

'THANKS VERY MUCH WILL TAKE HOLIDAY FROM TIME YOU RETURN ME TO MY HOME IN CALIFORNIA NIVEN.'

Poor, blameless Alex Korda, who wanted only to see his picture started, found himself in the middle of this lunacy. He offered me his yacht *Elsewhere* to go anywhere at his expense, but my mental imbalance was such that I forced Goldwyn to return me to the Pink House by boat and train: then, the next day, I flew with Hjördis to Bermuda for a delayed honeymoon.

Honeymoons are a great institution for getting to know one's spouse and the more I saw of Hjördis, the more amazed I was at my good fortune. The luck, the unbelievable luck that one man should meet, fall head-over-heels in love, marry within ten days and be blissfully happy – twice in a lifetime!

I revelled in Hjördis's forthrightness, honesty and laughter and the holiday sped by. Towards the end, a full-scale hurricane hit the island – a nasty reminder of the impending storm with Goldwyn.

Six weeks to the day from the moment I had been brought back to California, I reported to the studio for work. Rather naturally, Goldwyn did not wish to see me and I detected a certain coldness towards me all over the Lot. Conduct such as mine, spoiled brat behaviour of the worst sort, was idiotic, conceited, indefensible and unforgiveable: the sort of thing that helped bring Hollywood to its knees.

Goldwyn, of course, had no further use for me and all the direst predictions came true. When we came back from England upon the completion of *The Pimpernel*, I was immediately loaned out to play the 'heavy' in a Shirley Temple picture, a disastrous teenage pot-boiler.

'Big shots' at other studios counselled me to break my contract with Goldwyn – 'just walk in there and tell him –

the hell with it! ... tell him you want OUT ... then come and join us, we have a million properties for you!' I fell for that — it was not my finest hour. I asked to see Goldwyn and as he sat expressionless behind his desk, I said, 'Look, Sam, we don't see eye to eye any more. I have two years left of my contract — how about releasing me?'

He never took his eyes off me as he flicked his intercom lever.

'Give Niven his release as from today ... he's through.'

CHAPTER FIFTEEN

HJÖRDIS sounded doubtful when I told her the good news.

'Where will you work now?' she asked.

Where indeed? There is no question but that the Black List existed in Hollywood at that time but I have absolutely no proof that Goldwyn invoked its use in my case. On the other hand, the fact remains that the flattering studio 'big shots', who had painted such glowing pictures of my future with them once I was free of Goldwyn, were suddenly unobtainable. When I called their offices, the voices of their secretaries changed subtly from fawning to evasive or even to faintly hostile.

Headlines put out by the Goldwyn Publicity Department were no great help –

GOLDWYN DROPS NIVEN

NIVEN FIRED

BRITISH ACTOR NO LONGER GOLDWYN'S CUP OF TEA.

Hjördis was nothing short of stoic because only too soon there was a shortage of cash. Nothing was coming in, every thing was going out and the reserves were melting like butter on a hot stove. Friends such as the Astaires and the Fairbanks tried to cheer me by reporting that, at the latest Goldwyn dinner party, my photograph was still on the piano, but nobody suggested I should try a reconciliation.

Bogart, as usual, was down to earth.

'Let's face it, kid – you've blown it! Keep going somehow, mortgage the house, sell the kids, dig a ditch, do anything but for Christ's sake, never let them think they've got you running scared because somewhere in somebody's desk is a script that's right for you and when they dig it out – it's you they'll want and nobody else and everything'll be forgotten.'

Bogie's life was either black or white – he had little patience with the greys, so he simply did not understand when I accepted the first offer that came along after months of near panic.

'You should've held out, kid – this is crap,' he said when I showed him the script.

The film, *The Toast of New Orleans* at M.G.M. was a success thanks only to the fact that it launched Mario Lanza's golden voice and with the proceeds, Hjördis happily paid the bills one short step ahead of the sheriff. The next picture was even worse – an appalling travesty of a costume thriller. The result was so bad that the audience thought it was a comedy and as such it became faintly successful.

'Get outta town, kid,' growled Bogart. 'They gotta have time to forget that one.'

I took his advice, let the Pink House for a year, took the whole family to England, and moved into a haunted manor house in Wiltshire on the edge of the Downs.

Hjördis somehow remained calm and outwardly unaffected by the rapid changes in our fortunes but my new role as a country squire was hard for her to digest. I had a 'gun' in the local syndicate dedicated to the slaughter of pheasants. I had a 'rod' on the River Kennet for the purpose of killing trout and I had a private pew in the village church (complete with hidden stove) for the good of my soul.

In the autumn she came rushing to find me – 'Hurry! hurry! hurry! the garden is full of dogs and men blowing trumpets!'

Philip Hardwicke and Philip Dunne as joint Masters of the local foxhounds were merely following tradition. The opening meet was held each year at our Manor House. Hjördis, in tight, blue jeans and a white T-shirt with PALM SPRINGS RODEO written across her bosom, was a welcome if incongruous sight when I despatched her outside with bottles of port and slices of fruit cake.

In England, we were able to catch up with Trubshawe, Coote, with Noël Coward and with the Oliviers who had moved into an Elizabethan abbey, near Thame. Arguments waxed and waned at Notley; causes were defended or attacked with vigour and professional reputations came under withering fire but there were few tears and gales of laughter, particularly, when accompanied on the piano by an hysterical Vivien, Larry, dead seriously, would sing *The Messiah*.

Friends were always championed to the death. One weekend, Larry, Vivien, Bobby Helpmann and Noël were trying to put Hollywood into its proper perspective for me.

'It's all very fine for you,' I argued, 'you are all theatre people who occasionally make a movie ... I have nothing but movies.'

If I had trodden on a wasps' nest, I couldn't have stirred up more action: everyone started shouting at once and when it died down, it was obvious that steps were about to be taken to get me started in the theatre.

Within a week, John C. Wilson, the Broadway producer and longtime friend and associate of Noël's offered me a play – *Nina*.

Gloria Swanson, who, the season before, in a spectacular comeback, had been the toast of Broadway in *Twentieth Century*, had already been signed and the cast of three was to be rounded off by that excellent English character actor, Alan Webb.

'I'm terrified,' I said to Noël. 'I've only been on the stage once over ten years ago and I was fired for being gassed.' The Coward finger wagged immediately.

'You will do it,' he ordered. 'You will do it well, and above all, you will do it sober.'

The boys stayed on in the haunted manor with Evelyn Walne, their new governess, poised to join us if the play looked like running and in October, Hjördis and I flew to the United States. First stop was to spend a weekend, pheasant shooting, with friends in New England.

I had by now seen Hjördis under a variety of conditions and had come to realise that one of the joys of being married to a 'foreigner' is being constantly surprised – nothing is automatically predictable.

I was not thrown off balance, therefore, when she came down to breakfast on the first morning, dressed not for the chase but for spending the day with an apple and a good book.

'I am not coming to watch you shoot,' she announced, 'because I don't want to be shot.'

The high-powered hunters and their wives tried to persuade her that it was perfectly safe, but she was adamant.

'I *know* I am going to be shot – so I stay home.'

Finally, after much badinage about Scandinavian sixth sense, trolls and spooks, she reluctantly consented to join us.

'But I will be shot,' she said sadly.

Less than an hour later, two guns turned to fire at a bird that was going back low and Hjördis fell to the ground, hit in the face, neck chest and arms.

I rushed over and as I cradled her, moaning, in my arms, a terrible thought went through my head – it's happened again.

Her beautiful face was a terribly swollen mask of blood; when she asked for a mirror, we pretended nobody had one. Within half an hour she was in the local hospital, where it was discovered that she had over thirty pieces of lead in her, including one which to this day remains embedded in the bone of her eye socket.

She was given an anaesthetic and they were preparing to remove the pellets when some strange force propelled me, uninvited, into the operating room.

'Stop, please!' I said to the astonished white-clad group. 'I'm sorry, before you cut her – I want another opinion.'

I don't know what made me do it – some half-forgotten wartime whisper about shrapnel wounds perhaps; anyway, white gauze masks were lowered and I was asked, icily, if I wanted to accept the full responsibility. My host produced an ex-navy surgeon friend who was paged at the local football game. He came and examined her and gave it as his opinion that if the swollen tissues were operated on at that time, she would be scarred for life.

'Many will work their way out,' he said, 'the ones in deep we can get later. She should be X-rayed frequently to see if any move, especially the one near the jugular.'

Thank God for the U.S. Navy. Hjördis is, today, unmarked but now when she hears those little northern voices, I listen with great attention.

A battered Hjördis and I moved to the Blackstone Hotel, New York. In a tiny room next to us was lodged a doe-eyed waif, a young actress, also making her debut on Broadway that season – Audrey Hepburn. Together, we shook with fear as our opening nights drew inexorably nearer.

Nina was a translation from a big French success by André Roussin. It was directed by a comic Russian, Gregory Ratoff. In English, it was pretty bad.

Gloria looked marvellous and took great pains to remain that way by eating the most loathsome concoctions of yoghurt, yeast, wheat germ and molasses. She also had a fixation that every actor should have another string to his bow – some other profession capable of padding out the lean times.

'I have a clothing business myself,' she said. 'The Pilgrim Company ... all my clothes for this show will be made by Pilgrim.'

We opened in Hartford, Connecticut, in front of a heavily partisan audience, most of whom had come up from New York to cheer us on, but among them was the usual sprinkling of carrion crows sniffing for the first scent of possible disaster and ready to fly back to Broadway, the bitchy bearers of grim tidings.

The show, at this point, went over quite well and Otto Preminger, never a man to mince words, said he liked my efforts very much but by the time we arrived in Boston, a week later several scenes had been re-written and the show was half as good. Two weeks and many re-writes after that, we opened in Philadelphia. The carrion crows had every reason to be delighted – there was no question – we were headed for big trouble.

Rex Harrison and Lilli Palmer answered my S.O.S., and came down from New York to see the show and offer me some advice.

'Well, what do you suggest?' I asked over supper.

'Get out of it,' said Rex.

When we arrived in New York, Hjördis tried her best to appear optimistic and Garson Kanin suggested questionable aid for first-night nerves.

'Go to the top of the Empire State Building ... don't throw yourself off – just look down at all those millions of lights and remember that only one of them is the Royale Theatre.'

When the big night came, neither the producer nor the director made it to the theatre and the last run through was conducted by Biff Liff, the stage manager, who read out the final instructions with all the enthusiasm of an undertaker.

All the professional first nighters were there and the dreaded critics. Also, Alfred Lunt and Lynn Fontanne, Tallulah Bankhead and Rex and Lilli – gluttons for punishment.

The house lights dimmed and an expectant buzz faded into a pregnant silence. I stood quaking beside the stage manager who made an abortive effort to bolster my sagging morale as he signalled for the curtain to rise –

'Get out there, Dave – there's nothing you can do about it now – the horse has left the barn.'

For a panic-stricken moment, I toyed with the idea of rushing madly out of the theatre and throwing myself beneath the hooves of the mounted police, then I tottered on stage.

Webb and I played the first explanatory scene together, then the doorbell rang signalling the entrance of Swanson. Webb, the husband, took refuge behind the curtain and I, the lover, moved across stage to admit my mistress. I was ill prepared for what I saw.

She had, I thought, worn some rather odd garments in Hartford, Boston and Philadelphia but now the Pilgrim Company had really excelled itself. Swanson stood there enveloped in a black taffeta tent. She stepped forward and a gasp of horror mingled with the applause.

She smiled seductively at her lover and I was supposed to smile back. I tried but I was so nervous and my mouth so dry that my upper lip became stuck above my teeth and I stood there leering at her like a mad rabbit.

The Bedouin tent with Swanson's head sticking out of the top of it rustled across the stage and flung itself into my arms. Swanson is not tall. She is, to put it mildly, petite, so when I clasped her to me, the top of her head nestled just to the right of my breast-bone.

Unfortunately, in my terror of the whole situation, I squeezed too hard in that initial clinch. There was a loud report. This was followed by a twanging noise and about eight inches of white whalebone shot out of Swanson's chest, and straight up my nose.

The audience was delighted – something new at last – they roared with laughter. Swanson half turned to see what was happening, thereby stirring the whalebone around in my sinus. Tears of pain streamed down my face but in my innocence of things theatrical, I thought maybe it didn't show and with the whalebone crunching about among the scroll bones, and with my gopher teeth gleaming in the limelight, I carried bravely on with the scene.

286

The audience hooted, and the 'flop sweat' broke out all over me like dew. Down in the area of my navel, Swanson hissed, 'What the hell's going on?'

In the morning, Walter Kerr, the critic for the *Herald Tribune*, wrote –

'We understood from the programme that Miss Swanson designed her own clothes ... like the play, they fell apart in the first act.'

Nina trailed along for three months but by early spring, we were all mercifully back in the Pink House. The movie business still wanted no part of me.

Hollywood is like a bird dog. When things are going badly, it tenses and sniffs at you. It scrapes away at the camouflage. It knows.

Hjördis told me not to worry because, she said, it made me put out an aroma of defeat. I must have been particularly smelly because she suggested a few days on a boat to take my mind off things. We chartered a small sloop and set off for Catalina Island with Garbo and a gentleman friend, an ex-navy man, completing the crew. Garbo was cook, Hjördis stewardess, and as befitted his background the G.F. engineer and navigator. I was in charge of the sails.

When the wind fell away towards evening, I hauled them down and handed over to the G.F.

For an hour he tinkered with the engine. I hovered nearby with useless advice while the Swedish members of the expedition drank schnapps, and made crude Nordic jokes at our expense.

'I wonder,' said Hjördis sweetly, 'if you should give us a bearing because if we miss Catalina, the next stop is Japan.'

Finally the engine spluttered into life and as we chugged hesitantly west in the gathering darkness, the man pored over charts and poked about with calipers. Then he announced heavily,

'Something's screwy here – according to my reckoning, we are eleven miles north of the Grand Canyon.'

The seafaring Swedes showed no sign of panic. One of them – both claimed the honour – saw a pinprick of light far away to port. We changed course and hours later with faltering engine, dropped anchor in a sandy cove.

Garbo during the weekend made up for some patchy

uninspired cooking by exuding sparkling fun and swimming, unselfconsciously so, every day, Swedish style.

Television, in the early fifties, had begun to rear its ugly head. The major film studios, instead of grabbing it and making it their own, decided first to ignore it, then to fight it and wound up, a few years later, being swallowed by it.

I picked up some sparse but badly needed dollars by doing 'guest shots' on the Bob Hope and Jack Benny shows. Many people thought it was nothing short of suicide for a film star to fly in the face of the studio bosses and align himself with the enemy. I had no alternative. I was already dead. One well-known 'zany' red-head did a show with me and over a very inexpensive supper at the Brown Derby, confided that she was even more strapped for cash than I was. She turned out to be about as 'zany' as General Motors: within four years Lucille Ball had bought both the R.K.O. studios.

In the spring, unable to raise another dollar in mortgage on the Pink House, I decided the sad moment had come – the Regency furniture had to go. I mailed carefully authenticated lists to Parke Bernet in New York and to the Shabbie Shoppe in Dallas, Texas, and enclosed a letter to each guaranteeing that their establishment was the only recipient of this golden opportunity. Their replies were sharp.

My own carelessness had saved me from losing my beloved collection. I had put the letters in the wrong envelopes.

In October, I was offered a live TV show of *Petrified Forest* in New York. Hjördis and I worked it out and after deducting air fares and three weeks' hotel expenses, we looked like clearing three hundred dollars so we took off in a hurry.

It was a good show and thirty million people saw it – a record at that time. Robert Sherwood sat in the control room watching us and professed himself delighted with our playing of his famous work.

Alex Segal directed it beautifully and Lloyd Gough, Kim Hunter and Art Carney rounded out the cast, but by the end of it I was so exhausted by the tension that we decided to blow the three hundred dollars on a trip to Barbados whence Ronnie and Marietta Tree had bidden us come and visit them for two weeks.

288

The day after we returned to the Pink House, Otto Preminger called up and offered me the best part in his forth-coming picture, *The Moon is Blue*. Something he had seen in my performance in *Nina* at Hartford had persuaded him that I was the actor he wanted. Hjördis and I were beside ourselves with excitement but Otto had a great deal of opposition from United Artists who were financing the picture.

'Niven is washed up!' they told him ... 'get somebody else.' But Otto is an immensely determined individual and what Otto wants, he usually gets ... he got me ... bless him!

Many actors don't like working with Otto because he shouts even louder than Goldwyn and can be very sarcastic. I love it. Actors have a certain amount of donkey blood in them and need a carrot dangled in front of them from time to time. The directors I dread are the ones who say, 'You've played this sort of thing before – do anything you want' ... Otto dangles carrots.

A highly organised man, he made a German version of his picture simultaneously with the American one. The German cast arrived, the two companies rehearsed for a month and the entire film was completed in two languages in eighteen days. It was also far ahead of its day in its attitude towards sex, was promptly banned by the Catholic Church in the United States and helped enormously by the ensuing publicity.

The Moon is Blue became a very big success all over the world and I, personally, was highly delighted to win the Golden Globe Award from the foreign press – for the best comedy performance of the year.

William Holden and Maggie MacNamara played the lovers in the film but before we started shooting, Otto asked me to play *The Moon is Blue* for three months on the stage in San Francisco with Scott Brady and Diana Lynn.

While we were doing so, Charles Boyer was performing in an adjacent San Francisco theatre. The two of us were having supper together one night when Boyer told me that he and Dick Powell were thinking of forming a company to make films for television.

In view of the film studios' attitude towards the upstart television, I was surprised that two such big names were prepared to risk so much, but I myself had little to lose and the net result of that after-theatre snack was the formation of Four-Star Television Inc., which to date has made between two and three thousand films for home consumption.

The idea of Four Star Playhouse was to have four well-known movie stars each appearing once a month in an anthology series. Since, however, we were unable to persuade a fourth star to join us, most people still being too frightened of the studio bosses who uttered the direst threats against 'black-legs', a few staunch friends helped us out during the first season by doing 'guest' shows – Ronald Colman, Joan Fontaine, Merle Oberon and Ida Lupino among them.

The three of us took nothing in salaries and with the proceeds at the end of the first year, we bought the rights to Somerset Maugham's short stories and started a second series with Henry Fonda as host: he even had the guts to blow froth in the beer commercials. The third year, we purchased the Zane Grey stories and launched a third series, 'Zane Grey Theatre'. This in turn spawned 'The Rifleman' which spun off another new series, 'Wanted Dead or Alive', into which we put an instantly successful unknown, Steve MacQueen.

So it went on but it was not all smooth sailing by a long shot. Frequently, we overspent, or under-planned; often sponsors were weeks behind with their payments. Once on a Friday, I pulled all my savings out of the Bank of America to meet the studio payroll. The day before we were to start shooting a new series with Anita Ekberg as a female Tarzan, we received a very clear message from Howard Hughes's right-hand man informing us that the luscious Miss Ekberg had left town indefinitely for an undisclosed destination and would not be available in the foreseeable future. We took the high-powered hint and hastily re-cast another beautiful body in the leopard skin.

Several owners of today's biggest names started their careers with us as actors or directors and Jack Lemmon, Barbara Stanwyck, Steve MacQueen, David Janssen, Chuck Connors, Robert Ryan, Robert Taylor, June Allyson, Gig Young, Ida Lupino and many, many others made series for us. One year we were turning out fourteen different series at the same time ... as big an output of film as any of the major studios had made in their hey day. We had become big business; nerve-wracking big business.

My film career after *The Moon is Blue* also climbed back on to a most satisfactory plateau of important pictures.

The boys were growing fast and had settled down well in California though I always felt a tiny bit out of place with my polite hand-clapping Hollywood Cricket Club back-ground when I found myself at Chavez Ravine, wedged between two cap-wearing, gum-chewing, mitt-thumping, raspberry-blowing little Dodger fans.

The days were full of promise and the friends with whom I could savour them were nearby.

Fred Astaire is a pixie – timid, always warm-hearted, a sentimentalist with a Lefty-Flynn-type penchant for school-boy jokes. He is also a racehorse aficionado who owned a winner of the Hollywood Gold Cup.

Early one Sunday he called me.

'I've done a terrible thing – I don't know what possessed me, but at four o'clock this morning, I got out of bed and drove all over Beverly Hills, painting the city mail boxes with my racing colours.'

Freud might have had an explanation for Fred's behaviour – well-to-do ladies often abduct sausages from supermarkets – so when one day a voice on the telephone said,

'Good morning – I am the Bishop of Los Angeles.' I replied knowingly, 'And I am the Mother Superior – how's your cock?'

A quick intake of breath followed by a longish pause alerted me to the fact that it was not Fred. When the Bishop had recovered from the unaccustomed greeting, he told me what was on his mind.

'We have a Convention of several thousand Anglican clergy coming to Los Angeles from all over the world, we are holding a service in the Hollywood Bowl and we would be very happy if you would read the Second lesson.'

He explained that it was several weeks away and when I enquired why he had selected me, he told me that as the Archbishop of York was coming from England, it had been decided to invite what he kindly described as a prominent British resident of Los Angeles.

The day approached and what had for some time seemed no more than a minor chore, now assumed the proportions of a major hazard. I had meetings with the Bishop and enquired about my wardrobe for the occasion ... dark suit.

We discussed the 'script' ... Galatians, Chapter IV.

I did not understand it ... 'What is *un*circumcision?' He explained patiently and told me with a smile not to worry about who was to read the First Lesson – 'You won't have to follow Bob Hope ... I will be reading that myself.'

On the night before my appearance at the giant Hollywood Bowl, I was so nervous I was unable to sleep. In the morning, I had a high fever and had completely lost my voice.

Hjördis telephoned the Bishop and explained while I listened on an extension ... I could tell from the disappointment in his voice that he was having a hard time being a believer so I went down there anyway to let him hear me croak, I think. He said gently, 'You could try it, they will understand that you have something wrong with your voice and they will be terribly bored if I read them both lessons.'

When the moment came, with my knees clanking together like castanets, I walked out on to the desert-like stage while the thousands of clerics rustled themselves into seated comfort. A massed choir of hundreds stood in tiers behind me as I turned to face the vastness of the Bowl.

'Somebody' up there loved me that day. I opened my mouth to whisper the announcement of the Lesson and out of my hitherto totally constricted throat came the deepest and most resonant sounds I had ever heard.

On the Fourth of July in the United States American friends point out, with unholy glee, that the crack of each firework is symbolic of the breaking of a redcoat's neck. Bogart was always at his most sardonic on this occasion but once, in celebration, he broke all his rules and invited women aboard *Santana*.

'Betty', calling her husband 'Captain Queeg' after the half-mad sadist he had portrayed in *The Caine Mutiny* came along to keep Hjördis company. We dropped anchor in Cherry Grove and Frank Sinatra moored alongside us in a chartered motor cruiser with several beautiful girls and a small piano. After dinner, with Jimmy Van Heusen accompanying him, Sinatra began to sing.

He sang all night.

There were many yachts in Cherry Cove that weekend and by two in the morning, under a full moon, *Santana* was surrounded by an audience sitting in dozens of dinghies and rubber tenders of every shape and size. Frank sang as only he can, with his monumental talent and exquisite phrasing undimmed by a bottle of Jack Daniels on top of the piano.

He sang till the dew came down heavily and the boys in the listening fleet fetched blankets for their girls' shoulders.

He sang till the moon and the stars paled in the pre-dawn sky – only then did he stop and only then did the awed and grateful audience paddle silently away.

Noël Coward was about to appear in Las Vegas. He was sitting in a deep sofa at Bogie's one evening, discussing the problems of his show.

Bogie and I were facing him in two easy chairs. Suddenly, we realised that little Stevie, the five-year-old Bogart son and heir, was stalking Noël from behind, his target, obviously, the top of Noël's head. In his hands he bore a large brass tray.

The impending assault was so horrible that Bogie and I just sat there unable to move like two dogs watching a snake.

Little Stevie raised the tray high and brought it down with a crash on Noël's unprotected cranium. His head almost disappeared into his shirt.

Noël never looked round. His voice never changed nor did the rhythm of his speech alter.

'Bogart, dear,' he said, 'do you know what I am going to give darling little Stephen for Christmas? A chocolate covered handgrenade.'

The famous 'Sinatra Rat Pack' should now be put in perspective. All sorts of people were for years stuck with this label, Dean Martin, Sammy Davis, Shirley MacLaine, Peter Lawford, Tony Curtis and Janet Leigh to name a few. They were guiltless.

During Noël's appearance at the Desert Inn, Sinatra invited a few friends to go with him to Las Vegas for the opening. When anything is organised by Sinatra, the arrangements are made with legendary efficiency and generosity. We boarded a bus outside Bogie's front door. Caviar and champagne sustained us during the drive downtown to the Union Station and there, with a cry from our leader of 'yellow armbands, follow me', we trooped aboard a private coach on the train for the overnight trip to Las Vegas. The group consisted of Betty and Bogie, Mike and Gloria Romanoff, Ernie Kovacs and his wife, 'Swifty' Lazar, Sid Luft and Judy Garland, Angie Dickinson, Hjördis and myself.

Sinatra provided individual apartments for everyone at the Sands Hotel and a large communal suite with hot and cold running food and drink twenty-four hours a day: a big bag of silver dollars was presented to each girl in the party to gamble with.

We saw Noël's triumphant first night and on subsequent evenings we visited all the other shows in Las Vegas. We gambled endlessly, only occasionally poking our noses outside to sniff the desert air and gauge the time of day. After three days, Judy Garland slipped me something that she promised would keep me going. It was the size of a horse-pill and inside were dozens of little multi-coloured 'energy' nuggets, timed to go off at intervals of forty minutes.

After four days and nights of concentrated self-indulgence, the only one of the party who seemed physically untouched was Sinatra himself. The rest were wrecks and it was then that Betty Bacall, surveying the bedraggled survivors, pronounced the fatal words – 'You look like a Goddam Rat Pack!'

A week after we returned to Los Angeles and forced ourselves back into some semblance of good health, the Rat Pack gave a testimonial dinner to Sinatra in the private room, upstairs, at Romanoff's. A surprise package, tied with pink ribbon and flown down by Jack Entratta, the entrepreneur of the Sands Hotel, awaited every one of us. Inside each was a white rat. Several escaped during the unpacking and hot-footed it into the restaurant – sowing instant alarm among the chic clientele and eagle-eyed columnists belowstairs – thus heralding the end of the short, happy life of Sinatra's Rat Pack.

So much has been written about Sinatra, of his talent, his generosity, his ruthlessness, his kindness, his gregariousness, his loneliness and his rumoured links with the Mob that I can contribute nothing except to say that he is one of the few people in the world I would instinctively think of if I needed help of any sort. I thought of him once when I was in a very bad spot: help was provided instantly and in full measure without a question being asked. It was not, incidentally, money.

On New Year's Eve of 1956, Annie and Charlie Lederer stretched a striped awning across their back garden, boarded over their swimming pool and gave a very beautiful party for a couple of especially glamorous visitors, the Shah and the Empress of Iran. 'Le tout Hollywood' turned out in force.

Hjördis and I were dancing and beside us, 'Betty' Bacall, a particularly active and dedicated exponent of modern dancing, was gyrating, bumping and grinding round the guest of honour – a comparatively subdued performer.

In an effort to re-establish some sort of contact with his partner, the incumbent of the Peacock Throne said,

'You are a wonderful dancer, Miss Bacall ... you must have been born to dance.'

'Betty' tossed back her mane of tawny hair, gave one more convulsive heave and answered loudly in her husky-sexy voice.

'You bet your ass, Shah.'

Betty Bacall was the perfect wife and companion for Bogie. I don't know how long she knew he was seriously ill but she was courageous and dedicated through the whole heartbreaking period. I had heard his nightly coughing bouts on my last trips with him in *Santana* but he said it was just his smoking, nothing more. Then, he began to lose weight but he never had been much interested in food.

Suddenly, there was an emergency seven-hour operation and the slow slide began.

'If I put on weight – I've got it licked,' he told me.

Hjördis and I went away to Rome for three months while I made *The Little Hut* with Ava Gardner and Stewart Granger and afterwards we spent a short time together in Sweden.

From there, I brought back the radical plans and specifications of a new yacht that I thought might interest Bogie and took them to his house. I was shocked at the change.

We spent a day aboard *Santana*, but she remained tied up alongside her dock. She never put to sea again with Bogie.

He no longer referred to his illness and with Betty in permanent attendance, preserving somehow, God knows how, her marvellous gaiety and fun, he slowly wasted away. When he became too weak to make the trip downstairs for his ritual evening drink with his friends – now invited only one at a time and carefully selected by Betty – they converted the little service elevator, took out the shelves, and sharp at six o'clock, Bogie would have his terribly emaciated frame carefully dressed and be lowered below, sitting in his wheelchair.

One of us would always be waiting – Huston, Sinatra, Harry Kurnitz, Nunally Johnstone, Joe Hyams, 'Swifty' Lazar – a few others, and on special occasions, 'Dum Bum'.

At four o'clock one morning, Betty called us and said very quietly, 'My darling husband is gone.'

CHAPTER SIXTEEN

ONE Sunday afternoon, the phone rang in the Pink House.

'This is Mike Todd. 'I'm over at Joe Schenck's. I wanna see you. Get your ass over here.'

I was halfway through a polite excuse before I realised that he had long since hung up. I had never met Todd but I had heard a hundred stories about the legendary master showman, gambler, promoter or con man — everyone saw him from a different angle.

We had a houseful of friends that afternoon and the consensus of opinion was that, whatever else, Todd was always interesting and I should indeed get my ass over to Joe Schenck's.

When I arrived, Todd was by the pool. Of medium height and perfect proportions, he was tanned dark mahogany. He wore the briefest of swimming slips. On his head was a white ten-gallon hat, in his mouth was a cigar of grotesque proportions.

He had no time for preliminaries.

'Ever heard of Jules Verne?'

'Yes, of course.'

'Ever read *Around the World in 80 Days?*'

'I was weaned on it.'

'I've never made a picture before but I'm gonna make this one ... How'd you like to play Phileas Fogg?'

My heart bounded. 'I'd do it for nothing.'

Todd tossed aside his hat and cigar.

'You gotta deal,' he said and disappeared beneath the surface of the pool.

From that moment till the time, six months later, that the picture was finished, I lived in an atmosphere of pure fantasy. Nobody knows where Todd raised the necessary seven million dollars and he certainly didn't raise it all at once because several times production ground to a halt while strange, swarthy gentlemen arrived from Chicago for urgent consultations. For weeks on end we went unpaid. Todd induced S. J. Perelman to write the screen play and employed John Farrow to direct it.

The Mexican bullfighter comedian, Cantinflas, arrived to play my valet, Passepartout, and Shirley MacLaine was signed to play Princess Aouda.

'But who the hell do we get to play Mr. Fix the Detective?' said Todd, chomping on the inevitable cigar.

'How about Robert Newton?' I suggested.

Todd was enchanted with the idea and immediately put in a call.

'But I warn you, Mike,' I said, feeling every kind of heel, 'Bobbie is a great friend of mine but he does drink a lot these days and you must protect yourself. Lots of people are scared to employ him – he disappears.'

'I want to see Newton,' said Todd firmly, 'and when he comes in, I want you here in the office.'

'For Christ's sake, don't tell him I said anything,' I begged, 'he'll never forgive me.'

A little later, Bobbie Newton shuffled in. I hadn't seen him for some weeks and it was obvious that he had been on a bender of heroic proportions.

Todd went into his routine.

'Ever heard of Jules Verne?'

'Ah, dear fellow,' said Newton, 'what a scribe.

'*80 Days Around the World?*'

'A glorious piece, old cock.'

'How'd you like to play Mr. Fix?'

'A splendid role,' said Bobbie, rolling his eyes. 'Do I understand you are offering it to me, dear boy?'

'I might,' said Todd and I felt like the slimiest worm when he continued, 'But your pal, Niven here, says you're a lush.'

'Aah!' said Newton, 'my pal, Niven, is a master of the understatement.'

He was hired immediately and gave his word of honour to Todd that he would go on the wagon for the duration of the picture. He stuck manfully to his promise.

On location at Durango, Colorado, Bobbie and I went off every evening after shooting to catch big, fighting rainbow trout in the mountain lakes. One cold autumn sunset with streaks of blue wood-smoke clinging to the surface of the water and the last rays of the sun falling on the glorious colours of the aspens and beeches, Bobbie confessed to me that his promise to Todd had not really been all that difficult because that very morning his doctor had warned him that one more session with the bottle would almost certainly be fatal. Two weeks after we finished the picture, Todd called some of us back for an added scene on a ship. Bobbie Newton was only required for one day but when he arrived for work, a roaring delivery of 'Once more unto the breach ...' announced alarming news. 'Oh, Bobbie,' I said, 'what have you done to yourself.'

He put his arm round my neck and tears rolled down his swollen cheeks.

'Don't chide me, dear fellow, please don't chide me,' he said.

Within a very few days, the doctor's warnings to that warm-hearted, talented and wonderful soul proved tragically correct.

If Todd had difficulty in raising money for his epic, he seemed to have none persuading the biggest names in show business to play small 'cameos' for fun. We started shooting in Spain with Louis Miguel Dominguin playing himself in the bullring, and there, after a falling out, Todd replaced the director, John Farrow, by the young Englishman, Michael Anderson.

In London, more cameo parts were played by Noël Coward, Beatrice Lillie, Hermione Gingold, Hermione Baddeley and Glynis Johns, and back finally in California for the major portion of the work, I became inoculated against surprise when I found myself playing scenes almost daily with different distinguished visitors – among them Ronald Colman, Charles Boyer, Marlene Dietrich, Frank Sinatra, George Raft, Red Skelton, Victor McLaglen, Andy Devine, Joe E. Brown, Cedric Hardwicke and Buster Keaton.

Somehow Todd also found time to collect someone specially for himself and, radiant with happiness, Elizabeth Taylor became a permanent fixture.

Nothing 'phased' Todd ... when a flock of several hundred sheep stopped our car on the way to location in Colorado, he bought the flock.

'Great idea!' he said. 'We put the sheep in front of the train to hold it up.'

The sheep had been on their way to market so now feed had to be provided at great expense to keep them alive till their big moment. When it came, far from stopping the train, they scattered before it like chaff.

'Sell the goddam sheep,' ordered Todd, 'we need a herd of buffalo.' He found them too, in Oklahoma, and the scene was reshot with several hundred gigantic beasts stampeding in every direction.

In Paris, shooting with Todd-luck on the only sunny day in five weeks of continual rain, we were joined by Fernandel and Martine Carol. Todd needed all the luck at his disposal when he took over the Place Vendôme and ordered cars towed away in the early morning which might interfere with his day's shooting.

One of the offending vehicles turned out to be the property of a Cabinet Minister who was spending the night away from home. Todd was ordered to stop shooting and the police moved in to enforce the order. Todd promptly paid two taxi drivers to stage a head-on collision in the rue de Rivoli and during the ensuing diversion, he completed his work.

In London, he 'stole' a shot of a company of Guardsmen marching out of Wellington Barracks and separating on either side of his camera by the simple device of camouflaging the machine on a vegetable barrow and pushing it directly in front of the oncoming soldiers at the last second ... that, not surprisingly, proved to be our final day's shooting in the streets of London.

At Balboa, Todd converted an ancient sailing yacht into a paddle steamer of the period by building on deck a large superstructure which housed the ponderous engine of a San Francisco cable car to turn the paddle wheels. Not only was the yacht now dangerously top heavy, but, as we chugged out of the harbour, full laden with actors, crew, lights and cameras, it was made clear to us that a nasty passage was ahead. I pointed to the storm warnings being raised by the coastguards at the end of the breakwater.

'I can't see a goddam thing,' said Todd, 'I'm Nelson.'

In the event the boat proved too dangerous to turn round in the heavy seas and we had to go all the way to Catalina before we dared try it.

With gorgeous Elizabeth by his side, Todd remained undefeated to the end even when the sheriff of Los Angeles locked up the finished footage of his picture, thereby immobilising his only asset within the State of California till various local creditors had been mollified.

Todd was allowed to assemble and score the film during the day time under the watchful eye of a sheriff's deputy but at night, back it went into the vault.

'Somehow, Todd staved off the enemy and, at last, the picture was ready for presentation. The sheriff was persuaded to allow the film to travel to New York for its big gala opening at the Rivoli Theatre.

'You gotta get your ass back East,' Todd told me. 'You gotta be there at the pay-out window.'

Todd sent air tickets and installed us in the most expensive apartment in the St. Regis Hotel. There was a present for Hjördis when we arrived and the rooms were full of flowers; champagne and caviar were waiting for us.

The opening was a Todd bonanza; mounted police held back the screaming crowds as the audience of a thousand famous people in evening dress filed into the theatre. Every member of the audience received a beautifully bound and illustrated programme embossed in gold on the cover with the name of each recipient. After the showing, Todd gave a champagne supper for fifteen hundred at the Astor Hotel.

Where did he get the money for all this?' The answer, according to Bennett Cerf of Random House, who produced the programme, was that he didn't. The morning after the opening, his cheque made out to the publishers – bounced.

No matter, Gambler Todd had got right to the wire with his last penny and when the audience had finished cheering and the ecstatic reviews were being read, there he was standing happily at the pay-out window.

The picture won the Academy Award as the Best Picture of the Year and became one of the biggest money spinners of all time.

Todd married Elizabeth and gave her a diamond the size of a skating rink. He bought himself a twin-engined plane.

Hjördis and I, with peculiar logic, decided that with a lot of good pictures now being offered to me, it was the ideal moment to go away from Hollywood for a few months so we flew off around the world.

Shirley MacLaine came with us to Tokyo and, with her

301

husband, Steve Parker, as guide, we saw the best of Japan. The four of us went on to Hong Kong.

Shirley is a great traveller and a spectacular companion. She is also a lady of formidable crusading opinions and her anti-Establishment observations reverberated round the crown colony.

When she and Steve flew back to Japan, Hjördis and I continued on to Thailand, India and Turkey. In Greece we decided to spurge so we chartered a small ketch and the boys flew out to spend their holidays with us in the Islands of the Aegean and Ionian Seas. Hjördis caused a stir in every land we visited not only because of her spectacular beauty but because her idea of travelling light was to order a local costume in each country in turn. Somehow, her purchases always seemed to be delivered on the day of our departure, consequently, she contrived to be a country behind in her clothing. Her cheongsan from Hong Kong, was, however, a huge success in Bangkok and her sari from Jaipur nearly caused a riot in a football match in Istanbul.

Back once more in the Pink House via Sweden and England, I made *My Man Godfrey* at Universal before we decided to visit the scene of the Rat Pack inauguration.

The operator at the Sands Hotel located me at a black jack table and told me Mike Todd was calling me from New York.

'Get your ass over to Palm Springs,' he said, 'Liz and I are flying out tomorrow. Come and spend the weekend.'

I explained that although Las Vegas is separated from Palm Springs by only a hundred miles as the crow flies, the bird would have to cross a hundred miles of mountains and desert to make the trip.

'Hold the 'phone,' said Todd.

After a while, he was back on the line.

'Okay, I'm sending the plane out there to pick you up — we'll come on out on a commercial — see you tomorrow night for dinner.' He hung up.

The following day, Todd's twin-engined, twin-piloted pride and joy arrived from New York, picked us up and half an hour later, we were in Todd's Palm Springs pad.

Elizabeth Taylor has always fascinated me. I met her first when she was fifteen and got to know her well during her marriage to the gentle, self-effacing Michael Wilding. Her incredible beauty, her talent and her violet eyes have been the subject of endless paeons of praise; less well known are her courage, her down-to-earthiness and her staunch defence of friends. That she is completely unspoiled and natural is a miracle when one remembers that with all the attendant sycophantic adulation, she has survived being a major world movie star since she made *National Velvet* at the age of ten.

She was gay and relaxed during the weekend but made no secret of her annoyance that she would have to stay behind and work in Hollywood when Todd flew back to New York in a few days' time to attend some testimonial dinner.

On the Sunday evening, we all returned to Los Angeles in Todd's plane. Hjördis and I needed little persuading when Todd suggested that we pick up our car and drive back to Palm Springs to relax in his beautiful house till the following weekend when he would be back again.

On the day we reinstalled ourselves in his desert home, Todd called us and said how he wished he could be with us and how little he relished the idea of going back to New York.

'Get out of the dinner,' I said, 'come on down.'

He said he couldn't as he had promised to attend. With typical thoughtfulness, he called again just before he took off to make sure we had everything and repeated once more, how much he wished he didn't have to go.

Four hours later, his plane crashed in New Mexico.

The word 'playwright' is spelled that way for a very good reason. Shipwrights build ships, wheelwrights fashion wheels, and playwrights construct plays. If they construct them badly, they quickly fly apart at the seams.

Terence Rattigan is an actor's playwright. To perform the characters he has invented is a joy because they are so well drawn and the plays that present them are so well constructed that so long as you can remember your 'lines' and don't bump into the furniture, you can't go wrong. *Separate Tables* is one of Rattigan's best plays and 'The Major' is one of his best written characters, so I was, naturally, overjoyed when I was offered the part in the film version. Burt Lancaster, Deborah Kerr, Rita Hayworth, Wendy Hiller, Gladys Cooper, Cathleen Nesbitt, Rod Taylor and myself rehearsed for two weeks under the expert eye of Delbert Mann – one of the best of the new brew of young directors who had been making names for themselves in 'live' television in New York.

It was a dream company to work with.

When the shooting was completed, Hjördis, who had just suffered through yet another miscarriage, was particularly delighted when we took off for a long-planned two weeks' holiday with Noël Coward at his home near Port Maria in Jamaica. On the first evening over rum drinks, having just heard sad news from England, I said to Noël,

'It's terrible – I've arrived at the age when all my friends are dying.'

'Personally,' said Coward. 'I'm delighted if mine last through luncheon . . .'

'Incidentally,' he added, 'you don't look too good yourself.'

I wasn't, it is true, feeling very well – feverish, and Hjördis had just discovered some spots on my back – they itched. By the next morning, more spots had appeared on my face and chest – and my fever had soared.

'I'm terribly sorry, Noël,' I said, 'but there seems to be a faint possibility that I may be coming down with chickenpox.'

Noël eyed my flushed face with mounting distaste then spoke very slowly and distinctly.

'I want to make one thing crystal clear – you cannot come down with it here.'

The next day when Hjördis counted my proliferating spots and reported to Noël that on my face and chest alone she had found over two thousand, Noël sighed resignedly.

'It's high time I wrote another play,' he said, 'and painted some more of my excellent pictures, so we will now pull up the drawbridge, fly the Yellow Jack . . . and the hell with it.'

He then fetched the bottle.

'The village postmistress,' he said 'swears that pure rum will stop the itching and bring down the fever.'

While Hjördis watched apprehensively, he anointed my spots and gave me a hefty tot to drink for good measure.

The result of this piece of folklore was instant delirium and two attempts, bravely frustrated by Hjördis, to climb out of the window into the sea.

By the time, weeks later, that I was well enough to travel, Noël had indeed painted many excellent pictures. He had also, written a very successful play – *Nude with Violin*. His real resilience, however, is demonstrated by the fact that he invited us to stay with him again.

Children's diseases are not to be recommended to adults. It was weeks before I could go back to work. When I did, I started *Ask Any Girl* with Shirley MacLaine.

On the set one day, Shirley was called to take a phone call from New York; she let out one of her traffic-stopping shrieks.

'Hey, David! come here quick!' she yelled. 'You've just won the New York Critics' Award for *Separate Tables*.'

It was a tremendous surprise, I didn't even know I was a candidate. There were, I believe, fifteen voters and apparently after three ballots I had just scraped home over Spencer Tracy in *The Old Man and the Sea*. Bosley Crowther, the influential voice of the *New York Times*, had voted against me which, of course, he had every right to do, but finding himself in the minority, he behaved like a spoiled brat and devoted his Sunday article to saying what a disgrace it was that I had won.

Shirley got me all excited.

'If you win the New York Critics, you are almost bound to be nominated for the Academy Award! Hey! you may get the Oscar! !'

I tried to be cool and accepted congratulations all over town as unsmugly as I could but the weeks before the announcement of the five nominees for best performance by an actor were endless. When it finally came over the radio, I was on my way home from work and my receiver was on the blink. The attendant at a gas station gave me the good news when I stopped to fill up. When I arrived at the Pink House, Hjördis had the champagne out. The phone never stopped ringing. Basically, the awards system is a good one . . . for the nomination, five in each category, one's peers vote. The actors nominate the actors, the directors nominate the directors, the writers the writers, the cameramen the cameramen – and so on. Then the whole lot, all three thousand members of the Academy, vote for the winners.

The other nominees in my category were Spencer Tracy, Paul Newman, Sidney Poitier and Tony Curtis.

I had ten weeks to wait before the final result and I started out by telling myself that at best, I was a four-to-one shot. I also felt a bit of a fake because playing the role of 'the Major' had, thanks to the way it was written and directed and the formidable help I had received from that high-powered cast, been far easier than I could have imagined.

As the ten weeks dragged by, the pressures built up. The winner of the Academy Award is supposed to add a million dollars to the potential of the picture he is in. His next film, too, is supposed to benefit largely. The advertising campaigns start in earnest one month before voting day. Film companies and some individuals spend thousands of dollars pushing their wares, everyone is speculating.

'Tracy will win because everyone loves him ... Newman will win because he is always so good – and it's time he did ... Poitier will win because he's black and Hollywood is colour-conscious ... Curtis will win because he's Jewish ... you can't win because you're British and they gave it to Alec Guinness last year,' etc., etc. It was all very nerve-racking but as the day came nearer, I found that I wanted that Oscar desperately.

My estimate of my chances was not very high at the best of times but it dropped to zero on the very day that the three thousand voters received their ballot sheets ... there in the *Hollywood Reporter*, the local Bible which would be read by all of them, was a reprint of a story by the eminent film critic and columnist of the *Washington Daily News*, Jim O'Neill. It stated that a well-known Hollywood producer had told that newspaper's columnist that the one person he would never vote for would be me, because I had copied Eric Portman's stage performance entirely, had seen the play forty times and had haunted Portman's dressing room till I had to be bodily thrown out of the theatre.

I was sunk. I cabled O'Neill in Washington and pointed out that not only was I not clever enough, or stupid enough, to copy anybody's performance – but it so happened that I had seen the play precisely once, four years before in London.

O'Neill checked with Portman, who kindly corroborated

this and wished me luck and O'Neill then, very graciously, apologised to me in print for 'irresponsible reporting'. He quoted Portman's cable and for good measure, told me, over the phone, the name of the Hollywood producer, 'as the very least I can do'.

It was far too late to hope to put the record straight, the votes would already have been cast and I had really given up any hope. However, I called the 'well-known producer' and thanked him for his help.

After a lot of spluttering, he said, 'Jesus; I'm trapped. I did it but I heard it from So-and-So. So-and-So told me it had come from "thingummibob"' – and so it went on.

Out of curiosity, I tracked it back through eight people and there I found who had originated the story – a publicist in the publicity department of a rival studio whose job it was to further his man's chances had decided that the best way was to chop down the opposition.

When there is a million dollars at stake, Hollywood has never believed in kid gloves. The actor, of course, had no idea it had happened, he would never in a million years have condoned it.

The night before the 'Awards', someone gave a large party for Ingrid Bergman, who, after years away from Hollywood and a romance on Stromboli which had shocked or titillated the world, had reappeared to make one of the presentations. Everyone at the party seemed to have voted for me; they didn't say so in so many words, they were content to signal the fact across the room by making a cross in the air and pointing to their own chests and winking knowingly.

I was greatly encouraged until I caught the eye of Rosalind Russell, a nominee for best actress for whom I had not voted – and found myself winking, pointing and drawing crosses in the empty air.

The night of the awards finally was upon us. I was slightly anaesthetised because for the hour-long show, Bob Hope, Jack Lemmon and I had been pressed into service as the three masters of ceremonies and this preoccupied me with a great deal of hard work. At Grauman's Chinese Theatre on Hollywood Boulevard, the scene was set.

The traditional searchlights weaved back and forth across the purple night sky and the bleachers were jammed with thousands of excited fans as the bearers of well-known faces arrived and popping flash-bulbs blinded their well-known eyes.

I had to be there early. Before I left home, our Celtic and Nordic blood sent us dashing superstitiously about the house gathering up good luck charms. Distributed about my person were several rabbits' feet, a silver pig that one of my sons had given to me, some heavy Swedish coins, a Hebrew inscription on beaten bronze which I hoped might have captured the Jewish vote, a Buddha with a tiny diamond in his navel which Hjördis had found in Thailand, and my other son's first fallen tooth.

Hjördis looked spectacular and munching tranquillisers like popcorn, arrived later with Suzanne and Peter Ustinov.

My chores as a master of ceremonies over, I found my seat with them and sat knotted with indigestion as the show dragged on. I watched wretchedly as the happy recipients of Oscars made their carefully prepared acceptance speeches (more superstition had stopped me from preparing even one line – just in case). Ranged around the walls of the packed auditorium were five television cameras, each focused on a nominee and each ready to capture and flash to millions of viewers all over the world, looks of expectancy, disappointment, joy, studied indifference or tears.

Irene Dunne was finally introduced and I carefully composed my generous-hearted-loser face for she it was who would open the big white envelope, sealed in guaranteed secrecy by Price Waterhouse and Company and containing the name of the winner of 'The Best Performance by an Actor'.

She opened the envelope and, after an interminable pause, read out my name. There was a roar. I didn't wait to diagnose whether it was a roar of approval or rage. I kissed Hjördis, leapt to my feet and with tail coat flapping, I cantered down the aisle – I thought 'I've got to get there quick before she changes her mind.'

Such was my haste to get on that stage that I tripped up the steps and sprawled headlong. Another roar rent the air. Irene helped me up, gave me the Oscar, kissed me on the cheek and left me alone with the microphone. I thought the least I could do was to explain my precipitous entrance, so I said ... 'The reason I just fell down was ...' I had intended to continue 'because I was so loaded with good luck charms that I was top heavy ...' Unfortunately, I made an idiot pause after the word 'loaded' and a third roar raised the roof.

I knew that I could never top that, so I said no more on the subject, thereby establishing myself as the first self-confessed drunk to win the Academy Award.

So many ingredients go into one individual's winning an Oscar – the material, the direction, the other actors, the photography, the editing, even the music, that in reality it's a team effort, but whatever the background and however sentimental the vote, it's a lovely feeling to accept first prize.

Cables and messages and scripts poured in from all over the world ... King for a day? ... Certainly! After that, it's back to the old drawing-board.

The message I cherished the most was an invitation to go and see Samuel Goldwyn at his home. He opened the door himself and put his arm around my shoulders. It had been eight long years since we parted company.

In the drawing room, Frances caught me looking, surreptitiously, at the piano: there in its silver frame stood my photograph in uniform sent from England during the war.

'Sam never took it down,' she smiled.

Live television, during its reign, proved one thing – that many actors are masochists. Without exception, the most ghastly torture ever invented for people in my profession, it incorporated all the worst features of films, radio and the legitimate theatre.

Before an unseen audience of millions, over-dressed and under-rehearsed actors struggled with badly written scripts in front of cameras which collided with sickening regularity and scenery that wobbled and often collapsed while the whole mess was directed by egomaniac directors, drunk with power in front of consoles studded with switches and buttons.

The actor's nightmare was ever present – the dread of forgetting the lines without any possible hope of being prompted back on to the track. My partner, Dick Powell, was the genius who overcame this on one occasion. When

309

forgetfulness set in, he continued mouthing silently and all over the country hundreds of thousands of viewers frantically twiddled their dials and phoned their repair men.

Fortunately, film and tape gradually eliminated the live monster, leaving it to cope most efficiently with the news, 'talk-shows', and sports, but while it was in its final throes, masochist me could not resist one more exposure to its well-known dangers, so off I flew to New York.

It was an important show but the material was the usual gibberish: I was a spy or a doctor or a Congressman, I forget which – it would not have made the slightest difference. The strange thing was, I didn't really need the money that badly ... it was an irresistible urge to be frightened ... like skiing, but this time I was determined to be calm. After all, I was the star of the show and the major part of the burden was mine. My idea of being calm was this: I left my hat, coat and briefcase (my spy, doctor or Congressman equipment) in my little dressing room just off the sound stage and with only five minutes to 'air time', I wandered nonchalantly about in shirt sleeves.

An hysterical assistant rushed up, 'David! ... for Christ's sake! ...'

'Calm yourself, please,' I said, trying not to throw up, 'we have five, lovely, long cool minutes before we have to act this very bad play in front of several millions of people but, in the meanwhile, let us all relax ...'

'David! for Chriss. ...'

'Please, I said, 'don't raise your voice, all I need is two minutes during which I will go to my room, put on my coat and hat and pick up my briefcase.'

The man nearly disintegrated as I sauntered about, perhaps for the first time what Americans have always hoped a true Britisher might be – an ice-cold Gibraltar.

'David!' the assistant pleaded. '*Please* – you've just got two minutes!'

'Okay,' I said, 'no sweat', and followed by a forest of admiring eyes and with the slow measured tread of a London Bobby, I stalked to my little dressing room.

I had locked myself out.

Immediately, I was transformed into a shrieking, babbling, banshee.

'HELP! HELP!'

A quivering announcer started to extol the sponsor's wares against a background accompaniment of studio firemen hacking down my door and eventually, I made my entrance with my hat on back to front, my coat wrongly buttoned and covered in wood chips. I couldn't remember a word.

Orson Welles once said to me, 'We have now acted in theatres, on radio, in films and on live television – they *can't* think of anything else, can they?

Oh! God! I hope not.

I stayed on in New York to make a film.

In this journal, I have, by now, firmly established myself as a name-dropper so I can, with equanimity, record that apart from re-establishing contact with McClain, the New York Giants and many other old friends, the only occurrence of note during the time I was filming in New York was my good fortune in getting to know Senator J.F.K. of Massachusetts and his beautiful wife, Jackie.

One night with a small party, we visited El Morocco and were seated at J.F.K.'s request in the Champagne Room at the back. I was dancing with Jackie in the main room and remarked on the fact that her husband remained out of sight all evening.

'Why's that? Doesn't he like to dance?'

'He wants to be President,' she replied.

The picture finished, I returned to the Pink House just in time for the boys' summer holidays. I had many offers. Four Star was mushrooming, the mortgage was paid off and the Oscar was gleaming on the mantelshelf. I should have known from experience that I was headed for trouble.

The astute reader will have noticed fewer references to Hjördis in the pages covering the last few months. Unfortunately and almost imperceptibly, this had become the pattern of our lives at that time.

I had fallen into the well-known trap of becoming so wrapped up in my career, myself and, lately, my success, that I had been taking the most important thing in my life for granted.

Hjördis told me that she was leaving me.

CHAPTER SEVENTEEN

WITH complete honesty, Hjördis explained that she had to find out if she was still an individual, a human being in her own right, or just the trappings of someone else. It was very painful. Once Hjördis makes up her mind – that's it! She rented a small house nearby and moved into it to live alone and find out if she still 'existed'. The boys were nonplussed and refused to believe it had happened. Irreverently, they named her new residence 'The Summer Pink House' and visited it daily on their bicycles.

Hollywood is an impossible place to work out family problems. There, several hundred resident correspondents peer through their microscopes at an ever-changing handful of goldfish who are news. Rumours flew; so we put out the traditional nauseating statement about a 'trial separation' and voiced our pious hope that 'friends would understand while we attempted to reconcile our differences'.

Looking sadly at an empty chair was no way of spending the summer holidays so I took the boys to Honolulu to try our luck on the surf boards. Forty-eight hours later, the Los Angeles papers were full of pictures of me being helped from the sea with blood streaming down my face – the result of a head-on collision with a rock.

Urgent enquiries from Hjördis – a good sign.

After six weeks, I returned to the Pink House and diplomatic relations were re-opened between the two establishments, mostly in the form of S.O.S. messages, relayed by the boys.

'The boiler's burst – she wants to know what to do.'

'Somebody's stolen the mowing machine and the landlord is suing her – who does she call?'

I went to work at M.G.M. with Doris Day making *Please Don't Eat the Daisies* and, three months to the day from the start of our trial separation, I took my lunch box at midday and paid my first visit to the Summer Pink House. Hjördis was sunbathing in the garden when I walked in demanding beer to wash down my sandwiches. By the time I went back to the studio, the war was blessedly over.

It was a horrible experiment but by anyone as completely honest as Hjördis it could never have been undertaken except as a last resort. Most importantly, it worked and a whole new lease of life was given to our happiness entirely thanks to her having had the courage of her convictions.

As soon as I was through with the picture, we took off on a second honeymoon.

We had been invited to Brazil as guests of the Government. I was to be presented with the key of the city of Rio de Janeiro by President Kubitschek. We went via New York and while Hjördis busied herself finding clothes for the visit, I misguidedly enrolled myself at the Arthur Murray School of Dancing for a crash course in the tango.

For hours, closeted in a tiny cubicle, I nestled between the bosoms of a large, dark lady and swooped and dipped like a madman.

If anybody was still dancing the tango in Brazil they certainly were not doing so during our visit. I never had a chance to display my virtuosity.

North American hospitality is justly famous: the South American variety is exuberantly overpowering. It was a fascinating experience. Very few Hollywood faces had, thus far, been seen in that land of ardent moviegoers and we were fêted, cheered and mobbed wherever we went.

When the President, at the palace, presented me with a colossal key, Hjördis said, as a joke, 'What about me? Can't I have a little one too?'

With great gallantry, he ordered a small, golden replica to be made specially for her and delivered the same afternoon.

A fascinating man with a most attractive family, his pride and joy the controversial city of Brasilia, which was then only half built. On the spur of the moment he said,

'We'll go up there together tomorrow.'

We flew up in the presidential plane accompanied by his wife, daughters and the architect of Brasilia – Oscar Neymeyer, who sat white-faced and miserable throughout the trip – he is frankly terrified of flying.

When we arrived in Brasilia, the President put us in his helicopter and pointed delightedly as we flew between the half-built skyscrapers of his new capital, landing finally on the lawn of the only finished structure in the city, his own

'Palace of the Dawn', there to spend the weekend. 'Tomorrow,' he said, 'you and I will officially declare the lake to be filled with water.'

In a dinghy with an outboard motor, dodging in and out of the half-submerged tree trunks, we made the grand opening tour of the huge half-filled man-made waterway.

After another week of being royally entertained in São Paulo, we spent a few days by ourselves in Bahia.

Soon after we got back to the Pink House, my birthday loomed up and Hjördis said, 'Let's go down to some little place on the beach and have lunch together.'

It was a Sunday and the weather was glorious, and dreading the bumper-to-bumper traffic, I advanced every excuse, but she was adamant. So I took my place resignedly behind the wheel and we headed out towards Malibu.

She pointed excitedly, 'Let's go in there ... it looks sweet.'

'The Frigate Bird' was a well-known whore house with a very unsavoury reputation. I explained this to Hjördis.

'Oh, *please*,' she said. 'I've never been in one before. Please, do take me in there ... and look ... it says Dining Room!'

Still chastened by our short separation, I gave myself a good mark, for being attentive to my wife though luncheon in a brothel seemed a strange way to demonstrate it, and turned into the driveway.

As we entered, a parrot in a cage gave a wolf whistle and a sleazy madame greeted me with,

'Look who's here! Well, hullo there, Dave! ... Long time no see' – a libellous and erroneous statement as it happened but I pretended not to hear and pressed grimly on towards the dining room. There I froze. In the gloom, I saw the well-known back of a close friend. His arm was around a blonde girl's waist ... Laurence Olivier.

'Quick!' I hissed to Hjördis. 'We've got to get out of here.' Then as my eyes became accustomed to the semi-darkness, I spotted another even more easily recognisable form ... Peter Ustinov was pinning a dark girl to the wall. My head spun. My friends had gone mad – what a lunatic risk to take! I grabbed Hjördis by the arm and dragged her down the passage; the parrot whistled again, a peal of well-known laughter followed Patricia Medina!

314

Only then did I catch on. My surprise birthday party in surprise surroundings was a complete success.

In the spring of 1960, we had an overpowering urge to move. This urge became more and more pronounced and we knew with certainty that this was not something being signalled to our brains by out pathologically itchy feet. We knew that we wanted to make a big and permanent change. When I told my agent and my business manager that we were thinking of moving back to Europe to live, they were dumbfounded and lost no time in pointing out that my career had never been in better shape, and asked what sort of pictures I thought I'd make over there.

'You'll be sitting on top of some goddamned mountain,' they said, 'praying for the phone to ring.'

They talked ominously about the boys' schooling, hinted darkly about my obligations to Four Star ... they told me quite frankly that they reckoned I had gone mad, but the more they reasoned with me and the more valid their arguments sounded, the more certain I became that we would be going.

Hollywood had changed completely. The old camaraderie of pioneers in a one-generation business still controlled by the people who created it, was gone. The mystique had evaporated. Wrong it may have been, but when Joan Crawford, Norma Shearer and Marlene Dietrich had graciously consented to give interviews to the press, it was on the strict understanding that the copy would be submitted and could be altered to their taste before it was published. They created and perpetuated their images and – they became immortal.

Now, the inevitable reaction had set in and upon us was the era of the vicious, apparently law-suit proof columnist, of *Confidential* magazine and the telephoto lens. The pipe dream was gone – the lovely joke was over. The asphalt jungle of highways was proliferating everywhere through the once lovely Californian countryside; the famous sunshine was dimmed by automobiles and industry and the scent of fear was attacking the smog-filled lungs of the professional film makers, already resigned to the fact that their audience was brainwashed by television. It was time to go, but even so

315

and with our European roots tugging at us, it was a tough decision to make. Although we had lately received a nasty shock from the tax authorities who had taken all our savings to pay off a hefty reassessment of taxes from four years before, we still needed a clear sign that we should actually start making our reservations.

The message was delivered nearby in tragic and brutal fashion ...

On a bright Sunday during the Easter holiday, David and Jamie were on the patio helping me with the barbecue, Hjördis was indoors baking the potatoes. The garden was vivid with blossom and the yellow orioles had come back to nest once more. Around us the hills were misty and the blue jacaranda trees were in full bloom. In the distance Mount Baldy on one side reared its snow-topped head above the industrial haze of the Los Angeles basin, in the opposite direction. Catalina and the Santa Barbara Islands floated in ghostly isolation far out in the Pacific.

I don't think we even heard it ... if we did we would have dismissed it as the backfire of an automobile. It was a revolver shot. Four youths, 'junkies', had come up from Downtown in a taxi. After paying the fare, they had 'cased' our street for suitable victims and had settled on a neighbour's house a few yards away.

They rang the bell. The son of the house, a boy about the same age as mine, opened the door. They shot him.

While he was dying in agony on the threshold, they held up the distraught parents, took their available cash and then, inexplicably, allowed them to call a doctor.

They were all arrested within half an hour, and, receiving the sentences reserved for juveniles, have, presumably, long since been once more let loose on society.

Los Angeles is a violent city so I don't mean that we stampeded in panic as a result of this single tragedy, but it certainly tipped the scales, because we had lately decided to adopt and we wanted to bring up a new family somewhere in peace and quiet.

Finding a good home for the Pink House was our primary consideration. Many unknowns wanted it badly but we sold it much less advantageously to an old friend who loved it and who has lived there happily with his family ever since.

I resigned from the Board of Four Star, put the Regency furniture in storage and when the boys went back to boarding school, we flew off to find a new home and a new life in Europe.

First stop – Klosters in Switzerland – to catch the tail end of the skiing and to ask the advice of Deborah Kerr and her husband, Peter Viertel. They were adamant that we should follow their example and make Switzerland our base so when my agent finally trapped me after days of frantic search offering me several months in Greece and England making *The Guns of Navarone*, I left for the island of Rhodes and Hjördis stayed behind combing the Alps for a suitable chalet. She was brilliant and within a few weeks found exactly what we wanted, a comfortable cuckoo clock in a quiet farming village fifteen minutes from the ski resort of Gstaad.

The Guns of Navarone was a long and physically very arduous picture culminating with five weeks in England in November simulating a storm at sea by working nine hours a day in a huge tank of filthy water.

After nine months, Gregory Peck and I were left alone with two weeks of exhausting night work still to do, shooting from dusk to dawn, filming the actual finale of the picture – blowing up the guns. As my character had been built up as 'a genius with explosives ... the only man who can do it', it will readily be appreciated that without my presence during those crucial last two weeks, the colossal seven-million-dollar epic could never be finished. With only three days to go, I picked up a fearsome infection via a split lip and at two o'clock one morning, was carted away with, what in the grim times before antibiotics, was known as general septicaemia. I lay dangerously ill for days while the experts from Guy's Hospital struggled to identify, isolate and eliminate the bug that had struck me down.

The picture ground to a halt amidst general consternation. The 'Big Brass' of the company arrived post-haste from America. They called a meeting with Carl Foreman, the producer, Lee Thompson, the director, the head of the finance department, representatives of the banks and insurance companies and various assistants.

One of those present reported the scene to me later.

Foreman read out the latest ominous bulletin from the

doctors: murmurs of sympathy and alarm arose on all sides. After a suitable pause, the Biggest Brass spoke, 'We gotta problem here, fellers ... so David is very, very sick ... that's tough on him ... and we all love him ... but wadda *we* do if the sonofabitch dies?'

'The sonofabitch', pumped full of drugs, went back to work against the doctor's orders far sooner than was prudent, completed the crucial three days' work and suffered a relapse that lasted seven weeks.

The Big Brass never even sent me a grape.

While I was recuperating in the Chalet, Hjördis busied herself looking for the baby girl we had both set our hearts on. One day the miracle happened. A little round bundle, a few weeks old, was delivered into her arms. It promptly went purple with rage and tried to scream the house down, but one look at the Madonna-like serenity of Hjördis's face was all I needed. We were entering a period of pure joy.

Two years later, another little creature appeared and while Hjördis remained calmly confident, relentless competition for the affection of these two diminutive blonde bombshells set in between myself and my two sons. It continues, unabated, to this day; no holds barred.

After a while in Europe, the twin calls of sun and sea increased in volume. Hjördis, once again, was brilliant and this time, after combing the whole northern Mediterranean basin till she knew every rock by name, she found an old monstrosity, perched in an olive grove on a little promontory of its own on Cap Ferrat.

Any actor who voluntarily supports two residences should have a psychiatrist permanently installed in both of them.

However, the Regency furniture was sent for and the house was officially declared open by the more-beautiful-than-ever Grace from next door in Monaco who sat on a packing case with her enchanting husband and ate sardines by candlelight.

During the next few years, we returned a few times to Hollywood including once to make a picture about two crooks with Marlon Brando and once to shoot the pilot of Four Star's most ambitious television series, *The Rogues*. The eye must really have been 'in' on the day when producer,

Collier Young, and I did the casting because we chose as my leading lady, a complete unknown – Sally Kellerman.

Brando, contrary to what I had heard, was easy, sympathetic and generous to work with and a great help on a tricky political occasion.

Hjördis and I had received a message from the White House. Jackie was giving a very small surprise party for the President.

The producer of the picture, a staunch Republican, saw no particular reason to arrange the schedule to get me off a few hours early on Friday evening. Brando, a super Democrat, viewed it quite differently and the matter was quickly arranged. We flew to Washington; on arrival, we were smuggled by Fifi Fell into a small hotel where we changed and then boarded the Presidential yacht at a heavily guarded dock.

Apart from Fifi, ourselves and a senator from Florida, it was entirely a family affair – the R.F.K.s the E.F.K.s, the Shrivers, the Smiths and so forth. Jackie had provided a small orchestra. When it struck up 'Happy Birthday to you' as the President boarded for what he thought was a quiet dinner alone with his wife, his face, luckily, lit up with pleasure.

We cruised up and down the river, followed by a secret service launch ... a gay, happy family evening. We gave presents and in the early hours of the morning, played some fairly strenuous Kennedy games.

During one of these physical encounters, the entire left leg of Senator E.K.'s trousers was ripped off at the crotch. At four a.m. we came alongside for landing and it was evident that several marines, secret service men and others, were standing there to receive us.

'Please take my pants,' I said, 'it'll cause no stir if an actor comes ashore half-dressed, but it might look odd if you do.'

'The hell with it,' laughed Teddy Kennedy, 'it happened didn't it?' and with white underpants on the port side flashing bravely, he stepped jauntily ashore.

The next day, J.F.K. was in his office at eight sharp before attending a Decoration Day Service with his small son. At eleven, we had a rendezvous in his oval office.

'See how it feels,' he smiled and I sat for a moment at the Presidential desk.

With Jackie and the two children, we were whisked away in the Presidential helicopter to spend the rest of the weekend swimming, walking and skeet shooting at Camp David.

On the way up there, with a secret service helicopter in attendance, I noticed, at the President's elbow, a brightly coloured telephone. He saw me staring at it and started to laugh.

'Is that *the* one?' I asked. He nodded.

'The one you pick up if you want to blow up the world?'

'That's it,' he said, then he looked down at the glorious, green countryside passing below us, glanced at the attendant chopper flying beside us and laughed again.

'You know,' he said, 'a guy could get to like this!'

Countless volumes have been written about this extraordinary human being and the earthshaking moments he lived through and often controlled. I shall never forget him for his simplicity, his humour, his kindness, his interest in other people and, above all, his love of life.

The end of the journal is now in sight so I will attempt to reward the reader's patience and loyalty by bringing it swiftly to a close without making it sound like my obituary.

Since the war, Trubshawe, long since married to the glamorous Mrs. Tower, had tried his hand at many things, including becoming a publican. He had been the landlord of several hostelries including a small inn – The Lamb, at Hooe in Sussex. The honest burghers of Brighton, taking their Sunday drives over the Downs, were astonished to see a newly erected billboard that stated simply –

TRUBSHAWE HAS A LITTLE LAMB

12 miles.

Now he has given up that line of business and become an actor – a very good one too. He swiftly made a name for himself in television and one of his earliest screen appearances was in *The Guns of Navarone* – a lovely bonus for me.

Bill Rollo died. He died exactly as he would have planned it, except that he had every intention of living for ever. He worked hard all his life and put all he could afford into his delightful small farm in Rutland. Fox-hunting was his joy and his extravagance. He spent all the time he could spare with Dinie, his second wife, at Barleythorpe. At the age of seventy, mounted on his favourite hunter, on a glorious autumn morning, with the scent breast high and the Quorn hounds in full cry, he put his horse at a big thorn fence. It fell. Bill's neck was broken.

I was filming in Spain. Hjördis was visiting her family in Sweden, David was at the University of Florence and Jamie at school in Switzerland. We converged on London and the next day drove north for the funeral.

In London, it had been a happy family reunion, but as the miles sped by and Barleythorpe came nearer, the terrible sadness of the reason for our coming together swept over us. We had all adored him. He had been indestructible. The little village church was packed with his old hunting and shooting friends sitting silently and stoically in their grief. In the family pew, the Niven contingent wept unashamedly. After the service, we walked miserably out into the pale sunshine. The Duke of Beaufort, a close friend of Bill's, approached.

'I take it you will be spending the night with Dinie?'

'I can't, I'm afraid,' I said. 'I have to go back to Spain – I'm shooting in the morning.'

'Ah' he said, 'they've got a nice lot of birds down there this year, I hear.'

I didn't try to explain.

The boys completed their education in Switzerland, France, England and Italy. Jamie returned to the U.S. and after leaving Harvard, married a very special girl from Philadelphia. He now works in New York, David in London.

Lately, Betty Bacall arrived to spend some time at Cap Ferrat with us. She brought with her the score of *Applause* and for ten days sat at the end of our promontory, belting out her numbers. The fishermen deserted the rocks below, the sea gulls departed and certain species of fish are no longer to be found in our waters, but when she opened on

Broadway, she scored the greatest triumph that has come to any actress in the last ten years.

Well, that about rounds it off ...

What else is there? Oh! yes! ... the Movies! I almost forgot about them. Well ... in the ten years since I left Hollywood, my itchy feet have spurred me, usually accompanied by Hjördis and the girls, to make films in Greece, Spain, England, France, Israel, Ireland, United States, Monaco, Switzerland, Austria, Mexico, Italy and the Lebanon – and more than one film in many of these countries.

During that time I have been directed by the highly intelligent such as John Huston, John Frankenheimer, J. Lee Thompson and Peter Ustinov and by other professionals, also by the heavy-handed, the hysterical and the half-wits. I have worked with drunkards and those who preferred 'pot', 'speed' or 'horse'.

As a result of these travels and all these exposures nothing really fatal happened but there was one extremely painful near miss.

We were shooting *The Pink Panther* in the Italian Alps; the following day I was required to do something very simple on skis and the producer, not knowing that I would rather ski than eat, told me to take the afternoon off and practise with a ski teacher. So anxious was I to profit from his rash instruction before he realised I might break a leg, that I bustled off up the mountain in my thin movie ski outfit, halfwittedly ignoring the fact that on the top it was 35° below zero ... so cold in fact that no one else was skiing. Halfway down and travelling fast behind the instructor, I suddenly got a feeling of absolutely nothing in precisely the spot where I should have been the warmest ... something was badly amiss amidships. A neon-sign flashed on in my brain FROSTBITE and cupping my hands over the danger area, I inadvertently put myself into the racing position and flashed past the astonished instructor. At the bottom three morose and mauve-coloured guides were warming themselves over a fire of fir branches.

'Catso gelato!' I yelled in my shaky Italian.

The men were galvanised into instant action. This was a fate worse than death.

'Put it in the snow,' they shouted, plucking feverishly at my zipper.

'You put yours in the snow,' I gibbered, 'mine's cold enough.'

My instructor arrived. 'Alcohol!' he commanded. 'We put it in alcohol!'

We all clambered into his ancient car and I was driven through the main street of Cortina d'Ampezzo, one of the choicest resorts in the Alps, lying in the back with four horny-handed mountaineers, trying to keep the circulation going in my stricken friend.

In the bar of the Hotel de la Poste, smartly dressed clients finishing late lunch, gaped in amazement as we clumped to the bar and yelled at the barman to fill a brandy glass to the brim with whisky 'prontissimo!'

In the lavatory, while the Italians formed a solicitous clucking semi-circle, I faced the agony of the thaw and prised out of my ski pants a pale blue acorn. Into the whisky it went and the pain was excruciating. This moment was chosen by a smart Milanese nobleman whom I happened to know to enter with a view to relieving himself. He took in the tableau at a glance.

'David,' he asked in a horrified voice, 'what *are* you doing?'

'I am pissing in a brandy glass,' I muttered between clenched teeth, 'I always do.'

Apart from that, nothing much happened on my wanderings.

I have been knifed (by mistake) in a Spanish production and nearly shot dead by a bedouin in Israel when the World War II rifle he was handling still had one up the spout. The bullet passed between our heads as I was talking to Duncan Macrae.

I have been knocked senseless by falling scenery in an English studio and overturned in a canoe into the loathsomely infested waters of a Mexican jungle ... all in all, about par for the course.

The results, too, have been average. Some pictures the critics loved and the audience hated; some despised by the experts were greatly appreciated by the paying customers. One effort became one of the great money-takers of all time;

323

another broke the record at the Radio City Music Hall and a third was so bad that it never got shown anywhere – even on the airlines.

The whole movie industry, at the moment of writing, is in disarray – some say it will never recover.

When it was booming, nothing was put into research. With people, today, cavorting about on the moon, it is incredible to think that films are still made and distributed in much the same way as they were in the days of D. W. Griffith, Chaplin and Buster Keaton. If the film companies had been making motor cars or false teeth, they would have been bankrupt forty years ago. When the business men took over from the old-time movie makers and started chasing 'trends', disaster followed as the night the day and now there is little money left with which to make new pictures. Fingers of blame have been pointed freely in every direction including at the people who pulled in the customers.

Sitting in their yacht in Monte Carlo harbour, I was discussing the situation with the Burtons.

'What about the people who got a million dollars a picture?' I asked.

Elizabeth's reply was as down to earth as usual.

'If someone was stupid enough to offer me a million dollars to make a picture – I was certainly not dumb enough to turn it down.'

The movie business has often proved its resilience and it will do so once more. In these days of super communications, it makes no sense to think that the greatest form of mass entertainment ever invented will just fade away.

Actors have a problem – often we don't know how to get 'off'.

'How do I finish this story?' I asked a writer friend.

'Quite simple,' he replied, 'just bring it up to date, then stop writing.'

After he had departed I was left in my London hotel staring at a blank sheet of paper digesting his brilliance and wondering how to avoid being sentimental while at the same time underlining my wonder at the ease with which two baby girls had altered my priorities and changed the whole process and meaning of my life when the phone rang.

'Uncle David!' said a sweet voice, 'this is your god-daughter!'

Noël Coward has twenty-seven godchildren – five more than I (eighteen of mine are girls).

Noël would never have floundered as I did ... his record for patience and helpfulness is legendary ... example –

Uncle Noël! Look at those two little doggies! What *are* they doing?'

'The little doggie in front,' said Godfather Noël, 'has just gone blind, and his friend is pushing him all the way to St. Dunstan's.'

'I have a friend with me,' said my unidentified goddaughter. 'He's dying to meet you ... can we come up?'

When she walked in and embraced me I remembered her. Eighteen years old, long, blonde hair, Indian head-band, willowy wasp-waist figure, suede jacket, fringed skirt, green eyes and a gorgeous smile.

Her companion was considerably less prepossessing.

'This is Big Top,' said my goddaughter offhandedly, as she indicated a morose, bearded creature lurking behind her. He sported an Afro hair-do, a grave error for a red-haired Caucasian. He, too, was festooned with love beads and his heliotrope bell-bottoms were kept up by a broad leather belt, the buckle of which was fashioned in the shape of a penis. Dirty, horned toenails jabbed out belligerently from between the thongs of his questionable sandals.

'You wanna blow some grass, man?' he demanded, his flat Lancashire voice winning easily over a phoney American accent. He ignited a joint and passed it to my goddaughter.

'You dig today's pictures?' he asked me. 'How come you only work for these creepy has-beens, man! I've got something that'll really blow your mind, very groovy.'

'What's it about, Big Top?' I asked, groaning inwardly.

'Just be cool,' he said. 'Be cool ... if you wanna be in something really far out, really specific, something really against your bag ... I have this story about this old guy, rich and weirdo: his daughter has freaked out, see, and shacked up with a spade who drops acid, who's a big wheel in some corny new African state ...' He droned out the rest of the well-known rubbish and then delivered a homily.

It was cats like me, it seemed, who had ruined the movie business with our bad taste and lack of imagination. The only way we could atone for our sins, was by coming up with some 'heavy bread' for his production company.

He finally withdrew, leaving my room smelling like a haystack. I opened the windows.

'Isn't he awful?' giggled my goddaughter. 'I won't do that to you again ... I got trapped.' She looked at me speculatively and took a long draught of champagne.

'Want to take me to a party? It's just around the corner.'

In the lobby many heads turned in her direction as she clung to my arm.

The party was located in a studio above an antique shop. A glassy-eyed transvestite admitted us and pointed limply into the gloom of a sickly-sweet haze ... 'There's wine over there.'

The place was illuminated by carriage lamps; on the walls were garish posters, large, coloured numbers and blown-up photographs of Che and Mao. Through an open bedroom door to the right, I could see two young lesbians making slow, unhurried love. Our host offered us some pills from a Georgian snuff box.

'We have it all, man,' he said. '... California Sunshine even.'

Out of the gloom a tall girl rose, kissed me on the lips, said 'Peace', and sat down again.

Round the walls couples sat and smoked and stared at nothing in particular. From a record player, a female voice, Joan Baez, I think was singing a sad ballad about children.

Not much happened for an hour, then a 16 mm. film was thrown on a portable screen. It was about homosexuality in Algerian prisons. The warders played prominent parts and the close-ups were quite repulsive. As the film unfolded, my blonde-green-eyed Godddaughter became aware of my increasing restlessness.

'This isn't your scene is it?' she giggled. 'Do you want to split?'

She was giggling a lot by now and in the reflected light of the screen, I saw that her eyes were brightly out of focus.

326

'Gratefully, I grabbed the offer and ducking under the beam from the projector I went quickly down the stairs. In the street, like a man who has just run a four-minute mile in thick mud, I leaned against the railings, gulping down great draughts of clean, windy spring evening.

After a while, I looked up at the scudding clouds above and suddenly and unexpectedly, up there above the chimney pots, I beheld an old childhood friend, sailing calmly and confidently through a clear patch of sky ...

> who knows if the moon's
> a balloon, coming out of a keen city
> in the sky – filled with pretty people?
> (and if you and I should
>
> get into it, if they
> should take me and take you into their balloon,
> why then
> we'd go up higher with all the pretty people
>
> than houses and steeples and clouds:
> go sailing
> away and away sailing into a keen
> city which nobody's ever visited, where
> always
>   it's
>   Spring) and everyone's
> in love and flowers pick themselves

Index

330

311, 312–13, 314, 316–17, 321

Niven, Jamie (son), 262, 266, 272, 277, 291, 312, 316, 321

Niven, Joyce (sister), 16, 23, 39, 154, 220

Niven, Max (brother), 16, 23, 39, 65, 99, 154, 214, 220, 225, 232

Niven, Mrs. Max (Doreen Platt), 232

Niven, Primula (first wife), 223, 232, 236–8, 242–3, 245, 247, 249–50, 253, 262–3, joins author in California, 266–7, accidental fall and death, 267–70, 272

Niven, William Graham (father), 13, 34

Niven, Mrs. W. G. (mother) – see Comyn-Platt, Lady

O'Neill, Jim, 306–307

Oberon, Merle, 184, 192, 194, 196, 290

Olivier, Laurence, 124, 194, 196, 197, 205, 213, 214, 245, 249, 267, 282, 314

Paget, Barbara, 38

Paget, Edmund, 38

Paget, Joan, 38

Paget, Peter, 38

Palmer, Lilli, 245, 270, 289

Paramount, 168–9, 173, 184, 189, 266

Parker, Dorothy, 207

Parker, Steve, 302

Parsons, Louella, 182, 209

Patton, General Mark, 255, 259

Peck, Gregory, 317

Perelman, S. J., 297

Petrified Forest, The (TV film), 288

'Phantom' squadrons, 238–41, 242–4, 247–8, 252, 256

Phipps, Paul, 139

Phipps, Tommy, 139, 155, 167–8, 193

'Pinkie', 267, 268, 269, 270, 273

Please Don't Eat the Daisies (film), 312

Pleydell-Bouverie, Anthony, 90, 92, 101, 107, 154, 163–5

Pleydell-Bouverie, Audrey, 277

Poitier, Sidney, 306

Pope, Group Captain, 205, 219

Porter, Cole, 207

Portman, Eric, 306–307

Powell, Dick, 289, 309

Powell, Michael, 262

Powell, William, 173, 183, 184

Power, Tyrone, 199, 265, 267

Preminger, Otto, 285, 289

Pressburger, Emeric, 262

Prisoner of Zenda, The (film), 202–204

Raffles (film), 210, 213

Rantzman, Harry, 136

Rathbone, Basil, 183, 205

Ratoff, Gregory, 284

Rattigan, Terence, 303

Real Glory, The (film), 199

Reed, Carol, 245

Rifle Brigade, 224, 229, 231–2

'Rifleman' TV series, 290

Riscoe, Arthur, 244

RKO, 173, 184, 189

Roark, Aiden, 175–7

Robinson, CSM 'Robbo', 56, 57–8, 63

Robson, Flora, 197

Rogers, Ginger, 207–208, 226, 267

Roland, Gilbert, 184

Rollo, Andrew, 250

Rollo, Kathleen, 270

335

336